Fighting Financial Crises

Fighting Financial Crises

Learning from the Past

GARY B. GORTON AND
ELLIS W. TALLMAN

The University of Chicago Press
Chicago and London

The University of Chicago Press, Chicago 60637
The University of Chicago Press, Ltd., London
Published 2018
Paperback edition 2021
Printed in the United States of America

30 29 28 27 26 25 24 23 22 21   1 2 3 4 5

ISBN-13: 978-0-226-47951-4 (cloth)
ISBN-13: 978-0-226-78620-9 (paper)
ISBN-13: 978-0-226-47965-1 (e-book)
DOI: https://doi.org/10.7208/chicago/9780226479651.001.0001

Library of Congress Cataloging-in-Publication Data

Names: Gorton, Gary, author. | Tallman, Ellis W. (Ellis William), 1958– author.
Title: Fighting financial crises : learning from the past / Gary B. Gorton and
    Ellis W. Tallman.
Description: Chicago ; London : The University of Chicago Press, 2018. |
    Includes bibliographical references and index.
Identifiers: LCCN 2018011958 | ISBN 9780226479514 (cloth : alk. paper) |
    ISBN 9780226479651 (e-book)
Subjects: LCSH: Financial crises. | Financial crises—United States—History. |
    New York Clearing House Association. | Clearinghouses (Banking)—New York
    (State)—New York. | United States—Economic conditions—1865–1918.
Classification: LCC HB3722 .G673 2018 | DDC 338.5/420973—dc23
LC record available at https://lccn.loc.gov/2018011958

Contents

Preface

[The subject of banking panics] is thoroughly understood by few only; and most people, shunning the trouble of patient investigation, form hasty conclusions based on superficial impressions.

(B R O W N I N G 1 8 6 9)

History is important, especially for understanding financial crises. What is a financial crisis? How can we recognize a financial crisis? What should a central actor, like a central bank or a private bank clearinghouse, do to restore financial market conditions to normalcy? What does "restore normalcy" actually mean? The Panic of 2007–8 makes clear that we should know the answers to these critical questions. We have been through financial crises before, but history is selectively remembered. No committee determines what elements of history should be emphasized and what should be forgotten; rather it is a social process.

The Panic of 2007–8 showed that even the most advanced economy in world history is not immune to banking panics, which are bank runs on many institutions. Widespread financial distress perceived by investors and depositors compelled them to "get liquid" and caused the potential insolvency of the entire financial system, the collapse of which was prevented only by central bank and fiscal interventions. Before 2007 such a crisis was inconceivable to financial market experts, policy makers, and especially the general public. Perhaps this was because no one thought that banking would change in important ways, as in, for example, developing wholesale funding as a major source of funds. And yet it is a fact that the United States experienced a systemic financial crisis during 2007–8. At the time, the financial crisis was unexpected, unthinkable, and seemed to come out of nowhere. But it did not come out of nowhere. It only seemed that way because the financial history of the United States was not commonly known. In fact, financial history was not studied, and history was ignored. This history was unexploited and is only now being recovered. This book is part of that effort.

The Panic of 2007–8 was not supposed to happen because panics are events of "the past." Generally, "the past" is viewed as inherently different from "the present," so much so that the past is viewed as of little use in understanding the present. Of course, the line between past and present is a blurry one. A recent economics article is typical: "the structure of the economy has of course changed massively since the 1930s. Data from a long time ago may not be a good guide to what we expect going forward." And that statement comes from a paper published in 2013, well after the Panic of 2007–8. The authors, of course, do not explain what "changed massively" means. Had we held a different view of history, the Panic of 2007–8 might not have come as a complete shock. Our view is that market economies have inherent structure. And part of that structure is that short-term debt is vulnerable to runs—the potential for a widespread demand for cash rather than the short-term debt. The Panic of 2007–8 showed that the past and the present have much more in common than many may have believed.

Macroeconomics is a field that was born in the Great Depression, and the early macroeconomists who lived through the Great Depression had direct, lived experience of the enormous economic distress it caused. Randall Parker (2002) interviewed members of this generation for their memories of the events and the influence of those events upon them. Paul Samuelson: "I can remember a knock on the door in the evening when we were at dinner. There would be a person or even a child with a note, 'We are starving, can you give us a potato or ten cents?'" (29). And Moses Abramovitz: "There were sights to be seen in the streets of Manhattan which were very, very disturbing, to say the least. The apple sellers, unemployed men trying to pick up a few pennies to help support themselves and their families by buying a little carton of apples, putting it on a folding chair on a street corner, polishing them up and offering them for sale" (64). These experiences inspired them to become economists. Milton Friedman: "I guess the major role the Depression played . . . was in leading me to become an economist" (42).

This first generation of macroeconomists remembered directly. The next generation speaks of the Great Depression more abstractly, perhaps on the basis of stories from those who had experienced it, but they had no firsthand knowledge of the aftermath of the event (see Parker 2008). Nevertheless, in economics the Great Depression is well remembered, and economists have produced a huge and vibrant literature that still illuminates it. But the financial crises prior to the Great Depression are less prominent in the research literature and virtually absent in general mainstream macroeconomic discussions. And because the earlier financial crises are not commonly known, the Great Depression appears special, to some an aberration defying explanation with an equilibrium model. An explicit argument has never been made for why financial history prior to the Great Depression should be downplayed or even ignored, except for casual statements about the past being different. Usually, the key argument is that pre-Fed panics were ended by the existence of the Federal Reserve, and that the Great Depression panics were different because of the incompetent response of the Fed or the unwieldy structure of the Fed. We, however, take the view that market economies have an inherent structure—things like demand curves sloping downward—and that one of these inherent structures is the necessity for short-term debt that is inevitably vulnerable to runs. This vulnerability implies that all financial crises are at their root about short-term debt. This view makes previous history interpretable with respect to modern events and also relevant for understanding them.

In the study of financial panics, the period before the Federal Reserve System was in existence offers an excellent laboratory for investigating both the sources of panics and the methods taken to combat them. With these goals in mind, we study the US National Banking Era, 1863–1913. In that period, firms and households had no expectations about what actions the central bank would take, because there was no central bank. Lacking a central bank, firms and households reacted differently than if one had existed and taken actions to intervene. In this laboratory, we are able, for example, to differentiate the argument that government policies cause financial crises (e.g., moral hazard, "too big to fail") from the argument that there are root underlying causes of crises, which government policies aim to address. Being able to make such differentiations can help answer our motivating questions about crises.

This book began as a long paper about how confidence in banks gets restored after runs on banks. But we did not submit the paper, or a shortened version of it, to an academic economics journal because we cannot formally establish the causal link between the key actions taken to quell distress during a crisis and the restoration of confidence. We provide a narrative of what happens during the period between the loss of confidence (the first bank runs) and the restoration of confidence, which to us is compelling, but we cannot establish a causal link by the high standards of econometric practice. Sometimes important questions simply cannot meet those standards. Our view is that historical methods can arrive at understanding also; it is not just the province of econometric practice. The alternative is to not study crises, and to us, that is unacceptable.

It is ironic that we should proceed essentially with pure history, because we both received our PhD degrees from the University of Rochester Department of Economics (although we did not overlap). We each studied economic history, either formally or informally, with Professor Stanley Engerman. Engerman, an expert on slavery (among other topics), is a strong believer that the past is informative about the present and future. And Engerman, along with Robert Fogel, set the standard for using econometric methods in economic history, later coming to be called cliometrics. While cliometrics has become widespread, creating the standard for (or barrier to?) empirical evidence in economic history, Engerman never eschewed purely historical methods.

The question of whether there can be understanding or insight without standard errors is a philosophical issue that we do not want to address. We would point out that in studying financial crises there often is really no other way than through historical analysis.

We thank Maggie Jacobson and Charles Goodhart for comments on an early draft of this book. For comments and suggestions on the original paper, we thank Jeremy Atack, Howard Bodenhorn, Michael Bordo, Charles Calomiris, Andrew Coleman, Ben Craig, Stanley Engerman, Kinda Hachem, Eric Hilt, Gary Kornblith, Arvind Krishnamurthy, Jon Moen, Hugh Rockoff, George Selgin, Richard Sylla, Larry Wall, Warren Weber, David Weiman, and Eugene White, as well as the participants at conferences in honor of Elmus Wicker and of Hugh Rockoff, the 2015 Atlanta Fed Monetary and Financial History Conference, and the Monetary Economics Workshop at the 2015 NBER Summer Institute. Thanks to Bob Chakravorti and Mirjana Orovic for assistance with the New York Clearing House Association Archives. We also thank George Berry, Thomas Bonczek, Jialu Chen, Paulo Costa, Grant Goehring, Arun Gupta, Yiming Ma, Markus Shak, and especially Arwin Zeissler for research assistance.

For sharing data for figures and other information, we thank Augusto de la Torre, Guillermo Perry, Sergio Schmukler, Luis Servén, and Eduardo Levy Yeyati. Portions of chapter 6 appeared in "Too-Big-to-Fail before the Fed," *American Economic Review* 106, no. 5 (2016): 528–32.

Fighting Financial Crises:
Learning from the Past

Of course, it would be best not to have financial crises. Then there would be no reason to think about how to fight them. But the naive view that advanced economies are no longer vulnerable to financial crises was exploded by the Panic of 2007–8. So it is necessary to think (again) about fighting crises.

Financial crises are devastating events that have long plagued market economies and continue to be a problem. Indeed, crises like the Panic of 2007–8 are certainly not rare in US history (or, for that matter, in the history of all market economies). Before the Panic of 2007–8, the United States endured what might be perceived as a recurrent pattern of financial crises, with panics in 1797, 1814, 1819, 1825, 1833, 1837, 1857, 1861, 1864, 1873, 1884, 1890, 1893, 1907, 1914, and 1929–33. Each event combined financial distress with economic contraction; the final date in the list is the Great Depression, a monolithic enigma for economists. The depression—a watershed event for policy responses to crises and the aftermath—stimulated extensive inquiries into its causes. The social distress observed in the depression—unemployment rates above 25 percent and the contraction of real output by more than 30 percent—left an indelible impression on many of those who lived through it. As that population has dwindled over time, the social memory of the event faded and it was assumed that such an event could not happen in the world's most advanced economy.

Financial crises are runs on short-term debt—bank money. Through history, the runs have been on various forms of bank money, private banknotes and demand deposits, and then in 2007–8 on short-term debt like sale and repurchase agreements (repo), various forms of commercial paper, and money market funds. All these forms of short-term debt issued by banks are money-like. They are used for transactions and as very short-term stores of value. As such, they have the common feature that they are designed to be information-insensitive; that is, their value does not change when information arrives. And no one spends resources to try to determine something about the debt that others do not know. The reason for this is that it is most efficient if the short-term bank debt is always viewed as being worth par, that is, $10 is worth $10.

Market economies allocate resources via the price system. Prices go up or down and consumers and producers respond. In Adam Smith's "invisible hand" allegory, the price summarizes the supply and demand for the good. Similarly, stock prices are thought to be "efficient," meaning that they embed all the relevant information. New information arrives about each company, and their stock prices respond, going up or down. The stock market is a reasonable contrast to the case for bank money. We want stock prices to reveal information because the value of the stock is meant to reflect the value of the company that issued it. Bank money is different—the value of money should not move, and it is meant to be a numeraire—the medium used to determine prices for other goods. Bank money is best if the price system *does not* work. This is its defining characteristic. The price should *not change* so that transactions are straightforward. If the price of bank money does not change, it is not sensitive to new information. Then there are no arguments over the value of the money: $10 is $10. But the problem is that such debt is vulnerable to runs, situations where the debt becomes information-sensitive. This happens when holders of the debt suspect that the backing portfolio of loans or the backing bond collateral value has deteriorated. Suddenly, the price of bank money changes, but no one knows what it should be—a crisis. This structural commonality is the root of financial crises. To be clear, financial crises are always about short-term debt that debt holders no longer want. To be safe, they want cash, and what we mean here is whatever form of payment is indisputable.

The history of market economies is replete with many, many instances of financial crises. Crises occur in countries with and without central banks, with and without deposit insurance. They occur in emerging markets and they occur in developed economies. Central banks are supposed to fight crises, and the US Federal Reserve System took actions in 2007–8 to combat the crisis. And before the Federal Reserve System was established in 1913, private bank clearinghouses fought crises as best they could with the limited powers they had available.

At the center of a financial crisis or banking panic is a widespread scramble for cash. Something happens to make depositors "act differently" and find reasons to question the value of their deposits or other short-term bank debt. In a run on a single bank, depositor withdrawals threaten the viability of only one bank. Financial crises are events that spread beyond a few banks and affect the entire system. Hence the term "systemic." In crises, the holders of short-term debt seek to withdraw their money. In the standard case of bank checking accounts, depositors want to exchange their deposits for cash. In a historical context, holders of private banknotes, as in the antebellum banking system, want to exchange the banknotes for specie, that is, gold or silver coin. In the case of sale and repurchase agreements (repo) or commercial paper, as in the 2007–8 crisis, holders of short-term debt instruments simply refused to redeposit their money. Or in the subtler case, the holders of short-term debt would have engaged in such a mass run had not explicit or implicit government or central bank intervention occurred or was expected to occur.

A financial crisis is a systemic event; in a banking panic *all* banks are at risk, and the financial system is about to collapse. For example, during the 2007–8 crisis Ben Bernanke in his testimony before the US Financial Crisis Inquiry Commission (2011, 354) said that of the thirteen most important financial institutions in the United States, "12 were on the verge of failure within a week or two [after Lehman]." One hundred and eighty years earlier, the United States had experienced the Panic of 1837, and the situation was the same, as described by William Gouge (1837, 5):

> At the present moment [during the Panic of 1837], all the Banks in the United States are bankrupt; and, not only they, but all the Insurance Companies, all the Railroad Companies, all the Canal Companies, all the City Governments, all the County Governments, all the State Governments, the General Government, and a great number of people. This is literally true. The only legal tender is gold and silver. Whoever cannot pay, on demand, in the authorized coin of the country, a debt actually due, is, in point of fact, *bankrupt*: although he may be at the very moment in possession of immense wealth, and although, on the winding up of his affairs, he may be shown to be worth millions. (emphasis in original)

So a financial crisis is not just a bad event. The 1987 stock market crash or the US Savings and Loan mess would not qualify as financial crises because these events never threatened the entire financial system. Stock market crashes alone do not threaten the solvency of the banking system.

In a financial crisis, holders of short-term bank debt, like demand deposits, but also other forms of short-term debt, like sale and repurchase agreements (repo), want cash instead of their bank debt, because they have doubts about whether the issuing bank will be in business all that long. Further, unlike a bank run on one institution, depositors are unsure about the solvency of any bank and that is why cash and not a deposit in another bank is what depositors are after. Yet sometime later the very same lenders/depositors are comfortable and ready to hold short-term bank debt again. Why do depositors' (or, synonymously, lenders') beliefs switch from panic to not panic? Causing such a change in beliefs is called "restoring confidence." With renewed confidence, short-term bank debt can again be used as usual. But how does this happen? How can depositors be convinced that the banking system is solvent and viable?

This book is about fighting financial crises. Why is such a book necessary? Don't we already know how to fight crises? We have Bagehot's rule. This is the time-honored way to fight crises. The rule was stated by Walter Bagehot in 1873 and says that to end a financial crisis, the central bank needs to lend freely, against good collateral, at a high rate. In the recent crisis, the heads of central banks said that they followed Bagehot's advice (see King 2010; Draghi 2013; and Bernanke 2014a, 2014b). It is not known why this rule should restore confidence or, in fact, that it does. Everyone pays lip service to Bagehot's rule. Is Bagehot's rule useful because it encapsulates everything we need to know about fighting crises? Or, is it that nothing has been learned about fighting crises since 1873? Opening emergency lending facilities has never in itself ended a financial crisis. So the reality is that no lessons have been distilled for fighting crises since 1873. We will see that there is more to restoring confidence than Bagehot's rule.

The gist of Bagehot's rule is to provide cash to banks with high-interest loans from the central bank that are collateralized with the borrowing bank's assets. The relatively high interest rate on the borrowed cash prevents banks from taking advantage of the emergency lending opportunity. The banks can then hand out the cash to depositors who withdraw it, and other depositors see that their cash is available. There is a crucial piece of this rule that is implicit and missing from the rule as typically expressed. Bagehot failed to mention it because he was English. The financial structure of banks in Britain kept the identity of borrowing banks secret. This is the crucial missing piece: secrecy. Secrecy about the borrowing banks' identities hides weak banks, preventing runs against them, which would lead to runs against the next weakest, and so on. This secrecy focuses the attention of households and firms on the key question; is the banking system solvent? In a systemic event, convincing bank debt holders that the system is solvent is what reestablishing confidence means.

To understand a crisis and how to fight a crisis, we focus on the US National Banking Era (1863–1913). There are three reasons for this. First, once the Civil War ended and the National Banking Acts had fuller impact, it is a homogeneous period during which there were five notable banking panics.

Three were very serious events. So we can study the experience of multiple panics occurring in the same system. Of course, many casually dismiss the past as irrelevant, but how else do we learn if not from history? With respect to financial crises, it really is, as Marx put it, a case where "History repeats itself, first as tragedy, second as farce." The reality is that financial crises have occurred throughout the history of market economies. There is a common root problem: short-term debt. Short-term debt is necessary for the economy to work, but it is vulnerable to runs. This is clearest to see during the National Banking Era.

Second, this period is particularly interesting because there was no deposit insurance and no central bank, and so expectations of possible future central bank interventions during a crisis are not an issue. During modern crises, firms and households expect the central bank or government (Treasury) to intervene by, for example, issuing blanket guarantees against bank debt, nationalizing the banks, bailing out banks, and so on. In most modern crises, there are bank runs, but they come later in the sequence of events than we observe in the earlier period, as people often wait to see what is going to happen. This makes modern crises very difficult to study. Because of the public's expectations about interventions, some conclude that the interventions themselves are the problem. And further, because delays in actions by authorities can take place earlier or later in the event sequence, it may appear that crisis events have nothing in common. In that circumstance, researchers and regulators seize on idiosyncratic aspects of each crisis and miss the essential common features.

Third, crises typically do not happen frequently enough for there to be a learning process about how to fight them or to develop some clarity about the nature of a financial crisis. Lessons from fighting previous crises are lost. Without multiple observations, crises are attributed to all sorts of factors. That's why Bagehot is still invoked. Our view is that by studying a period that avoids these modern complications but exhibits the same short-term debt problems, we can distill the essence of fighting crises. We can state some common principles or guidelines for fighting crises. And it is important to note that crises during the National Banking Era cannot be due to "moral hazard" or "too big to fail," so some clarity about the underlying cause of a financial crisis can be gleaned.

During the crises of the US National Banking Era, banks would suspend convertibility of deposits into cash, that is, banks would refuse to repay amounts in depositors' checking accounts. Suspension was an intervention meant to disrupt widespread liquidity drains from the banking system. Suspension was always illegal, but it was tolerated as necessary to save the banking system (a lesson that was lost and could not be recovered during 2007–8). We study how depositors' beliefs change during the period of the suspension of convertibility—as a laboratory to uncover what caused the change in depositor sentiment.

Prior to the Federal Reserve System and without deposit insurance, people in the United States could rely only on private bank clearinghouses to fight crises. Among those institutions, we focus on the New York City Clearing House Association, an organization of private banks. New York City had become the key financial center of the United States by the mid-1860s, and by that time, the New York Clearing House was at the center of the US banking system during the National Banking Era. The clearinghouse also was the leader in fighting banking panics prior to the existence of the Federal Reserve System (the central bank). It is instructive to study the period before the Federal Reserve was in existence because we will see that the clearinghouse engaged in many of the actions that central banks engage in today to fight crises. We will seek to understand these actions and why they are successful in the fight against a crisis.

The Federal Reserve System was, to a large extent, modeled after the New York Clearing House and the existing clearinghouse system across the country (as well as the Bank of England). With regard to liquidity provision, an essential innovation of the Federal Reserve System was the establishment of a permanent discount window, one that was open all the time, where member banks could borrow money by depositing collateral. The Federal Reserve's discount window was always available, whereas the clearinghouses' emergency lending facilities were open and functioning only during banking panics. The panic had to happen first in the clearinghouse case, whereas it was hoped that with the Federal Reserve's permanent discount window perhaps the panic could be avoided.

But there was something else that the Federal Reserve System learned and retained from the history of private bank clearinghouses: secrecy about the identities of the banks borrowing from the discount window and management of the information environment more generally. This is a hallmark of fighting crises. During the most severe crises, the pre–Federal Reserve clearinghouse actions were similar to those of modern central banks—for example, bank-specific information is suppressed rather than made public and only limited aggregate information is released. Keeping information suppressed helps restore confidence, especially if the information might reveal what could be temporary weakness among a few banks.

During the 2007–8 financial crisis, the government (Federal Reserve System, US Treasury, and the Securities and Exchange Commission [SEC]) adopted five policy responses. First, new anonymous short-term (or temporary) lending programs were put into place, including the Term Auction Facility, the Term Securities Lending Facility, and the Primary Dealer Credit Facility. These programs were designed to make loans in secret, protecting the anonymity of borrowers in order to avoid identifying weak banks, which might then face runs. The Federal Reserve's discount window is regarded as being unable to maintain the secrecy of borrower identity. Borrowers become stigmatized if their name is revealed.[1] Second, in an attempt to prevent revelation of weak financial institutions, the SEC instituted short-sale bans on the stock of 797 financial firms starting on September 18, 2008.[2] Third, the Federal Reserve conducted stress tests on large banks and publicly summarized the results with the amount of new capital each bank needed to raise.[3] Fourth, some financial institutions were effectively bailed out, notably the investment bank Bear Stearns and the insurance company American International Group (AIG). And fifth, the Federal Reserve lowered the policy rate to near zero. These policies together with the Troubled Asset Relief Program appear to have been successful in avoiding another depression.

During a severe banking panic, the clearinghouse engaged in policies analogous to the first four policy responses mentioned above. First, there was anonymous temporary lending via clearinghouse loan certificates, which were ultimately the joint liabilities of the clearinghouse members and came into existence only during panics. Member banks could deposit specified collateral with a clearinghouse committee and receive loan certificates that could be used in the clearing process and in later panics were also handed out to the public in small denominations (from clearinghouses other than the New York Clearing House). The borrowing amounts of each bank were typically kept secret. In addition, the clearinghouse suppressed their normal requirement that member banks release balance sheet information to the press each week. Like the short-sale constraints, this suppression of information avoided revealing weak banks. The clearinghouse also conducted special examinations of banks during the suspension period (similar to the stress tests) and then announced publicly only that the bank was solvent; no details were supplied. Finally, the clearinghouse effectively organized (and funded) depositor bailouts of member banks. The clearinghouse's management of the crisis reestablished confidence in the banking system.

The panics that we will study are listed in table 1.1, which shows the National Bureau of Economic Research (NBER) recession dates, peak to trough. The shaded recessions were recessions that had a banking panic where the "panic date" is the date that the New York Clearing House authorized the issuance of clearinghouse loan certificates. The major panics were those of

TABLE 1.1. National Banking Era panics

NBER business cycle dates, peak–trough	Panic date	%Δ(C/D)	%Δ(pig iron)	Loss per deposit $	% and # of US national bank failures
Oct. 1873–Mar. 1879	Sept. 1873	14.53	−51.0	0.021	2.8 (56)
Mar. 1882–May 1885	June 1884	8.8	−14.0	0.008	0.9 (10)
Mar. 1887–Apr. 1888	No panic	3.0	−9.0	0.005	0.4 (12)
July 1890–May 1891	Nov. 1890	9.0	−34.0	0.001	0.4 (14)
Jan. 1893–June 1894	May 1893	16.0	−29.0	0.017	1.9 (74)
Dec. 1895–June 1897	Oct. 1896	14.3	−4.0	0.012	1.6 (60)
June 1899–Dec. 1900	No panic	2.78	−6.7	0.001	0.3 (12)
Sept. 1902–Aug. 1904	No panic	−4.13	−8.7	0.001	0.6 (28)
May 1907–June 1908	Oct. 1907	11.45	−46.5	0.001	0.3 (20)
Jan. 1910–Jan. 1912	No panic	−2.64	−21.7	0.0002	0.1 (10)
Jan. 1913–Dec. 1914	Aug. 1914	10.39	−47.1	0.001	0.4 (28)

Source: Gorton (1988).

1873, 1893, and 1907. The next two columns show the percentage change in the currency-deposit ratio and the percentage change in pig iron production, both measured from the panic date to the trough of the recession. The currency-deposit ratio provided a good indication of the degree of intermediation in the economy, and sharp spikes upward typically signaled depositor concerns about the health of the banking system—a "show me the money" moment. Even though these panics involved suspensions of convertibility, still the currency-deposit ratio rose quite significantly during panics. National income accounting was not yet invented, and so economic historians look at pig iron production as a measure of real economic activity. Pig iron was used to make rails for trains among other things. By this measure, it is clear that the recessions associated with panics were very severe. However, while the recessions were severe, the losses per deposit dollar, calculated by the US comptroller of the currency for nationally chartered banks, were all less than a penny except for 1873 (2 cents per dollar) and 1893 (one cent per dollar). Also, the number of banks that failed during the panics (as a percentage of the total number of banks) was very small. Evidently, although the economic downturns were severe, the costs to the banking system—once through the panic—were very small.

How could a systemic bank run occur and nearly shut down the financial system and yet afterward losses on deposits are so small and the number of banks that failed is also small? During the crisis, depositors do not know which banks will end up insolvent or, indeed, whether the banking system is insolvent. Depositors (or short-term debt holders more broadly) observe unexpected information that a recession is looming and that the financial system is at risk. The threshold for financial risk is a widely observed financial shock that unsettles depositor confidence. Fearing that their bank might default in the recession, depositors run on their banks—all banks then face the potential of enormous demands for cash. In the National Banking Era, the response in the most severe crises was for banks to (illegally) suspend or severely restrict convertibility—that is, they refused to give out cash in exchange for their deposits. There is a shortage of cash and firms cannot meet their payrolls. Taxes cannot be paid. Purchases of goods and services become difficult or impossible.

What is to be done? Faced with the crisis, the clearinghouse took the lead in *managing information*. To convince panicky depositors that the banking system was solvent, the clearinghouse focused attention on itself (essentially the banking system, in the case of the New York Clearing House Association), *suppressing* bank-specific information. During the suspension period, only aggregate information about the clearinghouse was released, in particular the reserve surplus (reserves relative to required reserves). The clearinghouse then produced some information that was made public, namely through special bank examinations (like stress tests for selected banks). And bank bailouts of individual members were part of managing the information environment and hence expectations.

There was another aspect of the information environment that is very important. At the start of the suspension period, the clearinghouse transformed (legally) into a single institution by issuing clearinghouse loan certificates and certified checks, which were the joint liabilities of the clearinghouse members. These joint liabilities implied that the clearinghouse effectively combined the member bank resources into one big bank, a kind of temporary central bank. (See Timberlake 1984; Gorton 1985; and Gorton and Mullineaux 1987.) With the aggregate asset portfolios of the member banks, the clearinghouse could be perceived as safer than any single bank member. The clearinghouse itself was a kind of club that banks could join for a fee if they satisfied certain rules. But in a panic, member banks became a single bank until the conditions of panic were gone. When most of the clearinghouse loan certificates were retired and suspension of convertibility no longer applied, then bank-specific information became public again.

Also, during panics, certified checks, claims on the clearinghouse, were used as a transaction medium. But these checks were not as good as money. This resulted in a new market opening, where these instruments traded publicly at a "currency premium," for example, to buy $1.00 of currency required $1.05 of certified checks—a 5 percent premium. These prices (the premiums) were a source of information. Beliefs about the solvency of the financial system cannot be directly measured, but the currency premiums are a good proxy for beliefs, a market price. Prices aggregate and embed information, and a financial crisis is all about information. The currency premium was a measure of systemic bank risk, excess demand for cash because of fears that the clearinghouse might be insolvent.[4] It focused attention on systemic risk, rather than individual bank risk. The premium started high and over time it (nonmonotonically) declined. Eventually, convertibility was reinstated. In short, the information environment was managed by the clearinghouse so that systemic risk was reflected in the currency premium. When that went to zero, resumption of cash payments occurred.

The clearinghouse managed information: Some information was suppressed, and some information was produced and released by the clearinghouse. And finally the market for cash opens with an information-revealing price. How does this changing mosaic of information restore confidence? It is important that bank-specific information was suppressed, as well as the release of information about the clearinghouse, now that the members combined into one big bank. And the new market for cash revealed information about the solvency of the big bank—the entire New York Clearing House membership.

We show that there was a specific timing of events and sequence of actions that led the financial markets back to normalcy. For normalcy to return, the currency premium had to become zero, reflecting the belief that the clearinghouse was solvent, with the implied probability of systemic default going from roughly 5–10 percent to zero. When the currency premium became zero, fears that the banking system was insolvent had faded. Only then does resumption of convertibility occur. The currency premium went to zero because there were observable improvements in the state of the clearinghouse. Before the premium hit zero, the reserve surplus (total clearinghouse reserves in excess of required reserves) looks healthier, partly because of gold inflows. The special bank examinations turned up no insolvent banks, and this was observable. And finally, individual bank data starts being published again, but only after a delay of about a month. Notably, the reserve surplus, which becomes negative at the start of the panic, does not have to be positive prior to resumption but merely display an upward trend. In the aftermath there were few bank failures and no losses to the clearinghouse on loan certificates.

During the Panic of 2007–8, the Federal Reserve System made public the total amount of resources it made available to the banking system, but the identities of the banks that used the emergency lending facilities were not revealed. Preventing the identification of "weak banks" put the onus on the banking system and the question of its solvency. Then the key issue was whether the Federal Reserve did, in fact, have the needed resources and the wherewithal to shore up the financial system. It was the same during the National Banking Era. When a financial crisis took place, the New York Clearing House played an analogous role for the financial market. In both cases, fighting crises was about information—having the information and managing the amount and the form in which it was released.

The New York Clearing House Association

A clearinghouse is an important part of the plumbing infrastructure of the financial system that is jointly owned by its member banks. One specific clearinghouse—the New York Clearing House Association—will be the central player in what follows. The Supreme Court of the State of Pennsylvania defined a clearinghouse as follows:

> It is an . . . ingenious device to simplify and facilitate the work of the banks in reaching an adjustment and payment of the daily balances due to and from each other at one time and in one place on each day. In practical operation it is a place where all representatives of the banks in a given city meet, and, under the supervision of a competent committee or officer selected by the associated banks, settle their accounts with each other and make or receive payment of balances and to "clear" the transactions of the day for which the settlement is made. (*Crane, Parris & Co. v. The Fourth Street National Bank*, Kress 1896, 578)

Many writers have explained clearinghouses in the following way. Imagine that there are two banks in a town. To bring some historical texture to the discussion, we use the names of banks from the past—Corn Exchange Bank and Butcher's and Drover's Bank—as the two operating example banks. In the course of daily business, many checks will be written, some on the Corn Exchange Bank and some on Butcher's and Drover's Bank. Suppose a shopkeeper receives a check written on Corn Exchange Bank, but the shopkeeper has a bank account at Butcher's and Drover's Bank. The shopkeeper need not take the check to Corn Exchange Bank to receive cash. Instead, he deposits the check in his own bank, Butcher's and Drover's Bank. Butcher's and Drover's Bank will present the check to Corn Exchange Bank for the cash, which will then be recorded as an increase in the shopkeeper's deposit account. This is "clearing." The shopkeeper's bank, Butcher's and Drover's Bank, acts as an intermediary for the shopkeeper.

On any day, the Corn Exchange Bank will hold many checks drawn on Butcher's and Drover's Bank and vice versa. One way to clear these checks held by Corn Exchange Bank and drawn on Butcher's and Drover's Bank is for Corn Exchange Bank to send a clerk, called a "walk clerk," to take the checks to Butcher's and Drover's Bank and receive or pay cash. The walk clerk has to carry money in case he needs to pay. And if he receives cash, then he returns to Corn Exchange Bank with the cash. Meanwhile Butcher's and Drover's Bank sends its own walk clerk to do the same thing. As the number of banks grows, it is clear that this quickly becomes a very cumbersome procedure. As soon as there are many banks, all the banks have to send their walk clerks to each of the other banks. And the walk clerks end up carrying large sums of money around.

You can imagine the complication that evolved. Robert Holland Martin (1910, 268–69), in an article for the National Monetary Commission in Washington, wrote:

> in consequence of the number of the London bankers this method would prove awkward, and about the year 1770 we find that the walk clerks from the city [of London] and West End banks had made a practice of meeting at lunch time at a public house [a bar] called the Five Bells in Dove court, Lombard street [where] each day after lunch a rough system of exchange of checks was carried on between the clerks from each bank, the balances being settled in notes and cash. This rough system of clearing grew to such an extent that the bankers became alarmed at the large amount of notes involved and rented a room for their clerks to meet and exchange drafts. . . . [This was] a private room at the Five Bells [tavern] . . . [and] according to a clearing book dated 1777 . . . there seem to have been 33 banks in the Clearing House.

This story, maybe apocryphal though often repeated, explains the origin of the clearinghouse.

Squire (1888, 9–14) describes the efficiency of a clearinghouse relative to each bank's sending a representative to every other bank each morning to settle accounts of the previous day:

> Each Delivery Clerk advances to the next desk [inside the clearinghouse] at which he delivers the exchanges and receipt list; each Settling Clerk upon receipt of the exchange, receipts for it, and enters it on his settling sheet opposite the name of the bank from which he received it; thus the exchanging continues until every bank has been visited, and the Delivery Clerk has returned

to the desk occupied by his bank. . . . In about ten minutes the exchanges have been made, and the Settling Clerk has entered on his settling sheet, opposite the name of the banks, the various exchanges he has received, thus having a record on his sheet, of the amount brought, and the amount received from each bank. . . . [H]e foots up the aggregate he has received from various banks, and then makes a ticket called Debit Ticket, which is sent to the Proof Clerk on the platform. . . . The differences are generally announced in about half an hour. . . . By three o'clock the settlements of the transactions are completed.

With experience, settlement evolved away from direct transfers of cash or specie between bank representatives to avoid the daily risk and expense of moving currency and coin around. Instead, the clearinghouses devised a structure to hold deposits of clearing members (clearing balances) and in exchange gave member banks the equivalent value in certificates that were claims against those cash deposits. Then banks would settle through the use of the certificates. Gibbons (1859), Squire (1888), Cannon (1910a), and Thrall (1916) provide further details of the clearing process. These certificates were different from the "clearinghouse loan certificates" issued during panics, discussed later.

The New York Clearing House Association was founded on June 6, 1854, when its constitution was adopted (see Gibbons 1859, 296–302). It was founded because the volume of transactions that used demand deposits had grown significantly, especially in large cities.[1] The number of banks in New York City had grown from twenty-four in 1849 to sixty, making the costs of clearing with walk clerks very high. The idea for the clearinghouse was not new: the first one was established in London at least as far back as 1773 (see Cannon 1910a). And Albert Gallatin had proposed one for the United States in a pamphlet in 1831, "Suggestions on the Banks and Currency of the Several States in Reference Principally to the Suspension of Specie Payments."

The statutes of the constitution evolved as the clearinghouse association learned which policies were necessary to maintain the integrity of the institution. For example, the Clearing House Committee could require any member of the New York Clearing House to submit securities "of a sufficient amount" to protect the clearinghouse membership from exchange positions of a member that might threaten it. The clearinghouse might request additional asset collateral from a member in response to a large and unanticipated payment exposure. Further learning took place in the operations of the Clearing House Loan Committees, whose establishment in emergencies preceded the issue of any clearinghouse loan certificates.[2]

The substitution of collateral, securities "of a sufficient amount," and, as we will see, financial reporting requirements for member banks represent methods to address the risk faced by each bank in the clearing process. A bank might owe a large net amount to another bank during clearing, and there was the risk that the debtor bank would be unable to make the payment. This is the essential meaning of counterparty risk—the risk that a counterparty cannot make a required payment. Member banks had the incentive to monitor each other because those net exposures could arise quickly. Further, the clearinghouse members were in the best position to monitor other members because the outsiders, market participants, were not in a position to monitor the banks' risks. The counterparty risk in the clearing process was the source of the incentives for banks to monitor each other. And the valuable reduction in walk-clerk-type costs meant that a bank did not want to be thrown out of the clearinghouse for not abiding by the rules.

We focus on New York City, the center of US finance in the nineteenth century and home to the New York Clearing House Association. Just prior to the Panic of 1873, seven New York City banks (out of fifty) held between 70 and 80 percent of all banks deposits (net banker balances) of the country (Sprague 1910, 17). According to Sprague (1910, 15), "These 7 banks were directly responsible for the satisfactory working of the credit machinery of the country." Sprague (1910, 126), citing *Annual Reports* of the US comptroller of the currency for 1889, 1890, and 1891, says that of 3,438 national banks in 1890, all but three drew drafts on banks in New York City, and the total amount of these drafts was 61.3 percent of all the drafts drawn on banks in the United States.[3] Camp (1892, 686), the manager of the New York Clearing House, relates that "It was asserted by a prominent bank president, at a meeting of the Association, during the panic of 1884, that the influence of the New York Clearing House in this country was greater than that of the Bank of England in Great Britain, and those experienced in its history accord with that opinion."

Although the New York Clearing House Association was founded in 1854 when the clearinghouse constitution was adopted, we will focus on the National Banking Era, 1863–1913. The National Banking Era was inaugurated with a series of acts of Congress, starting in 1863. The legislation established national banks that possessed the power to issue national banknotes backed by US Treasury bonds. National banknotes soon became the dominant form of transactional currency. The new system replaced the previous state-regulated banking systems, which allowed banks to issue their own private monies. Banks could continue to be chartered at the state level, but private banknotes disappeared as a result of a prohibitive tax on their issuance.

Information and the Process of Clearing Checks

Check clearing creates counterparty risk. Even though the process of clearing occurred on every business day, each bank could still accumulate an enormous volume of claims to be paid by a particular bank—say, the Corn Exchange Bank—and end up exposed to the risk that Corn Exchange Bank would not be able to honor its obligations. The fact that these obligations could be sizable for any member bank at virtually any time has very important information implications. To see the source of these risks and the related incentives, we emphasize that checks need clearing in this way.

Prior to the prevalence of demand deposits, the dominant form of bank money was privately issued banknotes. The process of clearing notes was quite different from the process of clearing checks, and the difference highlights how the increasing predominance of check payments altered the information requirements and the information mechanisms among banks and between banks and the nonbank public.

Banknotes were money printed and issued by individual banks. Banknotes were the obligation of the individual banks that printed the money. They were not linked to an individual person. A check, on the other hand, is an obligation of a person (who must have the money in a bank account) and the bank (which must have the money to transfer to the bank of the recipient of the check). Instead of clearing through banks, banknotes cleared through markets. Banknotes were not "final payment," that is, the legal satisfaction of a debt. Final payment was most often specie, typically gold. A holder of the banknote would receive gold in the amount of the banknote upon presentation at the bank of issue. Suppose the shopkeeper received a $10 banknote rather than a check. The banknote was an obligation of a bank other than the bank where the shopkeeper had an account. The shopkeeper need not deposit the note in his bank. Rather, he could sell the banknote to a note broker, who operated in the banknote market.

In the banknote market, the $10 note might not sell for $10, but for something less if the issuing bank was some distance away. It might sell for, say, $9.90, and so there would be a discount of ten cents on $10.00 or a 1.0 percent discount. This discount reflected the cost of returning the banknote to the issuing bank and the risk that the bank might not have the gold when the note broker got to the bank. Note brokers made a market in banknotes in much the same way that market makers operate today in the stock market. The note brokers traded many banknotes and had a keen awareness of the market value of the banknotes they received. In trading with many market participants, one might think that the brokers held an informational advantage over the average banknote recipient. But information about banknote discounts was readily available.

The shopkeeper would check a newspaper, a "banknote reporter," to determine the discount on the note that he was being offered. Think of it as comparable to a price-seeking application on your Internet browser. Seeing that the discount was 1.0 percent, he would sell only that amount (value of $9.90) of goods in exchange for the $10 (face value) note. The main point is that the banknote market established prices (discounts) and revealed information about the issuing bank. The note discounts were informative about the issuing bank's risk (Gorton 1996, 1999). But, while informative, this feature also made the notes difficult to use as transaction media because of disputes about their value.

In the banknote market the counterparty risk was borne by the market makers outside the banking system. The shopkeeper sold the note to the note broker and received the discounted sum. The note broker was the one who bore the risk if, upon presentation of the note, the bank failed to pay the full amount. In contrast, the clearing of demand deposits puts the counterparty risk upon the other banks, and this change in structure is important. In the check-clearing system, clearinghouse member banks had strong incentives to monitor members (mutually) and to screen new members. The potential for counterparty losses was the basis for the clearinghouse to enforce regulations like the one mentioned above in which the clearinghouse demands that a member bank submit additional securities in the event of unfavorable exchanges. It was also the basis for clearinghouse bank examinations, which we detail below.

Once checks become a preferred means of exchange, the clearing system must change. Individuals and firms do not write enough checks for brokers to make a market in the checks of one person or firm written on one bank. And checks are not typically issued in standard denominations. So checks have to be cleared in a clearinghouse. But then the informative prices, the note discounts for individual bank issues, disappear and important sources of information are lost. The market outside banks can no longer discipline banks and place higher discounts on weaker banks. The discounts are not visible and no one can detect which banks at a distant location are weaker than others. The value of bank portfolios and banks themselves as well become opaque.

Bank opacity is at the root of the role that the clearinghouse will take on, a regulatory and central-bank-like role.

Banks and Opacity

Banks create private money—short-term debt that facilitates efficient trans-actions. That is the output of banks. It is efficient for the money to be able to trade at par, that is, payments take place at full face value without discounts like those discussed with regard to private banknotes (see Gorton and Pennacchi 1990 and Dang, Gorton, and Holmström 2013). Dang, Gorton, Holmström, and Ordoñez (2012) argue that banks are optimally opaque so that the value of the debt banks produce does not fluctuate. This property of nonfluc-tuating value—fixed nominal values—is what makes bank debt most useful as money. But to maintain the value of bank debt at par, information can-not leak out about the condition of a bank. Efficient private money involves no discounts, and so there can be no disputes about relative values between monies. Because when note markets disappeared, the condition of the banks could no longer be observed there. But what about bank stock prices?

Stock prices provide information, and so sharp deviations in bank stock prices could reveal weak banks. Then discounts would arise again. Bankers during the National Banking Era also made this point. For example, one banker in 1910 commented that if the public thought of bank stocks the way they thought of the stock of nonbanks, then the resulting fluctuations in prices could cause runs on the banks (*Bankers' Magazine*, September 1910, 337). This may explain why banks paid low dividends and tended to have high stock prices (i.e., they did not split their stocks). Bank stocks then tended to be purchased by rich investors (see "Bank Stocks as Investments," *Forum*, July 1925, 6). During the National Banking Era it seems that banks endog-enously acted to make their stock prices less revealing by making their stock highly illiquid. That is, the banks themselves *suppressed* information that would be revealed from liquid bank stocks.[4]

Whatever the reason, during the National Banking Era bank stocks were "not widely traded" (see O'Sullivan 2007, 517). Bank stocks were listed on the New York Stock Exchange prior to the Civil War but afterward migrated to the over-the-counter market because they were so illiquid (see O'Sullivan 2007, 517–18). This observation is consistent with Goetzmann, Ibbotson, and Peng (2001), who collected stock price data for the period 1815–1925 for *active* stocks. Theirs is the most comprehensive set of stock prices that covers the National Banking Era. For the post–Civil War period, their data come from the *New York Times* and the *New York Herald*. Goetzmann et al. (2001, 6) write that "In 1815, the index was about evenly split between banks and in-surance companies. By the 1850s however, banks, transportation firms (pri-marily canals and railroads) and insurance companies were all about equally

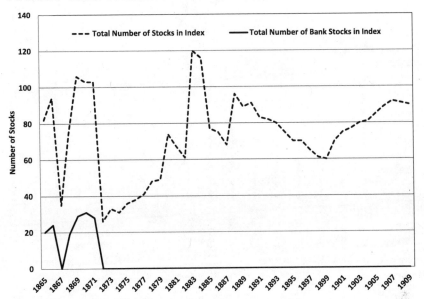

FIGURE 2.1. New York stock market, 1863–1909
Source: Data from Goetzmann et al. (2001).

common. By the end of the sample period, insurance, bank, mining and util-
ity companies had nearly disappeared from the price lists."[5]

Figure 2.1 shows the overall number of stocks in the Goetzmann et al.
stock index and the number of bank stocks. What is most striking is that
after 1872 there are *no* bank stocks in their data set. This is the same result
that O'Sullivan found. In 1885, 81 percent of the stocks traded on the New
York Stock Exchange were railroad stocks, and there were no stocks listed in
the finance, insurance, and real estate sector, according to O'Sullivan (2007,
495), as shown by data from the *Financial Review* and the *Manual of Statistics*,
a stock exchange handbook compiled by Manual of Statistics Company New
York. Banks' stocks were sometimes listed as "Stocks More Active" by, say the
New York Tribune during this period. But, taking an observation from a typical day, say May 1, 1891, the listing shows only the Western Bank, which traded
twice, and the Continental Bank, which traded once on that day.

The volumes of bank shares traded in New York were also extremely low.
For example, figure 2.2 shows that the trading volume for bank stocks relative
to the total trading volume around the Panic of 1893 was minuscule.[6] Prior
to the Civil War, it did not matter if bank stocks traded and thereby revealed
information because banknote discounts already provided similar information (see Gorton 1996, 1999). But, in order for demand deposits to trade at

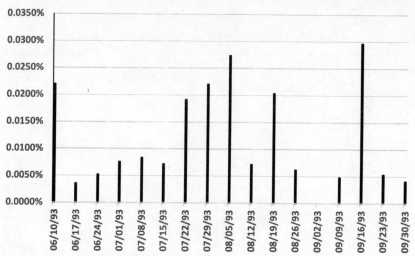

FIGURE 2.2. Panic of 1893: volume of bank shares versus volume of New York Stock Exchange shares
Source: Data from New York Stock Exchange; Goetzmann et al. (2001).

par, it was necessary that information about the perceived risk of individual banks not be revealed in the stock market.[7] The lack of informative stock prices on banks during the National Banking Era provided the appropriate degree of opacity for bank short-term debt to trade at par during normal times. The New York Clearing House Association membership, however, required information on other members in order to assess their exposure to counterparty risks.

Clearing House Bank Examinations

With opaque banks, the clearinghouse membership had incentives to monitor and examine all member banks because of the counterparty risk they faced in the clearing process. The New York Clearing House Association was empowered to examine member banks in the normal course of affairs. In the clearinghouse *Report* (1873, 16), this was stated as follows: "Any Bank in the city, worthy of public confidence, may become a regular member of the Clearing House Association, and the Banks which compose it are bound, in duty to themselves and to the public, to withhold the special support of this body from any who cannot submit to, or safely pass through the necessary examination which entitles them to credit." It is worth pointing out that right after the Panic of 1884 took hold (May 16, 1884), the power of the New York Clearing House to examine its members was made explicit in an amendment to the New York Clearing House Constitution, adopted on June 4, 1884: "The

Clearing House Committee is also empowered, whenever it shall consider it for the interest of the Association, to examine any bank member of the Association, and to require from any member securities of such an amount and character as said Committee may deem sufficient for the protection of the balances resulting from the exchanges of the Clearing House" (7). Also, Bolles (1903, 379) wrote that

> One of the most important features of the association is the examination of every bank that applies for membership and watchfulness always exercised over it after its admission. Each member has a direct interest in every other, for it does not wish to run the risk of loss in giving credit to checks of an insolvent institution. So whenever there is any reason to doubt the solvency of one of their members, an examination is made under the direction of the governing committee of the clearing-house, and the truth is ascertained. Moreover, this examination is no sham, ignorant affair, but is likely to disclose the truth. If the business of a bank is in a bad way, the committee decides on a course of action that the bank must follow, or withdraw from the clearing-house. No bank wishes to withdraw, for to do this is to set the seal of condemnation upon itself. Everyone knows what this means, that the institution is no longer worthy of credit. To withdraw under such circumstances would be essentially the same thing as to close its doors.

A description of the examination process is provided by Laughlin (1912, 178) from a report on the method of bank examination in the Chicago and St. Louis clearinghouses:

> Without notice, the examiner of his own volition, and with his assistants, enters any bank or trust company and commences his examination. All information he asks for must be given him, and all books and papers placed before him as in the case of a national or state bank examination. When the examination is completed, he makes duplicate reports, stating all the essential facts obtained in his investigation—whether the institution has the required cash on hand, the amounts of its past due paper, the amount of its bad debts, if any, the amount due by the directors as payers, endorsers or as guarantors, and the amount due by corporations in which they are interested, the value of bonds carried and whether they are carried at a sum in excess of the market value, whether the amount shown as capital, surplus and undivided profits is represented not by bad, but by good assets; in other words, whether the published statements are true, and finally, a complete statement of the bank's condition is set out, with any suggestion which, in his judgment, sound banking requires him to make.

If the bank does not comply with the recommendations of the report, then the clearinghouse can suspend or expel that bank, a fact emphasized by Gibbons (1859, 19): "The matters inquired into by the committee are, whether the capital has been actually paid in, and whether the general organization of the institution is such as to merit public confidence. If they find any cause of suspicion on these points, they report adversely to the admission of the candidate; and such is the influence of the Clearing House with the public, that this would be a serious, if not a fatal blow to its credit. On the other hand, a favorable report would give it at once an honorable standing."

The results of the clearinghouse's bank examinations were not made public, as was consistent with the information management structure (who should know what) outlined above.[8] Clearinghouse member banks should learn about the condition of their counterparties, but the public need not have information to distinguish between banks. Bolles (1903, 379): "The extent of the supervision exercised by this association over its members the public will never know, because it is best that much of it remain secret. The banks thus associated learn more about one another than they ever would if acting entirely alone, and examinations are made, and warnings given, of which the public has no knowledge. The direct interest that every bank has in knowing the true condition of every other member is one of the great merits of the system."

Banks were also examined by state and federal examiners, but Smith (1908) described the government bank examinations during this period as "defective" relative to clearinghouse examinations.

> The examiners appointed by the Government and the various states, while carrying on their work as best they can, have to labor under difficulties which can be eliminated by this new method (i.e., special examiners appointed by clearing houses), and they cannot make as thorough an examination as the clearing-house examiners. . . . Excessive loans to a firm that is borrowing from several banks, both national and state, can be discovered much better by the clearing house examiner, because he knows the relations of a borrower with the other banks. Each bank might be loaning to this firm what would be safe if he borrowed nowhere else, and in case of trouble all would lose. (177–78)

Special Bank Examinations during Normal Times

The clearinghouse also conducted special examinations of member banks when the results were needed to alleviate rumors of the bank's weakness. In December 1871, the clearinghouse initiated a special examination during normal times to address concerns about the National Bank of the Commonwealth. In the New York Clearing House *Minutes*,[9] the following entry describes the instance: "The National Bank of the Commonwealth having been drawn upon very heavily by its depositors in consequence of unfavorable rumors in circulation in regard to its condition and fearing a further run upon it—as many of the Clearing House Committee as could be immediately summoned, and the Chairman of the Clearing House met at the Bank and made an examination of its condition, the result of which was the publication in the city papers of the following morning, of this notice" (*Minutes*, December 14, 1871).

Another entry in the *Minutes* explains the examination of the Tradesmen's National Bank in November 1881:

> Owing to unfavorable rumors affecting the standing of the Tradesmen's National Bank, the Clearing House Committee met at that bank at three o'clock this day, for the purpose of making an examination of its condition.
>
> . . . and finding its capital unimpaired gave the bank a certificate as follows:
>
> > The undersigned Clearing House Committee of the New York Clearing House Association have today examined the Tradesmen's National Bank of New York and find that bank entirely sound and its capital unimpaired.
>
> This certificate was furnished to the public through the press, and at once allayed the excitement and distrust in the community. (*Minutes*, November 14, 1881)

The Clearing House committee examining the bank typically provided such a certificate to the bank so that the favorable result could be publicized. The certificate provided no details of the examination, however. The Tradesmen's National Bank example is interesting for another reason because while the details of the examination were not made public, those details might well be important. On November 19, 1881, there is this entry in the Clearing House Committee *Minutes* regarding the Tradesmen's National Bank:

> The Committee find much that met their disapproval, and after examination was complete felt it their duty to plainly state to the officer[s] of the [Tradesmen's National Bank of New York] their opinion of the weak nature of many of its assets and securities, and the impropriety and imprudence of large loans to its officers, as well as on its own stock, and on investment in stocks of a speculative character, and to warn them that if a reform did not at once take place in the general management of the bank, disaster must eventually and surely result. (*Minutes*, November 19, 1881)

Had that information been revealed publicly with terms like "impropriety" and "imprudence" associated with the Tradesmen's National Bank, the bank likely would have then become subject to a bank run. The New York Clearing House Association *Minutes* contains a number of additional examples of special examinations.[10] In general, in addition to normal examinations, the New York Clearing House Association undertook these special examinations for the purpose of credibly monitoring its membership and keeping member banks from being unnecessarily subject to unfavorable rumors. Specific examinations during nonpanic periods aimed to uncover fraud or the potential for insolvency or to verify solvency and reinforce that conclusion publicly.

Required Revelation of Member Information to the Public

While the clearinghouse did not reveal the details of its bank examinations to the public, and while bank stocks were infrequently traded and hence not informative, the clearinghouse complied with New York State law that required some bank-specific information to be made public. Gibbons (1859, 322, 325) offers the following specific information requirements:

> Each bank in the city of New York is required by law[11] to publish "on the morning of every Tuesday, in a newspaper printed in the said city, a statement under oath of the President or Cashier, showing the average amount of loans and discounts, specie, deposits, and circulation, for the next preceding week." . . .
>
> It was only when the Clearing House records were brought to such perfection as to give the means of analysis and test beyond dispute that the positive integrity of these statements guaranteed to the public.

Section 16 of the New York Clearing House Association (1903) Constitution requires that "Each bank belonging to the New York Clearing-house Association is required to furnish to the manager weekly, for publication, a statement of its condition, showing the average amount of loans and discounts, specie, legal tender notes, circulation, and deposits. The capital and net profits are also given" (Cannon 1910a, 158). With weekly information of key bank balance sheet items, the New York Clearing House had reasonably timely information about the ongoing operations of its member banks to support the conduct of day-to-day clearing activities. In addition, the clearinghouse kept a daily ledger of interbank exchanges among its membership so that they were aware when exchange balances were getting out of line.

Summary

The chapter began with a brief description of how short-term bank debt serves as the predominant means for transaction exchanges. We then described how early forms of short-term bank debt—private banknotes—got cleared with final payment media (specie) and outlined the extensive information requirements associated with clearing banknotes. Transacting with them was costly because the notes did not trade at par, and notes did not trade at par because the market for private banknotes produced information that enabled market participants (mainly note brokers) to discount the notes of the weaker banks relative to stronger banks. Private banknotes had a risk that the bank issuing the note would be unable to make payment in specie upon demand, and the holder of that risk was the bearer of the note. In most cases, the risk was borne by a note broker but sometimes it was an average person holding a note. In this setting, banks were unlikely to bear much risk as a result of another bank's inability to make payment in specie.

Bank checks became the dominant form of transaction payments at about the time when the markets that were the source of information to discriminate among banks disappeared. Private banknotes were replaced with national banknotes, which were backed by US Treasury debt collateral that was mandatory for any bank issuing currency. National banknotes of all banks traded at par as a result. Bank checking account deposits also had to trade at par for these transaction accounts to be effective forms of money, but the clearinghouse had to take into account the institutional changes that check clearing required of clearinghouse members. Bank checking accounts exposed the other banks receiving the checks to the risk that the debtor bank would fail to make its required payment. This exposure of the other clearinghouse member banks to the risk of nonrepayment is an example of counterparty risk.

The counterparty risk inherent in the nature of clearing provided the clearinghouse member banks with strong incentives to examine and monitor each other. This self-monitoring incentive is very important for the efficacy of the clearinghouse during banking panics, which we turn to next.

The Start of a Panic

In the nineteenth century, as during 2007, unusual and discomforting financial events took place, but it was difficult to know whether the distress indicated the start of a panic or reflected the effects of an ongoing panic or were merely a tempest in a teapot that would ultimately calm down—a mild recession. For the Panic of 2007–8, most observers date the start of the panic as the failure of Lehman Brothers in September 2008, although the start was actually the first or second quarter of 2007.[1] The tumultuous event of the Lehman Brothers failure was the catalyst to galvanize a consensus that the events constituted a financial crisis. Only after Lehman's failure was it widely agreed that events were dire and that congressional action was required to address them. The same problem of distinguishing between panics and moderate distress existed during the National Banking Era. In fact, observers in that era also pointed to the failure of a large financial firm as the start or cause of the panic, as with Lehman. The failure of a large financial firm is typically an effect of a panic, not the cause, but because the failure of a firm is visible, it often becomes a signal that a panic is under way. In this chapter, we explore several issues about panics and financial disturbances generally. First, it is difficult to determine the start of a panic. The New York Clearing House did not announce the suspension of convertibility. How then did a generalized bank suspension of convertibility happen? Second, what is the cause of a panic?

The events just prior to a panic are chaotic and, as events evolve, it is not initially clear whether the events are really a panic. The Panic of 1873, the first severe panic of the National Banking Era, is a good example. A front-page story called "A Financial Thunderbolt" in the *New York Tribune* of September 19, 1873, reporting on the suspension of Jay Cooke and Company in Philadelphia on September 18, 1873, wrote, "The news of the failure of Jay Cooke and Co. spreading through the country, caused much excitement. . . . [M]any of the depositors of the Union Trust Company . . . became frightened, and congregating about the paying window of the Company, demanded their money. A large amount was paid out." Is it the start of a panic? Sometimes the events are, indeed, the start of a panic. For example, two days later, September 20, 1873, the *Commercial and Financial Chronicle* wrote as follows: "The disturbances of last week on the announcement of the failure of the New York Warehouse and Security Company, which were not regarded at the time as having any general significance, have this week been followed by one of the most serious financial crises ever known in our market [the money market]. . . . [T]he excitement in Wall street and vicinity was intense, and was heightened by a run on the Fourth National Bank and the Union Trust Company" (382). The *Chronicle* made no mention of the Jay Cooke failure but mentions instead another minor failure. The conclusion that the events were "one of the most serious financial crises ever known" seems related to the bank run. And, indeed, widespread bank runs are the defining moment publicly signaling that the events are a financial crisis.

Even with some early confusion, the start of a panic is sudden and cataclysmic. For example, Sprague (1910, 33) noted: "It seems to be invariably the case that the outbreak of a crisis comes as a surprise to the business community, and the crisis of 1873 was no exception to this rule, but the astonishing suddenness of the explosion." Still, it was not easy for the New York Clearing House bankers to tell whether the events that they were observing constituted a panic. The first loan certificates were issued on September 20, 1873. But the suddenness of the onset of the panic is illustrated by the fact that on September 17, 1873, the *New York Times* reported that "Money and Stock affairs in Wall Street are again reported free of exciting rumors to the prejudicing of public confidence" (2). In contrast, the *New York Tribune* mentioned no financial difficulties in the issues of September 17 and 18, 1873, although there was a front-page story on September 18 about the defalcation of Brooklyn Trust due to "injurious loans of $804 thousand to railroad interests." In retrospect, the failure and bankruptcy of Jay Cooke and Company on September 18, 1873, should have been enough to signal a serious crisis.

A Financial Thunderbolt

Suspension of Jay Cooke and Company—A Crash in Stocks
Startling financial disaster—Failure of the Great Government Bankers of Philadelphia and their Branches in this City and Washington—The Northern Pacific Railroad Temporarily Crippled—Two other Railroads Embarrassed— Failure of Richard Schell and a Run on their Union Trust Company

New York, the financial clearing house of the Republic, was shaken yesterday by the suspension of Jay Cooke and Company, one of the most prominent banking firms in the country, and of Richard Schell and Robinson & Suydam, well-known stock brokers. The uneasiness which has been increasing in monetary circles during the past ten days culminated in a series of disasters the effects of which are already felt throughout the country. The ramifications of the business operations of Jay Cooke and Company extend to many of the principal cities of the Union; and following swiftly upon the closing of their house in this city was the suspension of the same firm doing business in Philadelphia and Washington, and of the First National Bank in that last named city. (*New York Tribune*, September 19, 1873, 1)

As in 2007–8, it was not easy to tell whether disturbing events were a fullblown financial crisis. The difficulty explains several important points. First, action by the central bank or government—in the modern era—or by the clearinghouse or the Treasury of the United States previously can be legitimately undertaken only when there is widespread agreement that the continued operation of the financial system is at stake. When events are agreed to constitute a financial crisis, the rules of debt contracts change; debt contracts are not fully enforced. As we will discuss below, this was widely true during US history from the founding through the Great Depression. But few economists were cognizant of that history and those with the historical knowledge were not directly involved in policy making, and so during 2007–8 events were much more harmful that they needed to have been, as we will explain. Finally, the New York Clearing House, which was to take the lead in fighting the crisis, never led the way by announcing a general suspension of convertibility. As events unfolded, banks would suspend one after another until there was a general suspension, but that might not have occurred. When all banks suspend nearly simultaneously, there can be no doubt that there is a crisis.

Suspension of Convertibility

Suspension of convertibility (also restrictions on convertibility or partial suspension) refers to the refusal of banks to honor their contracts with demand deposit customers. The contract requires that the banks exchange legal tender (cash) for bank debt on demand. This refusal was akin to a suspension of the payment of gold upon presentation of banknotes during the antebellum state banking era. Partial suspension was a typical response to a severe banking panic, but it is a disruptive action that increases the cost of transactions and adds doubt and concern to the financial market. Suspension was only

implemented when necessary because it was always illegal, although penal-
ties were never enforced. In fact, in the period prior to the Federal Reserve
System, suspension was often publicly welcomed in New York City as helping to calm things down. Even after the establishment of the Federal Reserve
System, President Franklin Delano Roosevelt's announcement of a banking
holiday, another type of suspension, had a similar moderating effect on the
public. The legal authority for President Roosevelt's banking holiday was
shaky at best, but the "holiday" was legalized ex post facto. Even though both
suspension of convertibility and the bank holiday were effectively illegal, this
illegality never stood in the way of their occurrence. This fact illustrates a key
observation about fighting crises: public or private agents in market economies seem to always find a way to save the financial system, whether by suspension, bank holiday, blanket guarantees of bank debt, nationalization, or
bailouts.

The New York Clearing House Association confronted the question of
when events constituted a panic, and it is the same issue faced by modern
policy makers and researchers. We define a banking panic as follows. A banking panic is an event in which bank debt holders at all or many banks in the
banking system suddenly demand that banks convert debt claims into cash
(at par) to such an extent that banks suspend convertibility of their debt into
cash or, in the case of the United States, the clearinghouse also acts to issue
clearinghouse loan certificates, a form of emergency private money that we
will discuss later. In each panic, we know the date when issuance of clearinghouse loan certificates was authorized.[2]

Suspension of convertibility was ultimately necessary in the most severe
panics because bank loans could not be sold and so banks would quickly run
out of cash to hand out to their depositors and would be declared insolvent
although, in fact (if they could survive through the turbulence), they would
turn out to be solvent (Gorton 1988). Subsequent to the panic, very few banks
were insolvent; we investigate this observation for New York Clearing House
members in chapter 9. There was no suspension of convertibility during the
Panic of 2007–8, perhaps because this timeworn custom had been forgotten. There was some discussion of suspending the use of mark-to-market
accounting because of the contagion that it caused, and that action would
have informational consequences as the fire-sale prices would devalue other
banks' assets. The suspension of mark-to-market accounting would have
suppressed information about bank assets, eliminating the contagion from
fire sales, but it did not happen., As a result, in the Panic of 2007–8, financial
firms had to sell assets, pushing prices down and getting into trouble because

the bank asset portfolios were marked to market. This is exactly what suspension was designed to prevent: the forced sale of illiquid assets. Notably, the New York Clearing House, which took the lead in fighting the crises, never announced a general suspension of convertibility. Noyes (1894, 26) wrote, "That some of the New York clearing-house banks did thus suspend cash payments, is a matter of public knowledge. No formal or concerted action, indeed, was taken by the banks." Why did the New York Clearing House never announce suspension? The clearinghouse did not know whether early suspensions of convertibility would evolve into a generalized panic or not. If the events morphed into widespread runs on many institutions, then the New York Clearing House would authorize the issuance of clearinghouse loan certificates in response to signs of panic conditions.

The chaos of financial distress events, which sometimes turn into a generalized run and sometimes do not, means that a banking panic or financial crisis is not a verifiable event. That is, it cannot be described and defined well enough to be part of a legal contract. The demand deposit contract, in principle, could have a clause that said the depositor is entitled to withdraw his money any time the bank is open except when there is a banking panic. But what definition of "banking panic" is sufficiently detailed and clear that it could be part of a legal contract? Our definition above, for example, included the phrase "all or many banks," but what does "many" mean? Two? The decision whether events were, in fact, a panic was left to the New York Clearing House. By the time the New York Clearing House authorized loan certificate issuance, it was generally clear to all that it was a panic. Further, suspension of convertibility was costly—and if the suspension became market-wide, it could cause interior correspondent banks to take actions that would in the short run add to the volatility in the markets (see Wicker 2000, 32–33; and James, McAndrews, and Weiman 2013).

The Panic of 1893 is instructive about suspension of convertibility and the actions of interior banks that made the financial crisis more severe in the short run. This panic started in the western United States, and New York banks did not face runs as the events in the West deteriorated. Still, large New York banks knew of the events in the West because of the withdrawals of cash from New York City banks by their correspondent banks in reserve city banks. Those reserve city banks were responding to withdrawals of cash by their country bank depositors. This sequence reflects the pyramidal structure of reserve balances that was legislated in the National Banking Acts. When the New York Clearing House announced that it had authorized the issuance of clearinghouse loan certificates, it was taken as confirmation of a panic.

The action of the New York Associated Banks in deciding to issue clearing house loan certificates at the request of such banks, members of the association, as shall need the same, has been at once a surprise and a cause of gratification in financial circles. Up to this time such procedure on the part of the financial institutions of the country's money center has been confined to periods of actual panic. The fact that it has been deemed advisable at this moment to make the large amount of ready cash which is ordinarily absorbed in the settlement of clearing balances between banks available in the market . . . is direct evidence of a crisis. (*Bradstreet's*, June 17, 1893, 324)

In the Panic of 1893, the clearinghouse authorized the issuance of the first loan certificates on June 16, 1893. The panic hit New York City on June 21, 1893. The *New York Times* on that day in a front-page article titled "Run on the Irving Bank" wrote, "The doors of the Irving Savings Institution, 96 Warren Street, had scarcely been thrown open yesterday morning before depositors surged up the steps, bank books in hand, bent upon withdrawing their money."

An effective definition of a panic cannot be written down in a legally enforceable way. In the absence of verifiability, the New York Clearing House was the real time agent whose actions effectively determined that the event qualified as a panic with the authorization to issue clearinghouse loan certificate and to suspend convertibility. The credibility to do this depended on a public consensus in the 1857 and 1873 panics, in which all observers could agree that the events were a panic.

According to the legal precepts of the New York State banking superintendent, suspension of convertibility was illegal; a bank could lose its charter if it did not honor its depositors' requests for cash. But the issue of nonverifiability had been addressed in 1857 the Supreme Court, New York County, New York, in *Livingston v. the Bank of New York* (26 Barb. 304). The case involved a suit by a depositor who was refused legal tender when he went to withdraw from the bank. Judge J. Roosevelt wrote, "Is such the necessary inference from suspension, no matter what the bank's assets may amount to, in cases where suspension is general, and nearly universal, throughout the State and every other section of the Union? It seems to me that it is not. . . . [I]n the very organization of such institutions . . . in case of a panic or sudden rush, the banks, although amply and clearly solvent, may not have specie enough on hand immediately to satisfy all claims" (3). In a subsequent meeting of the Supreme Court, this interpretation was upheld unanimously: "The mere fact of suspension of specie payments (when it is general) is not of itself sufficient proof of fraud or injustice" (5). We infer that the court is saying that when suspension is general then we know it is a panic, a systemic event in which demand deposit contracts are not enforced because enforcing these contracts would put the entire banking system at risk.

Two key distinctions arise from this ruling. First, there is a clear difference between one isolated refusal to honor the demand deposit contract and the suspension of convertibility that spreads system-wide. Second, it indicates an appreciation for the difficulty of distinguishing between illiquidity—"may not have specie enough on hand immediately to satisfy all claims"—and insolvency, which is the "necessary inference from suspension."

How and Why Do Panics Start?

The New York Clearing House Association observed the public events of nonfinancial firm failures, the sequence of bank suspensions, and via the clearing process, drains on bank cash holdings from the ledger books that it kept on all intraday member transactions. The association might well have observed other information not observable to us today. Whatever the association bankers observed when the issuance of clearinghouse loan certificates was authorized, it is not immediately clear that it was those events that *caused* depositors to run. Perhaps the events were a manifestation of something else. What did cause the run? What specific information became available that caused depositors to want their money? That is, what information arrived causing depositors to doubt the value of banks' loan portfolios, causing deposits to switch from being information-insensitive to being information-sensitive? This last question suggests that runs were not irrational manifestations of depositors rushing to be first in line, because if they were last in line, then they would get nothing. Not all depositors actually ran on their banks and withdrew their deposits during panics, although depositors with large balances, like correspondent banks, were often the usual suspects (see Sprague 1910).

The timing of bank runs during the National Banking Era was not random. Financial crises are an integral part of aggregate macroeconomic activity. As shown in table 1.1 in chapter 1, panics tended to start near the peak of business cycles when information has arrived forecasting a coming recession. That financial crises are part of movements in the macro economy should not be a surprise. In fact, financial crises have occurred in all market economies throughout history, in economies with and without central banks, with and without deposit insurance, in emerging and advanced economies, and so on. These events are often preceded by credit booms and are related to technological change (see Gorton and Ordoñez 2016). What causes these crises? The National Banking Era provides a good laboratory to study the link between panics and macroeconomic activity because depositors had no expectation that a central bank could act and had limited expectations the state government or an agency of the federal government such as the US Treasury would act forcefully.[3]

During the National Banking Era, a threshold event—a trigger—started the run on the banks. At a date when panic starts, new, unexpected, information arrives in the form of a leading indicator of recession: a measure of perceived risk that reaches a critical threshold. "[T]he data support the notion of a critical or threshold value of the liability of failed businesses variable, and a threshold value of the perceived risk measure, at the panic dates" (Gorton 1988, 771). "[D]uring the National Banking Era, whenever the information measure of the liabilities of failed businesses reached a 'critical' level, so did the perceptions of risk and there was a banking panic" (778).

The unexpected information about business failures was what caused depositors to become suspicious that the backing for their deposits (bank loans) were potentially in trouble. After all, banks make loans to businesses and these were failing. As a result, information-insensitive debt can become information-sensitive, especially after a credit boom. This switch from information-insensitive to information-sensitive is the crisis. In an early description of this process, Henry Cannon (*Annual Report* of the comptroller of the currency, 1884, XXXIV) described the US Panic of 1884:

> It is apparent, however, that a repetition of some of the same circumstances which brought about the monetary crisis of 1873 has been largely influential in causing the present crisis. Property of all kinds had been capitalized, as it is called; bonds and stocks had been issued for the purpose of building railroads, carrying on manufacturing and other business; municipal and other bonds had been issued for public improvements. These bonds and stocks were put upon the market, and commercial credit was extended *until a point was reached where capitalists of this and other countries questioned the intrinsic value of these securities and the earning power of the property on which they were based, and also doubted the solvency of many firms in commercial business.* This lack of confidence induced them to decline to make farther advances or investments. A decrease in the earnings of railroads, manufacturing, and other enterprises followed, and the entire business of the country has consequently been restricted and deadened. (emphasis added)

The measure of liabilities of failed businesses was a leading indicator of downturns in economic activity. The liabilities of failed businesses led peaks by one cycle phase and led troughs by two cycle phases (see Burns and Mitchell 1946). This measure of future economic activity was widely discussed in the financial press of the time. For example, *Bradstreet's*, July 1, 1893, reported:

[The f]requency of business failures and embarrassments during the past quarter of the present calendar year, as announced in many instances in daily papers, but more particularly as reported from week to week in *Bradstreet's*, has prepared the public mind to receive a report showing a large number of failures of an unusually large number of financial institutions. . . .

The total number of failures in the United States reported to *Bradstreet's* during the six months December 29, 1892, to July 28, 1893, . . . is 6,239, which marks an increase of more than 16 percent. More than the total number reported in the first half of 1891. . . . As compared with the number of failures in six months of the five years 1886 to 1890, inclusive, the total number of failures during the past months shows an increase of 15.5 per cent. (406)

Dun's Review, August 3, 1907, stated: "While the number of failures last month did not show more than the normal increase that is to be expected with the growth of the country, and fell far behind the number in July of most years, . . . the amount of liabilities [of failed commercial businesses] rose well above average, and testifies to the difficulty experienced in making half-yearly settlements" (8).

Making the same point, Henry Cannon, the comptroller of the currency, wrote in the 1884 *Annual Report* that

Owing to the large number of mercantile failures which had occurred during 1883, considerable financial uneasiness was felt at the beginning of 1884, and the year opened inauspiciously, by the appointment on January 1 of a receiver for the New York and New England Railroad. Following closely upon this failure were the troubles of the Oregon and Transcontinental Company, and the appointment on January 12 of a receiver for the North River Construction Company. The months of February, March, and April were characterized by many commercial failures, rumors affecting the credit of various corporations, and a still further depreciation in price of stocks and bonds, and in fact of all products and commodities. This feeling of uneasiness and of uncertainty as to values culminated on May 6 with the failure of the Marine National Bank of New York whose president was a member of the firm of Grant & Ward. (XXXII)

Cannon illustrates an important point. The triggering event was the failure information. This led to the failure of several companies, including Grant and Ward. This was a financial firm involving former president Ulysses S. Grant, and its failure was important because the president of Marine National Bank was a member of Grant and Ward. In all panics, there is some financial firm that fails early on. Without understanding that the trigger for the runs is the information about failures, all traditional panic narratives focus on some important firm failing at the start of each panic. The start of the panic is then attributed to that failure.[4]

It is not surprising that there should be failures of financial firms. First, nonfinancial firms are failing, and these firms have borrowed from financial firms. But there is also a second reason, explained by comptroller Cannon:

> In times of financial disaster and of a stringent money market the acts of dishonest and corrupt officials in any bank or banking firm or private corporation are more liable to be discovered, and naturally during the last year the consequences of disastrous speculation, which had been for a long period carried on with impunity with the aid of misappropriated funds, have been brought to the surface. Men who were supposed to be worthy of the entire confidence of communities, whose character stood so high that they were entrusted not only with the management of corporations, but with the investment of private funds, have now been proven to have dishonestly betrayed their trust. Never were the instances of this kind more numerous than during the financial troubles of the present year. (*Annual Report* of the comptroller of the currency, 1884, XLIX)

The traditional panic narratives—that are repeated over and over—are wrong. The trigger for the panic is the arrival of unexpected information: an increase in the liabilities of failed businesses. The failure of a financial firm is the effect, not the cause. The same mistake was made during the crisis of 2007–8. The run on sales and repurchase agreements and on asset-backed commercial paper was not observed generally because there were no lines at banks. Instead, the public saw some large firms get into trouble, like AIG and Lehman. The crisis was then attributed to these firms, not to the run.

Depositors apparently paid close attention to macroeconomic activity, because in a recession, firms fail and so banks may also fail. Even if few banks fail, still depositors generally may have held their entire life savings in a single bank, and so if the risk of bank failure were perceived to be high, depositors would run to get cash as a precautionary measure. Noyes (1901, 190–91) writes, "Experience had taught depositors that in a general collapse of credit the banks would probably be the first marks of disaster. Many of such depositors had lost their savings through bank failures in the panics of 1873 and 1884. Instinct led them, therefore, when the same financial weather-signs were visible in 1893, to get their money out of the banks and into their own possession with the least possible delay, and as a rule the legal tenders were the only form of money which they were in the habit of using."[5]

Another event that has often been cited as related to the start of panics during the National Banking Era is "seasonal stringency" of currency and credit that would be reflected in rising interest rates. Many contemporary observers noted this. For example, Kemmerer (1910) noted that the stringent periods were the "spring revival" (March, April, May) and the crop-moving period of the autumn (September, October, November). Kemmerer noted that of the five panics prior to 1910, three occurred in the autumn and two in the spring. There was no threshold effect, however. Gorton (1988) notes that there were many other dates when the short-term interest rate seasonal increases were larger than those at panic dates. The evidence does not support the idea that seasonality in interest rates was a key driver of panics.

Financial crises are rational events. In modern financial crises, bank runs usually occur later than they would have without a central bank. Depositors wait to see what will happen, and if the central bank or government is late to act or appears unwilling to act, then they run.

Summary

Financial crises are infrequent events that create havoc in both payments and capital markets, preventing the completion of transactions, leading depositors literally to panic and run from short-term debt and demand cash and nearly force the financial system to shut down. And yet it can be difficult to detect whether an event is only a temporary financial disturbance or the beginning of a horrendous financial panic. When panics began during the National Banking Era, key financial market participants faced uncertainty about whether the event was going to develop into a full-on crisis. The decisive actions of the New York Clearing House Association to calm conditions are taken as our indicators for financial panic events. When an event becomes a panic remains debatable, although the failure of a large financial institution is typically thought to be the threshold point. For 2007–8, the term "financial crisis" was used after the failure of Lehman Brothers, yet events as early as February 2007 resembled financial crises of the past, as depositors were running from short-term debt and toward cash or cash equivalents. Whatever the reason for depositors to run, or more generally, holders of short-term debt to run, something must happen to convince them that conditions in the markets have changed, so that, in fact, they believe that their money is safe in the bank. Debt holders' beliefs change from causing them to run to beliefs that cause them not to run. In what follows, we focus on what causes beliefs to change.

4

What the New York Clearing House Did during National Banking Era Panics

In this chapter, we describe how the New York Clearing House Association responded to panics in order to quell the disturbance. To a large degree, these clearinghouse actions were designed to limit bank-specific information and turn the focus of investors and depositors instead toward the release of aggregate clearinghouse information. The release of bank-specific information to the public was not entirely stopped because the clearinghouse also sometimes examined individual member banks and released simple statements about these banks to confirm continuing operations or to close them. In response to panics, the New York Clearing House became in essence an information clearinghouse for its member banks, and the manager of information releases that were deemed important for depositors and the public.

We set the start of a panic as the date of the decision by the clearinghouse to authorize the issuance of clearinghouse loan certificates. We choose this identification of panic starts because contemporary market participants knew far more about ongoing financial conditions at that time than we can uncover with limited data observations. We infer that if the New York Clearing House decided to authorize the issuance of loan certificates, such an action was sufficient to signal that there were bank runs or bank runs were thought to be imminent. Based on this decision rule, we examine five banking panics: 1873, 1884, 1890, 1893, and 1907.[1] In the panics of 1884 and 1890, the issuance of loan certificates was, apparently, by itself enough to forestall runs, leaving 1873, 1893, and 1907 as the severe panics.

In each of the five panics, the New York Clearing House took two actions — issues of clearinghouse loan certificates and the suppression of information on specific bank balance sheet items. These two actions in effect turned the

New York Clearing House into a coordinated and legally unified entity. In the most severe panics (those taking place in 1873, 1893, and 1907), the New York Clearing House banks engaged in an unofficial restriction on the convertibility of deposits into cash that in effect made deposits in banks less valuable than cash. The action was often referred to as "suspending convertibility" of deposits into cash, even though suspension was rarely complete. These three actions aimed to forestall the financial panic and generate conditions to support a financial recovery, and all can be viewed effectively through the lens of a panic as an information event.

The start of a panic is chaotic and sometimes the events do not result in widespread bank runs. When the clearinghouse authorized the issuance of loan certificates, it was sometimes coincident with suspension, but a general suspension of convertibility only happens in the most severe panics.[2] In all five panics during the National Banking Era the temporary suppression of bank-specific information took place roughly coincident with the authorization of loan certificate issuance.

The suppression of individual bank information prevents the public from reading adverse information on a specific bank's balance sheet and choosing to run on that bank. Only the balance sheet totals of the entire New York Clearing House banking system were published during suspension periods. Clearinghouse loan certificate issues were both issued by the clearinghouse (i.e., the membership) and accepted as final payment by the clearinghouse membership.[3] The decision to issue this form of liquidity and aggregate dollar amounts—the amount to be issued as well as the amount outstanding—were typically announced in newspaper articles. In contrast, the identity of borrowers was usually kept secret akin to the suppression of bank-specific information. These two actions combined to legally make the New York Clearing House into a single institution. Individual bank information was held within the New York Clearing House, which included the requests for clearinghouse loan certificates and the distribution of them among banks. This allocation of information was in line with the "single entity" theme. In an indirect way, the "suspension of convertibility," often associated with a currency premium, was also consistent with the New York Clearing House as the coordinating entity. This single entity was "priced" by the currency premium. The premiums can be interpreted as partly an estimate of the probability that the New York Clearing House (that is, the entire membership) would fail. In chapter 7, we discuss in greater detail the premium on currency relative to an alternative substitute.

Background

In this chapter, we examine the actions of the New York Clearing House during National Banking Era panics, that is, those that took place after the passage of the National Banking Acts of 1863 and 1864. In the 1857 and 1860 panics, the New York Clearing House was just learning about its ability to combat financial crises.[4] Those panics are interesting in their own right, but for our purposes, the experience of those two panics led to the invention of clearinghouse loan certificates, discussed below, which helped to increase bank liquidity, as well as banking system liquidity, temporarily.

New York Clearing House banks were essential participants in a general suspension of payments, although suspensions were never announced by the New York Clearing House or by banks in general. Instead, suspensions were observed by financial market participants and economic journalists and publicized in newspapers and banking trade publications. In 1857, suspension meant the suspension of gold payments by banks in exchange for their banknotes, which was illegal at the time and could result in bank closure by the New York State superintendent of banking. But during panics, as we have discussed, general suspensions were tolerated. A suspension of gold payments had the effect of breaking the nominal parity (the fixed exchange rate) between paper currency and gold—just like breaking the parity between deposits and currency during the National Banking Era. We will talk further about how breaking the parity generates a premium for the scarce currency in chapter 7.

The National Banking Acts changed some institutional structures, yet financial panics were associated with similar events during the periods before and after passage of the acts. One characteristic condition prior to a panic was a shortage of gold (relative to loans and deposits) in New York City banks. In the terms used then as well as today, New York City banks might be "illiquid" if interior banks (a key source of New York City bank deposits) made a substantial (but not necessarily panic-sized) withdrawals of deposits. Shortages of cash and specie along with unusually large withdrawals often surrounded the start of panics. Those unusual large withdrawals may also come at a time of the failure of an interconnected or relatively large financial institution in New York City or with a large presence in the market, exacerbating the situation.

Contemporary economists[5] during the post–Civil War era thought financial crises and panics were signs of the inherent flaws of the national banking system. The system lacked a central bank, had no reliable way to expand the currency supply quickly to satisfy increases in the demand for cash, and was

unable to expand credit quickly or to get cash transported to interior banks
effectively during the crop-moving season (autumn). The conventional wisdom saw "the system" as the source of conditions that gave rise to banking
panics and the perceived key flaw was the inability of the banking system to
expand cash and credit supply to satisfy credit demand during the seasonal
fluctuations. But this cannot be the central element, because panics occur in
many different types of banking systems, including the United States after the
establishment of the Federal Reserve System.

Banks in the interior of the country held deposits at New York City correspondent national banks as a portion of their required reserves as permitted
by the National Banking Acts. Although it was controversial, New York City
national banks offered interest on deposits from their interior correspondent
banks, motivating interior banks to hold a substantial portion of their reserve balances in that form. New York City banks parked a large percentage of
these funds in short-term assets, such as callable loans on the New York Stock
Exchange so that they could be readily available if interior banks withdrew
them on short notice. For most normal times, deposit balances from interior
banks held at New York City correspondent banks were used to facilitate in-
terregional and international trade. In this structure, the New York Clearing
House member banks were effectively the clearinghouse for the entire country (see James and Weiman 2010).

Cash demands from the interior of the country increased during crop-
moving season, and those cash demands drained cash out of New York City
in order to finance the shipment of produce during harvest season.[6] New
York City banks held a large proportion of deposits from banks in the interior
of the country and the cash drain from the New York City money market
produced a seasonal increase in New York City interest rates in the autumn.
As a result, some of the cash that would otherwise have flowed to the interior
was retained in New York City. Think of this as New York City financial markets signaling to the interior banks that it would pay a higher interest rate as
a way to keep cash in the New York City banking system.

During a panic, the typical flow of cash back toward New York City would
not occur, and in fact the flow of currency from New York City toward the
interior banks—the seasonal cash flow—would magnify to volumes many
times larger than normal. In these cases, the panic magnified the seasonal
interest rate spike because the normal small "demand-based" increase was
augmented by concerns about the solvency of the banking system and an associated risk premium, and the interest rate shot way up. Then interior banks
would remove their deposit balances in New York City in the form of cash
and ship it to their interior locations to avoid the possibility that their funds

in a New York City bank would be locked up in a suspension, or lost in a failure. Cash withdrawals by interior (or country) banks from New York City banks were the main culprits in the depletion of cash balances among New York Clearing House banks in 1873 and in 1907.[7] The contrast between the nonpanic periods of seasonal cash flows and the panic cash flows is striking.

During banking panics, a sharp increase in the demand for cash makes sense, but modern readers—until 2007–8—rarely thought about systemic bank failures as a real possibility. Today, even if a bank fails, there is deposit insurance. Back then, there was no deposit insurance, and so being confident about the condition of the bank holding your deposits was important. During the National Banking Era, depositors might run on their bank if there was a reasonable chance of a suspension of convertibility of deposits into cash, even if their bank was solvent and liquid. When cash demand increased, the ratio of cash to bank deposits rose notably (cash rose and deposits fell), which is called "cash hoarding." Financial market volatility—larger fluctuations than usual in securities prices and returns—rose dramatically, and credit was typically unavailable. The drain of cash from New York City intermediaries and the lack of liquidity (or credit) on the call loan money market were the unambiguous signs of financial distress in National Banking Era financial panics.[8]

During its history, the New York Clearing House evolved to become the operational center for organizing banking interests to combat the financial panic. The two clearinghouse actions—suppression of bank-specific information and issuance of clearinghouse loan certificates—aimed to combat the drain of cash reserves from its member banks, the first by limiting the ability of depositors to identify weak banks, and the second by temporarily expanding liquidity available to the membership. Suspension of convertibility also occurred, but, as discussed in chapter 3, it was not officially organized by the clearinghouse. Bankers generally had an aversion to imposing suspension, but it was sometimes unavoidable. In 1873 New York Clearing House banks held legal tender reserves relative to deposits that were insufficient to satisfy interior demands once the panic struck (see Sprague 1910; Wicker 2000; and Friedman and Schwartz 1963). Even with a suspension, legal tender reserves fell from a high of $33.8 million on September 20, 1873, to a nadir of $5.8 million on October 14, 1873.[9] Even though the net deposits of those banks fell to around $160 million in October, bank cash was far below the required reserve ratio of 25 percent.

Suspensions periods are more accurately called partial suspensions or partial restrictions on payments, because some currency would be available to depositors, but there were obvious limits. In most transactions during the National Banking Era, there was a standard fixed exchange rate (at par) between currency and deposits.[10] In suspensions, that par value fixed exchange rate would be negated. The purpose of suspension was to limit the drain of cash reserves out of the banking system and, as a result, the available supply of cash would not match the demand for cash, and so the excess demand for cash would produce a currency premium. More about this will be discussed in chapter 7.

Issuing Loan Certificates and the Change in
the Organizational Form of the Clearinghouse

Among the innovative measures that the clearinghouse used to combat panics, clearinghouse loan certificates have an interesting legacy. The clearinghouse loan certificate issues were authorized by the clearinghouse when widespread runs had already happened or were expected to occur.[11] The logic of loan certificates was that they could economize on the use of cash among the banks in the clearing process.

The design of discount window lending at the Federal Reserve Banks is akin to the arrangements undertaken for clearinghouse loan certificate issues of the New York Clearing House. Unlike discount window loans, the mechanism to issue clearinghouse loan certificates was not a standing function. The New York Clearing House Executive Committee would meet and agree to create a Clearing House Loan Committee and, at least initially, set out a total dollar amount of clearinghouse loan certificates to issue. The issues were typically given ample headline space during panics and were on occasion described with upbeat pronouncements in the press. From our perspective, these issues were the catalyst for many of the most effective actions that were taken by the member banks to combat the crises.

Clearinghouse loan certificates were liabilities of the individual borrowing banks, but their repayment was effectively guaranteed by the clearinghouse membership jointly.[12] Because the clearinghouse loan certificates were ultimately liabilities of the membership jointly their issuance signaled that the clearing members were binding themselves into a single institution. This was a remarkable process, of turning individual privately owned banks into a single large bank.[13]

The details of the role that clearinghouse loan certificates performed for banks and the process to issue them is important, and so we spell them out here. The New York Clearing House issued clearinghouse loan certificates— the temporary form of liquidity that was invented to produce "near reserves" for clearinghouse member banks—that were to be used to settle balances between member banks at the clearinghouse. In these wholesale transactions, clearinghouse loan certificates were substitutes for legal tender and specie (gold) that was typically used to clear for final payment transactions between banks. In order to ensure acceptance of these liabilities "at par," the holder of the clearinghouse loan certificate received a payment of interest, about which we will have more to discuss later. In addition, the New York Clearing House insisted that all members be required to accept them as a form of final payment, and the clearinghouse provided mechanisms to ensure accountability.

The clearinghouse loan certificates were issued to borrowing banks, and the certificate would have the name of the borrowing bank prominently displayed on the certificate. At the same time, the repayment of certificates was effectively guaranteed by the New York Clearing House. There is a good reason for this unusual arrangement of accountability. The purpose of a clearinghouse loan certificate was to substitute for a means of final payment—one that had unquestioned and uniform acceptability. According to Curtis (1898, 253), "During the financial storm the . . . bank will pay its balance by means of loan certificates." Two things were arranged in advance. First, that member banks in the New York Clearing House must accept clearinghouse loan certificates in lieu of specie or legal tender, and further, that unpaid or unfulfilled clearinghouse loan certificates at termination would be paid by the New York Clearing House, which would charge banks by their proportional share of capital and surplus of the aggregate among the member banks. The latter condition provided the guarantee of payment and the former restriction guaranteed that clearinghouse loan certificates would be accepted as a final payment medium. As a result, clearinghouse loan certificates were a liability that could transfer between banks because the clearinghouse enforced their acceptability and ensured their repayment.

The implicit guarantee on clearinghouse loan certificates was explicit to the membership to the New York Clearing House. When the banks became members of the New York Clearing House, they agreed with the enforced acceptability of clearinghouse loan certificates for payment as well as the pro rata sharing of the possible losses from unpaid clearinghouse loan certificates. To keep losses to a minimum, the New York Clearing House would, through the Clearing House Loan Committee, manage and monitor the loans. The committee of four or five representatives from New York Clearing House banks would monitor the value of committed collateral supporting clearinghouse loan certificates. Like the present-day discount window or primary credit loans from the Federal Reserve Banks, clearinghouse loan certificates were collateralized loans. The composition of the collateral, though, was very different in the National Banking Era from what it is today.

The collateral posted for clearinghouse loan certificates was mostly commercial paper or commercial loans that had relatively short-term maturities. Loan certificates were issued subject to the approval of the Clearing House Loan Committee and subject to approved collateral with at least a 25 percent "haircut" on the fair market value of the collateral. The exact phrasing in the New York Clearing House resolution stated that the clearinghouse loan certificate issues "shall not exceed 75 percent of the market value of the collateral" put forward. Haircuts on the value of the collateral could vary; for example, there was a small haircut on high-quality government bonds, whereas there was a 25 percent haircut on commercial paper collateral. The haircut amounts varied with the form of collateral provided as well as the amount (and frequency) of clearinghouse loan certificates requested. The New York Clearing House would often request substitute collateral for clearinghouse loan certificates if the initial collateral was perceived as insufficient, or if that collateral was maturing. We cannot rule out the possibility that the financial condition of the borrower, as perceived by the Clearing House Loan Committee, was also relevant. The goal of collateral and steep haircuts on it was to ensure that the banks had sufficient incentive to make a full payment. That comes about because if the borrowing bank cannot fully repay the clearinghouse loan certificates, the lender (the New York Clearing House) had the right to take full possession of the collateral and liquidate it to extract the full repayment of the loan.

Minimizing losses to the New York Clearing House was not the main goal of the Clearing House Loan Committee—their main goal was to issue sufficient liquidity to the member banks to alleviate the financial stress of a banking panic. The Clearing House Loan Committee relied on the member banks to be willing to borrow with clearinghouse loan certificates, and although announcements of the New York Clearing House decision to issue clearinghouse loan certificates was public and publicized, only on a few occasions was the identity and amount of specific clearinghouse loan certificate issues ever made public (see the discussion below).

Like the discount window of Federal Reserve Banks, opening up the process for issuing clearinghouse loan certificates required banks to borrow that liquidity. The secrecy of clearinghouse loan certificate issues was important to ensure that member banks would borrow the needed temporary liquidity. Otherwise they would be perceived as weak and would have to face future high costs of borrowing even if they survived the panic. The modern concern about stigma comes from a perception that banks borrowing from the discount window are banks in trouble and that somehow that information would leak out to other banks and the public. Such a stigma likely would have been relevant in the National Banking Era. Modern banks, however, do not have the option to suspend convertibility of deposits into cash, which we have mentioned was the other potent tool for combating crises. Those panics without suspensions, however, show that when the identity of the borrower was revealed (as in 1890), it did not bode well for that bank.

The Clearing House Special Committee of Five, June 16, 1884 (Clearing House Committee *Minutes*, 1878–85, 158) stated,

> Resolved: That the experiences of the associated banks in the New York Clearing House during the recent panic, having again shown that every member of the Association, in a time of general and serious financial disturbance, is involuntarily compelled to make common cause with every other member in the risk attending any practical expedient for general relief, or any effective combination for the public good: it is therefore proper and necessary to enquire whether the methods of business, as conducted by the several members of the Association, are uniform and correct in their operation with the public and equitable to all banks which are thus bound together in the Clearing House.

To issue clearinghouse loan certificates, the membership of the clearinghouse had to vote, essentially voting on whether the crisis was significant enough to warrant their use. For example, The *New York Times* reported that "A special meeting of the Clearinghouse Association began at 1:30 pm. After meeting for more than an hour, the members unanimously adopted a resolution to issue loan certificates. This action brought a 'perceptible feeling of relief' to Wall Street" ("On the Verge of a Panic," *New York Times*, May 15, 1884, 1).

Similarly, in 1890: "The NY Clearing House 'recognized the critical situation' on the afternoon of Tuesday, November 11, and authorized a resolution to issue loan certificates after the Bank of North America (a clearing house member) was short $900,000 at the clearing house because of large advances made to Decker Howell, a brokerage firm that suspended earlier in the day. In total, three firms failed and three banks were unable to meet their clearinghouse obligations" (*Commercial and Financial Chronicle*, November 15, 1890, 667; also see "Firms Fail, Banks Shaken," *New York Times*, November 12, 1890, 1).

Consistent with the information blackout that we discuss further below, the distribution of loan certificate issuance among banks was kept secret in the most severe crises. For example, although the Clearing House Committee did not meet, the "Law" committee issued more than a million dollars in loan certificates. Some of the larger banks (on occasion) had a tacit understanding that they would apply for loan certificates, even though they did not need them, in order to "remove the suspicion that there was any confession of weakness in asking for them" (*New York Times*, November 18, 1890, 1).[14] And the next day the *Times* reported that "The fact remains that nearly every bank is very sensitive about it and that the members of the Clearing House Association consider themselves honor bound not to mention the name of any bank that may thus have sought to protect itself against troubles" (*New York Times*, November 19, 1890, 5). Unfortunately, such behavior was not entirely consistent because the *New York Times* reported on November 13, 1890, that a syndicate of banks extended loans to the Bank of North America, which then borrowed $900,000 in clearinghouse loan certificates to repay those loans. The article also revealed the identity of Mechanics' and Traders' Bank as a borrower of clearinghouse loan certificates. But 1890 was considered a well-managed panic. (See Sprague 1910 and Wicker 2000.)

Cannon also later noted that "Attempts on the part of the business community were made in vain to discover what banks had taken out certificates, but such information was very wisely withheld. For more than two months [during the Panic of 1873], covering the worst period of the panic, no weekly statements of their condition were made to [by] the clearing-house banks, the object being to prevent general knowledge of the weak condition of some of the members, which, if disclosed, would invite runs upon them" (1910a, 86). Outstanding clearinghouse loan certificates (circulating outside the requesting bank) accrued an interest charge to be paid by the banks that initially took them out from the New York Clearing House. In New York, the interest rate on loan certificates was 7 percent in 1873; 6 percent in 1884, 6.25 for thirty days; 6 percent in 1893; and 6 percent in 1907. Curtis (1898, 255) wrote, "Bearing a substantial rate of interest, a policy of speedy retirement was of course followed by the banks for whom they were issued. Self-interest dictated a short term of existence for the certificates, which have seldom been outstanding for more than four or five months at a time." The interest rates on clearinghouse loan certificates were about the same as the market rates for commercial paper, but the haircut on collateral can be considered as part of the cost. The collateral got a bank up to 75 percent of the collateral value in terms of liquidity. Then an interest rate charge of 6 percent on $75 generated a cash outflow that would be covered by the interest on the $100 collateral of 4.5 percent.[15]

Figure 4.1 shows the maximum amounts of loan certificates outstanding during each period of loan certificate issue and the duration for which there were certificates outstanding. For scaling purposes, we take these amounts relative to the average reserve holdings for the previous two years for the aggregate of New York Clearing House member banks. Three notable features distinguish the severe panics (1873, 1893, and 1907) from the incipient panics (1884 and 1890). First, the duration of outstanding clearinghouse loan certificates is much longer, nearly twice the duration of the other two (the extended

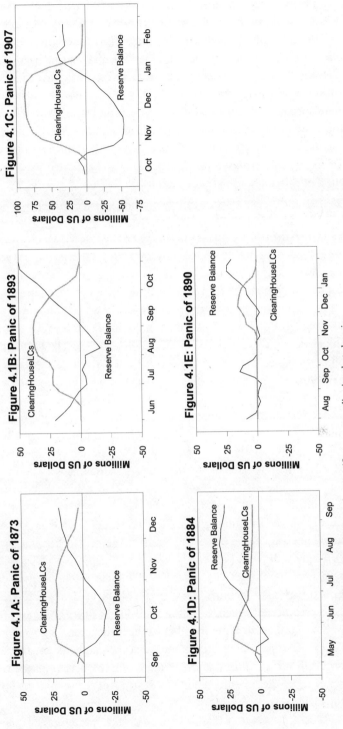

FIGURE 4.1. Reserve surplus versus clearinghouse loan certificates outstanding in selected panics
Source: Data from Andrew (1910) and Clearing House Loan Committee minutes (various dates), New York Clearing House Association Archives.

duration of 1884 reflects the outstanding balance of Metropolitan National Bank, which required nearly two years to settle). Second, and related to the first point, the outstanding balances of clearinghouse loan certificates in 1884 and 1890 reached a peak fairly quickly and then the outstanding balances declined relatively steadily, whereas for the more severe panics, clearinghouse loan certificates persist longer near their maximum amount outstanding. Third, there appears to be an association between the imposition of suspension of convertibility and the duration of clearinghouse loan certificate issues. In 1893 the issues of clearinghouse loan certificates spiked upward after early August when suspension was imposed, extending and apparently expanding the duration of clearinghouse loan certificates.

Panels A–E show the certificates outstanding as well as the reserve surplus. Except for the Panic of 1890, there is a clear pattern. Loan certificates were issued when the reserve surplus declined. So the reserve deficit and loan certificates outstanding are mirror opposites of each other. As reserves decline from runs, the clearinghouse issues loan certificates to economize on cash. The figures dramatically show the purpose of loan certificates.

In a report to the New York Clearing House after the Panic of 1907 (Special Report to the Clearing House Committee, n.d., unpag., New York Clearing House Association Archives), a table titled "Division of Collateral Originally Deposited against Clearing House Loan Certificates" distinguished between only two categories of collateral—Bills Receivable and Securities. For the aggregate amount of clearinghouse loan certificates issued ($101 million), bills receivable provided $107.6 million of the collateral, and securities comprised $44.1 million of the collateral. The total amount of collateral originally offered was $151.7 million, indicating that the average haircut on collateral value was slightly less than 35 percent. In the Clearing House Loan Committee minutes, certain banks (those in distress) were either willing to post more collateral in anticipation of needing more clearinghouse loan certificates in the near future or were required by the Clearing House Loan Committee to post collateral in excess of the standard haircut (25 percent) when borrowing amounts on a given day.

Additional collateral could be called for if the clearinghouse was concerned about a particular member. For example, "The Clearing-house committee is also empowered, whenever it shall consider it for the interest of the association, to examine any bank member of the association, and to require from any member securities of such an amount and character as said committee may deem sufficient for the protection of the balances resulting from the exchanges at the Clearing-house" ("The Storm Not Yet Spent," *New York Times*, May 16, 1884, 1).

Alexander Gilbert, president of the New York Clearing House Association, said in an interview "that the association had resorted to the issue of loan certificates on nine different occasions, the total certificates issued amounting to $260,000,000. Seventy-two per cent of the collateral was commercial paper and only twenty-eight per cent other securities. Not a dollar has been lost in connection with these transactions" (editorial, "A Menace to American Prosperity," *Bankers' Magazine* 76 [April 1908]: 479–80).

The New York Clearing House did not necessarily coordinate the timing of the two actions—clearinghouse loan certificates and informal suspension. For most of the financial crises, the New York Clearing House made the decision to issue clearinghouse loan certificates separately from the occurrence of generalized suspension, probably because suspensions were perceived as costly and imposed a breakdown in intermediation across regions that could ultimately slow down commerce. In addition, in the two panics that had no widespread suspension, clearinghouse loan certificates appeared to be sufficient to quell the panic. As a result, during most National Banking Era panics, clearinghouse loan certificates were issued before a general suspension took hold. In contrast, the Panic of 1907 was one time when these two means to combat panics were implemented simultaneously, and relatively late—essentially after the panic was in full force.

The Suppression of Bank-Specific Information

In every panic, the New York Clearing House not only issued clearinghouse loan certificates but also suppressed bank-specific information. As emphasized in chapter 2, New York State law mandated that the clearinghouse make public the balance sheet information of its members every week. Despite the law, the New York Clearing House cut off full publication of bank-specific numbers in order to prevent weak members from facing runs. In compliance with the law, the New York Clearing House accumulated the bank-specific information and published in the newspaper only the aggregates of the required data (net deposits, loans, specie and legal tender, capital and surplus, circulation, and total assets). The New York Clearing House expressed that the intent of the aggregate-only publication was to "prevent misunderstanding" of what might be unusual rearrangements of balances that arise as a result of clearinghouse loan certificate issues (see the quote from Tappan below). That is, there was no simple way to account for accumulations of clearinghouse loan certificates from the clearing activity instead of cash or legal tender, and it may have appeared that a given bank might be running out of cash balances when it was simply accumulating clearinghouse loan certificates. In addition, given that the interest paid on clearinghouse loan certificates was paid by the borrower to the bank holding the certificates, the accumulation of clearinghouse loan certificates may have been profitable in some situations.

From our perspective, cutting off bank-specific information upon issuance of loan certificates was intentional. By issuing clearinghouse loan certificates—a bank liability effectively guaranteed by the membership of the New York Clearing House—the member banks essentially combined into a single legal entity. Furthermore, weak banks were protected because they could not be identified. So the banking system would not unravel sequentially with the weakest bank being run on, and then the next weakest, and so on. Therefore, the intention to suppress bank-specific information was also practical: by reducing the likelihood of runs on banks that might be perceived as weak, the New York Clearing House generally benefited because it then reduced the dollar amount of loans that it would likely have to issue to support those banks if available information enabled depositors to identify the banks perceived as weak.

Curtis (1898, 260), with reference to the Panic of 1873, reported that "No weekly Clearing House statement of the condition of each bank was made from Sept. 22nd to Dec. 8th, as it was deemed inadvisable to call attention to the weak condition of any bank and so precipitate a run on it." And the *New York Times*, October 6, 1873, 2, stated, "The Bank Clearing-house has ordered the discontinuance of the Weekly Bank Averages until the return to Greenback payment. It is deemed proper and advisable, while the hybrid expedient of Clearing-house Certificates for settling their daily clearance is needful to be continued, to attempt Weekly Averages in the usual way. The Banks are now acting as a single corporation."

In each panic, it was announced that this cutoff of information would occur. For example, Sprague (1910, 16) wrote, "but these [weekly clearinghouse] statements for the individual banks were discontinued during the crisis of 1873." And on Saturday, May 24, 1884, Chairman Tappan of the Clearing House Loan Committee announced the halting of the detailed weekly bank statement: "The issue of loan certificates by the Clearing-house Association has so changed the relations of the banks to each other that the publication of the statement in detail would give an incorrect impression as to the actual condition of the banks" ("Not a Good Bank Showing," *New York Times*, May 25, 1884, 3).

The suppression of individual bank information lasted only one week in 1884. Further, the release of individual bank information on June 7, 1884, showed that Metropolitan National Bank had net deposits of $1.44 million, in contrast to its net deposits of $8.42 million on May 10, 1884 (data taken from the weekly statements, *Commercial and Financial Chronicle Bankers Gazette*). The banking crisis in 1884 was focused on the Metropolitan National Bank, which made it different from the more general and severe crises. (See chapter 7.)

According to the New York Clearing House Association *Minutes* for November 20, 1890, 2:00 p.m., the association voted to "discontinue the publication of the details of weekly reports." Similar instances took place in 1893 and 1907, and the release of individual bank information was among the last things to be restored. The New York Clearing House held tight control over information on its members and violated the legal requirement to release weekly details at times to prevent the release of bank-specific information in a panic. Some useful laws in normal times are problematic during panics, and so it is unsurprising that legal recourse was rarely sought.

The authorization of the issuance of loan certificates was public and this, in itself, was viewed as a positive informational event. The *New York Times* on September 20, 1873, announced that the New York Clearing House was to issue $10 million in clearinghouse loan certificates. In a sequence of articles in newspapers in 1893, the public was informed of the total volume of clearinghouse loan certificates borrowed by the New York Clearing House banks during the panic. This was also the case in 1873 and 1907; the amounts borrowed by individual member banks were not made public.

The Panics of 1884 and 1890

In the panics of 1884 and 1890, there was no suspension of convertibility. Wicker (2000) calls these episodes "incipient" panics. The New York Clearing House did stop publishing bank-specific information at these times, but in 1884 it suppressed the information only for the week of May 24. Clearinghouse loan certificates were authorized and issued in each of these panics. As is clear in figure 4.1, panels B and C, the reserve deficit (relative to required reserves) in 1884 and 1890 was brief and shallow. In both periods, the issuance of clearinghouse loan certificates aimed to assist specific institutions, rather than address a general situation (Sprague 1910, 143). In this sense, these two instances of financial distress appear more akin to a localized bank run than a widespread banking panic. Still, the actions of the New York Clearing House appear to have alleviated the need for a suspension of convertibility. According to Sprague (1910, 108), the 1884 panic was mostly confined to New York. Philadelphia newspapers made no mention of problems there, for example, but Bluedorn and Park (2015) find evidence of a response by Pennsylvania state banks.

Above we discussed the problems of the Metropolitan National Bank during the Panic of 1884. The *Annual Report* of the comptroller of the currency (1884, 33–34) stated,

> After consultation with the officers and directors of the Metropolitan National Bank a committee of examination was appointed to visit the bank and ascertain if some plan could not be arranged to permit it to open again for business. The greater part of the securities of the bank were found to be of such a character that loan certificates could safely be issued upon them, and in this way the Metropolitan National was enabled to resume business on May 15 and settle its balances at the clearing house. The prompt action of members of the associated banks and the resumption of the Metropolitan National Bank greatly assisted in allaying excitement and staying the panic, and although confidence was not immediately restored . . . there was no suspension . . . and the issue of loan certificates was confined to the banks of New York City, which were soon enabled to collect their loans and make good their reserves.

It was clear that in 1884 the Metropolitan National Bank was important enough to the correspondent system that the New York Clearing House would aid it, and we see that perspective in the views expressed by contemporaries. George S. Coe, president of the American Exchange Bank and participant in the committee to examine Metropolitan National Bank, wrote in a speech given in June 4, 1884, "When we examined its books, this most important fact at once appeared: that it owed some eight to nine millions of deposits, a large proportion of which consisted of reserves of interior banks, which could not be imperiled or locked up for another day without producing a further calamity of wide-spread dimension throughout the country" (from Sprague 1910, 372). One key distinction of the 1884 panic is that one institution, Metropolitan National Bank, took out nearly one-third of the total clearinghouse loan certificates issued. What is somewhat surprising, however, is that the Metropolitan National Bank lost such a large proportion of its deposits so quickly (dropping from $7.4 million to $1.7 million in the span of two weeks—May 17 to May 31, 1884). The New York Clearing House suppressed the release of bank-specific information for only one week. Then the public became aware of the large ($5.6 million) deposit withdrawals from Metropolitan National Bank upon release of the standard weekly balance sheet for May 31 (see *New York Tribune*, June 2, 1884, 4). The condition of Metropolitan National Bank by that time was readily apparent and was the subject of newspaper articles that, unlike the comptroller's *Annual Report*, suggested that the bank faced unusual challenges and the "remarkable shifting of accounts during the two weeks of excitement and disaster." Interior banks may have removed deposits from their correspondent bank in New York City (Metropolitan National) and likely moved those deposits to another New York City correspondent bank. There was no widespread and persistent draining of reserves from New York City banks in the aggregate. Bluedorn and Park (2015, 1) argue "that bailouts of [systemically important banks] by the New York Clearing House likely short-circuited a full-scale banking panic."

In the case of 1890, clearinghouse loan certificates were issued at an earlier point in the crisis, before there were many runs. Actions by the US Treasury over the summer had in fact delayed the onset of monetary stringency in 1890. The actions the US Treasury took from July through September 1890 added nearly $70 million to the net money in circulation. The actions in September alone added over $55 million.[16]

Sprague (1910, 142–43) speculated that the loan certificates were issued promptly because of news about troubles in London related to Barings. In the case of 1890, three clearinghouse members had problems: the North River Bank, the Bank of North America, and the Mechanics' and Traders' Bank. These three banks received clearinghouse loan certificates. Sprague wrote, "The prompt action taken by the clearing-house authorities did much to prevent the spread of panic" (142).

Suspension of Convertibility

Suspension of convertibility means that banks refuse to honor their debt contracts, that is, they refuse to exchange currency for demand deposits. During the National Banking Era panics, suspension of convertibility was never organized and announced by the clearinghouse.[17] It was also never legal, but the prohibition on suspension was not enforced (see Gorton 2012).

Noyes (1894) describes how banking conditions in 1893 deteriorated and led to the suspension of convertibility in New York City. The New York City banks were running out of cash after repeated shipments of cash to western correspondents and could use only clearinghouse loan certificates to settle debit balances at the clearinghouse. "[A] number of banks adopted the extreme measure of refusing to pay cash for the checks of their own depositors"; "the number of city banks refusing to cash depositors' checks had grown so considerably that well-known money-brokers advertised in daily papers that they would pay in certified bank checks a premium for cash." This description of how suspension arose may explain why we have been unable to find explicit declarations of suspensions of convertibility by the New York Clearing House—the market for cash forms in response to the circumstances as more and more banks impose a suspension.

The relationship between the dates of suspension of convertibility and the issue of clearinghouse loan certificates varies across the three panics. In two cases (1873 and 1907), the two events were basically coincident. In 1893, issuance started before suspension. In 1884 and 1890, issuance seems to have prevented the need for suspension.

Once one or more large banks suspend convertibility, all the other banks are forced to suspend convertibility as well because they are not receiving cash deposits from the public or from other banks that suspend. This was especially an issue because reserves were distributed unevenly (except for the Panic of 1873, when reserves were pooled), as noted by the 1873 *Report* of the clearinghouse. Sprague (1910, 181) wrote that "The real reason for suspension [in the Panic of 1893] was that which was pointed out in the report of the clearing-house committee of 1873. The drain [on reserves] had not fallen equally upon the banks. We have no means of knowing the exact positions of the few large banks which held the bulk of bankers' deposits at this time, but there can be no doubt that they must have suffered a far more serious loss of reserve than that of the banks taken as a whole." Sprague wrote that by the Panic of 1907 "the tradition seems to have become established among New York banks that the issue of clearing-house loan certificates and the suspension of cash payments are virtually one and the same thing" (171).

The Timing and Outcomes from New York Clearing House Actions during Each Panic

Clearinghouse loan certificates issued during the 1884 and 1890 crises, as noted above, were apparently sufficient to forestall the panic conditions. In the three severe panics, more action was necessary to calm financial markets. With clearinghouse loan certificates, a partial suspension of payments, and the suppression of bank-specific information, the combined actions allowed banks to continue to clear payments and checks despite the net drain of cash to interior banks. Further, banks were able to extend credit and help maintain transaction activity on the New York Stock Exchange in the 1893 and 1907 panics while also facilitating gold imports to increase the high-powered money stock.

During the Panic of 1873, the New York Clearing House suppressed bank-specific information and agreed to issue clearinghouse loan certificates on the same date (see table 8.1 in chapter 8). Two days later, the suspension of convertibility became clear to financial market participants. One key difference between the 1873 panic on the one hand and the panics of 1893 and 1907 was that the latter panics took place after the US Treasury had returned to the gold standard. Even though the Panic of 1893 arose in part from a fear that the United States might be forced to abandon the gold standard, the adherence to it in these latter panics contributed to the gold inflows motivated by the currency premium. Despite not being on a gold standard in 1873, there were still gold inflows from abroad that coincided with the currency premium, although the gold would not serve the purpose of increasing the monetary base. Instead, gold inflows financed the purchase of securities (by foreign investors) after a sharp decline in security prices.

The Panic of 1893 began in June 1893 when the New York Clearing House stopped publishing bank-specific information and issued clearinghouse loan certificates. These actions by themselves were unable to quell panic conditions, and in early August 1893, the banks in New York City implemented restrictions on the convertibility of deposits into currency. The suspension of convertibility generated a currency premium that motivated importation of gold with a value of nearly $40 million within three weeks, in contrast with imports of less than $5 million throughout June and July.

Concern over whether the United States would abide by the gold standard and the precarious position of the US Treasury gold reserve fund weakened the US liquidity position in 1893. By April 1893, the US Treasury gold reserve fund was below $100 million ($93 million). Dewey (1922, 447) noted that the US Treasury was forced to employ funds of the gold reserve fund to pay current expenses. As a result, the US Treasury was not a major actor in the resolution of the Panic of 1893.

For the Panic of 1907, the decision to issue clearinghouse loan certificates, suppress bank-specific information, and suspend convertibility all took place on the same date—October 26, 1907. Unlike the 1893 delay in gold inflows, gold imports during the weeks subsequent to October 26, 1907, were rapid, rising from $5 million during the week ending November 9 to more than $20 million during the following week. As displayed in table 8.3 in chapter 8, there was a cumulative net inflow of gold into New York City from abroad of over $85 million by the end of 1907. The increase in the high-powered money supply from gold arose from gold imports in 1893 (Muhleman 1908, 110).

The inflows of gold from abroad to the New York City money market took place during the three most severe financial crises. The gold shipments were signals of a willingness to transact in the US financial market, which was then perceived as unlikely to collapse. The first wave of gold shipments immediately following suspension of convertibility in 1893 and 1907 benefited from the currency premium of nearly 4 percent that generated a substantial return. Even during the 1873 crisis, when gold did not represent cash liquidity, the inflow of gold was an infusion of capital from abroad.

Summary

We examine each action taken by the New York Clearing House during the instances of financial panic, starting with the panic onset. In all five panics during the National Banking Era, the New York Clearing House imposed a temporary suppression of bank-specific information at about the same time as the authorization of clearinghouse loan certificates. Bank-specific requests for and amounts of clearinghouse loan certificates, in the most severe panics, were not publicly observable, and the absence of that information was complementary to the suppression of bank-specific information. The New York Clearing House engaged in this kind of information suppression to support the financial viability of the membership and, in essence, transformed the New York Clearing House into a single financial institution.

Information Production and Suppression and Emergency Liquidity

Managing the information environment during a crisis means not only suppressing bank-specific information but also producing some bank-specific information of a different sort. The bank-specific information that was produced during nineteenth-century crises came from special examinations of a few specific banks during the suspension period. The specifics were never released, but the banks were certified as solvent. Related to this bank-specific production were special clearinghouse loans that in retrospect appear to be essentially bailouts of banks. In this chapter we detail these clearinghouse responses to crisis.

The bank examination procedures during normal times laid the groundwork for special examinations during periods of information suppression. All five panics of the National Banking Era had periods of time during which the New York Clearing House suspended its normal weekly publication of key balance sheet aggregate measures (in the *New York Times*, as was required by the New York State superintendent of banking). While bank-specific information was cut off, the clearinghouse still engaged in some highly public special bank examinations. The clearinghouse examined some banks that were subject to unfavorable rumors, and they jointly aided and bailed out some other members.

In the case of a special examination during information-suppression periods, the results of the examination were publicized with only a certificate of health issued by the Clearing House Committee. The certificate gave no details of the examination but just stated that the bank was deemed solvent. In fact, the detailed results of clearinghouse examinations were never made public, even in normal times, although active lending to a distressed member bank (effectively bailouts) could be made public.

The clearinghouse also made emergency loans directly to individual banks, aside from lending via clearinghouse loan certificates.

In this section we examine the special examinations and loans during periods of suspension.

Special Bank Examinations during Suspensions of Convertibility

During suspension periods the only information coming from the clearinghouse was, first, the release and publication of the aggregate balance sheet of the clearinghouse and, second, the results of special examinations of member banks, often at a bank's request. Sometimes, the special inquiries were required precursors to the aid forthcoming from the clearinghouse; other times, the examinations were requested as a "seal of approval" from a credible authority. After these special examinations, the clearinghouse did not reveal very much information, only that there had been an examination by the clearinghouse and that the bank was certifiably sound. In fact, the clearinghouse supplied such a certificate to the bank that had been examined and the bank would display it to the press. This is not unlike modern supervisory examinations—even the comptroller examinations were held confidential. What other information would be warranted or expected? Too much information would cause borrowers and depositors to become concerned about why so much was being revealed.

Table 5.1 below lists the special bank examinations carried out by the New York Clearing House during each of the five panics, even though there was no suspension of convertibility in 1884 or 1890. There were not, however, a lot of special examinations: a total of thirteen, including three state banks in 1907, an average of fewer than three per panic. Of the thirteen, five of the examined institutions were not New York Clearing House Association members.

During the Panic of 1873, the National Bank of Commonwealth, a New York Clearing House member bank, received assistance from other banks and was advised not to suspend convertibility, but in the end it did suspend (*New York Times*, September 21, 1873, 1). A federal government bank examiner from the Office of the Comptroller of the Currency—the chartering and supervisory authority for national banks—and a receiver (an official who could take charge of the bank if deemed necessary) examined the bank. No official statement was released, but the receiver stated that depositors were very likely to be paid in full (*New York Times*, September 24, 1873). In early October, the director of the bank refused to accept the examination report of the receiver, saying that it was incorrect. He pleaded with the clearinghouse to examine the bank. The clearinghouse did appoint a committee on October 7 (*New York Times*, October 8, 1873, 5). The clearinghouse issued a statement: "Resolved. That a special committee of five be appointed, which shall with the President and Directors of the National Bank of Commonwealth, make an examination into its affairs and report at a future meeting of the Association" (Clearing House Committee *Minutes*, October 1, 1873, in vol. 1.1, March 11, 1854–December 10, 1894, unpag.).

There is no evidence that the special committee issued a report about the bank, and the National Bank of Commonwealth did fail. Sprague (1910, 43) reported that there was, however, no loss to creditors. Apparently, the failure was not viewed as important information. Sprague says that the National Bank of Commonwealth's "solvency had been long in question, and its business was of small proportions, with loans in question in the neighborhood of $2 million. Its failure, therefore, was not one of the serious factors in the situation" (43).

During the Panic of 1873, the New York Clearing House also examined nonmembers. On October 1, 1873, the Clearing House *Minutes* say that "The Clearing House Committee have made a thorough examination of three Banks during the year, suggested by unfavorable reports affecting their credit, in two cases finding the rumors unfounded and by a publication of a certificate signed by them to that effect, saving them from serious loss" (Clearing House Committee *Minutes*, vol. 1.1, March 11, 1854–December 10, 1894, unpag.). Sprague (1910, 151) says that the three banks were state banks and were not New York Clearing House members.

In one case during the Panic of 1893, a bank was examined and then liquidated. Seaboard National Bank, a New York Clearing House member, was the clearing agent for the National Bank of Deposit. The National Bank of Deposit had a significant reduction in its deposits, and its solvency was in question. Seaboard National refused to continue acting as clearing agent for the bank: "Notice of this intention was given yesterday afternoon by the Seaboard and was followed by a visit by the Clearing House Committee, and inspection of its assets and a recommendation that the bank go into liquidation." A statement by the clearinghouse issued at the Bank of Deposit at 9:00 p.m. after two hours of inspection stated, "The Clearing House Committee examined the assets of this bank this afternoon and were of the unanimous opinion that the bank should go into liquidation. The committee expressed the opinion that in all probability the depositors would be paid in full" (see *New York Times*, May 23, 1893, 1).

Three large New York Clearing House members were examined during the Panic of 1907. One was the Mercantile National Bank. According to the *New York Times* (October 18, 1907, 1):

An examination of the Mercantile Bank was made after the close of business last night [October 17] by a selected committee of the Clearing House Association. "It was virtually decided that if the examination proved the bank to be in sound condition, the Clearing House would stand by the Mercantile National and see it through any troubles which might follow the events of the last few days." At midnight, the Chairman of the Clearing House issued a statement saying that "the examination results show the bank to be perfectly solvent and be able to meet all its indebtedness. The capital of $3,000,000 is intact and with a large surplus." "The bank will reopen for usual business the next morning."

No further details of the examination were released. On October 18 (reported by the *New York Times*, October 19, 1907): "The Clearing House Committee met yesterday morning and formally voted to extend to the Mercantile any assistance which it may need. . . . [T]he subscriptions received to the fund for the help of the Mercantile included subscriptions of $200,000 from nine individual banks. This made a fund of $1,800,000." The loans were actually clearinghouse loans, which were like emergency loans from the New York Clearing House (as opposed to clearinghouse loan certificates). Then, on October 19, 1907, the clearinghouse voted to extend "$900,000 — in addition to the amount already advanced" to the Mercantile National Bank (Clearing House Committee *Minutes*, October 17, 1907, 337, handwritten).

As a prerequisite to the extension of this aid the Clearing House Committee asked for the resignation of all the Directors of the bank. . . . The Clearing House Committee felt that the new President of the bank should have a free hand in building up the organization. It was with this object in mind that the Directors were all requested to resign. Among the present Directors there are some gentlemen eminently qualified to serve as bank Directors, but the Clearing House Committee feels that the retention of the Board of Directors which has been responsible for the position in which the bank was placed would not serve to restore confidence in the situation. (*New York Times*, October 19, 1907, 1)

With respect to the Mercantile Bank, the *New York Times*, October 22, 1907, wrote, "The number of Clearing House member banks subscribed to the assistance fund increased from 9 to 25, with the new banks each contributing $400,000, making a total of $10 million. There are 53 members of the Clearing House, so just about half subscribed to the assistance fund" (1). Wicker (2000, 90) says that the Mercantile National Bank received $1.9 million from the assistance fund of the clearinghouse.

Commercial and Financial Chronicle, October 26, 1907, goes further:

Following the reorganization of the Mercantile last week the New York Clearing House on Saturday and Sunday extended its investigations to other quarters, two of the institutions being the National Bank of North America and the New Amsterdam National Bank, with which Mr. Morse had been prominently connected. At the conclusion of the examination of these banks a statement reporting their solvency was issued as follows:

"A committee of the Clearing House has examined certain banks of the association that have been under criticism and finds them solvent. The Clearing House Committee has decided to render them such assistance to meet their debits as the committee may think necessary." (1059)

The *New York Times* reported on October 19, 1907, that "The knowledge that the Clearing House stepped in to guarantee the solvency of the bank proved a great relief to the financial community" (1). The issuance of clearinghouse loan certificates was delayed until October 26, 1907, but the extension of loans to Mercantile National Bank indicates that the New York Clearing House was intent on addressing the problem at hand, which was deemed concentrated among the Heinze-Morse-Thomas banks.[1]

Examinations during Financial Distress Periods without Suspensions: 1884, 1890

The Panic of 1884 did not involve a suspension of convertibility. The panic began with the closure of the Marine National Bank, which was involved with the failed brokerage house of Grant and Ward. From an examination of the Marine National Bank, the New York Clearing House decided not to aid the bank and explained (publicly) that the assets of the bank were insufficient for it to reopen.

The next point of focus was the Metropolitan National Bank, which was forced to close temporarily on May 14, 1884. It was examined by New York Clearing House examiners, "a committee of examination" (*Commercial and Financial Chronicle*, December 6, 1884, 634) and was deemed to have sufficient assets in good condition to warrant aid in the form of clearinghouse loan certificates. The New York Clearing House met on May 14 to discuss the Metropolitan National Bank's situation and the Clearing House Committee issued this notice: "The Clearing House Committee have made an examination of the Metropolitan National bank and find the assets justify them in recommending to the Loan Committee to advance the amount required to enable it to immediately to resume business" (minutes of the joint meeting of the Clearing House and Conference Committees of the New York Clearing

House as well as minutes of the Clearing House Committee meeting held at Metropolitan National Bank, both on May 14, 1884; from the New York Clearing House Association Archives).

This case is also discussed in the next subsection on prompt liquidity provision.

The New York Clearing House was acutely aware that the Metropolitan National Bank was in trouble:

> The Chairman [of the Clearing House Committee] stated that he had called the meeting to consider the situation of the Metropolitan National Bank, as many rumors respecting that bank had been in circulation during the day.
>
> After an expression of opinion by all present, it was deemed best to cause an examination of the bank to be made immediately. Mr. [William] Nash [one of five members of the Clearing House Executive Committee] states that he had in readiness a corps of examiners attached to his bank. . . .
>
> The Committee appointed to examine the Metropolitan National Bank reported as follows: "The Capital of the Bank was found to be unimpaired. . . . [I]t was Resolved to extend aid to the bank to pay its debit balance in the sum of $400,000." (Clearing House Committee *Minutes*, vol. 1.1, March 11, 1854–December 10, 1894, 337, 338, handwritten)

The *New York Tribune*, May 15, 1884, published the New York Clearing House announcement subsequent to the May 14 examination as follows: "The Clearing House Committee have made an examination of the Metropolitan National Bank and find the assets justify them in recommending to the Loan Committee to advance the amount required to enable it immediately to resume business." The manager of the clearinghouse, William A. Camp, read the report around midnight May 14, and the representatives of the clearinghouse dispersed immediately after the report was read, refusing all requests to comment further.

In 1890, as shown in table 5.1, three clearinghouse members were examined. On Tuesday, November 11, 1890, three banks required immediate assistance from the New York Clearing House. At an early morning meeting, the presidents of nine of the Clearing House banks were informed of the difficulties facing the Bank of North America. The nine bank presidents each contributed $100,000 to the Bank of North America with securities as collateral, which it used to make its exchanges later that day so that the bank's "embarrassment" was only an "exceedingly temporary affair" (*New York Times*, November 12, 1890, 1).

On Wednesday, November 12, 1890, the New York Clearing House issued $1,495,000 of loan certificates: $900,000 to the Bank of North America, $500,000 to the Mechanics' and Traders' National Bank, and $95,000 to the

TABLE 5.1. Member bank examinations by the New York Clearing House Association during panics

	Date of examination	Clearinghouse member?	Some details
Panic of 1873			
National Bank of Commonwealth	Oct. 8, 1873	Yes	Clearing House examination carried out at the request of the bank's president, who deems receiver's report to be incorrect (*New York Times*, Sept. 20, 22, 23, 24, 1873; *New York Times*, Oct. 7, 13, 1873).
Three state banks	Oct. 1, 1873	No	Clearing House *Minutes*, Mar. 11, 1854–Dec. 10, 1894, vol. 1.1, unpag.
Panic of 1884			
Metropolitan National Bank	May 14, 1884	Yes	Clearing House Committee examines bank, issues notice that on the basis of the examination, the New York Clearing House Association will lend the bank money. Bank reopens on May 15.
Panic of 1890			
North River Bank	Nov. 13, 1890	Yes	Bank forced to close by state bank examiners on Nov. 12, 1890. The suspension was not expected, so the Clearing House Committee goes to the bank to investigate. They are "exceedingly doubtful" that the bank will ever open again (*New York Times*, Nov. 14, 1890, 5).
Bank of North America	Nov. 14, 1890	Yes	Clearing House Committee examines the bank and files a brief report, certifying that "its capital is intact, it has a large surplus, and its means are ample to meet all its obligations" (*New York Times*, Nov. 15, 1890, 8).
Mechanics' and Traders' Bank	Nov. 15, 1890	Yes	Clearing House Committee examines the bank and certifies that "its capital is intact. The bank has a considerable surplus and is fully able to meet all its obligations" (*New York Times*, Nov. 16, 1890, 2).
Panic of 1893			
Madison Square Bank	Aug. 9, 1893	No	Bank takes its books to the Clearing House in an attempt to prove its soundness. Clearing House Committee visits bank to examine it but makes no statement about results. Unofficial statement by an officer present says there is a deficiency (*New York Times*, Aug. 5, 1893, 5).
National Bank of Deposit	May 22, 1893	No	Clearing House member Seaboard National Bank refuses to act as Clearing House agent for National Bank of Deposit. Clearing House Committee examines National and recommends that the bank go into liquidation (*New York Times*, May 23, 1893, 1).
Panic of 1907			
Mercantile National Bank	Oct. 17, 1907	Yes	Clearing House examines bank, issues statement saying "the examination results show the bank to be perfectly solvent and able to meet all its indebtedness" (*New York Times*, Oct. 18, 1907, 1).
New Amsterdam National Bank	Oct. 20, 1907	Yes	Clearing House Committee examines bank, finds it solvent, and agrees to make emergency loan (*New York Times*, Oct. 21, 1907, 1).
National Bank of North America	Oct. 20, 1907	Yes	Clearing House Committee examines bank, finds it solvent, and agrees to make an emergency loan (*New York Times*, Oct. 21, 1907, 1).

North River State Bank (*New York Times,* November 13, 1890, 1). These were the three troubled banks. Two days later, on November 14, 1890, the Clearing House Committee completed its investigation of the Bank of North America, issuing a report stating that the bank's "capital is intact, it has a large surplus, and its means are ample to meet all its obligations" (*New York Times,* November 15, 1890, 8). The financial problems at these banks were apparent, and direct aid from the New York Clearing House with the explicit publication of the loan amounts was taken as a positive step.

On November 15, 1890, the Clearing House Committee finished investigating the Mechanics' and Traders' National Bank and issued a report again stating that the bank's "capital is intact" and that it "has a considerable surplus and is fully able to meet all its obligations" (*New York Times,* November 16, 1890, 2).

The North River Bank was closed by New York State superintendent of banking on November 12 and did not reopen; the other banks did not close during this crisis.

Special Examinations by Government Regulatory Authorities

Table 5.2 lists the examinations made by government bank examiners during each panic. There were a total of ten.

Among the government examinations, the most informative ones took place in 1884 and 1890, the two financial crises without suspensions. The examination of the Marine National Bank by the national bank examiner began on May 6, 1884. The results of the examination concurred with the one by the New York Clearing House, and the bank was permanently closed on May 14, 1884. Further, supplementary regulatory agency action allayed the fear of widespread bank insolvency. The Second National Bank, which suffered the defalcation of $3 million by its president (promptly replaced by the father of the president), was given a positive review on May 15. The *Commercial and Financial Chronicle,* December 6, 1884, described how the comptroller of the currency, on May 14, recognized the imminent financial distress and sent several reliable examiners to New York City to support the national bank examiner stationed in New York (635). The national bank examiner played a part in approving the plans to issue clearinghouse loan certificates and to reopen the Metropolitan National Bank. This point is conveyed in the description of the national bank examination of Metropolitan National Bank in table 5.2.

On Monday, May 26, 1884, the comptroller of the currency stated that the national bank examiner was "keeping an eye on the situation, and had reported to him that the national banks were all in good condition as far as

TABLE 5.2. Regulators' examinations of New York City banks during panics

	Date of examination	Clearinghouse member?	Some details
Panic of 1873			
National Bank of Commonwealth	Sept. 22, 1873	Yes	Government bank examiners examine bank, find "nothing startling" (*New York Times*, Sept. 23 and 24, 1873, 1). Bank refuses to accept examination report and requests that the New York Clearing House examine the bank. Clearing House agrees with government examiner (*New York Times*, Oct. 14, 1873, 5).
Panic of 1884			
Marine National Bank	May 6, 1884	Yes	National bank examiner arrives at the bank and begins his investigation (*Wall Street Journal*, May 6, 1884, 1). On May 7, the Clearing House suspends the bank for an indefinite period (*New York Times*, May 7, 1884, 1). Bank closes on May 14 (*Wall Street Journal*, May 14, 1884, 1). National bank examiner takes Receiver appointed May 13 (*New York Times*, May 14, 1884, 1). National bank examiner takes possession of the bank's property on May 14 (*New York Times*, May 15, 1884, 1).
Metropolitan National Bank	May 14, 1884	Yes	National bank examiner announces on May 15 that the bank's capital is unimpaired. Bank resumes payments (*New York Times*, May 16, 1884, 1). Bank starts voluntary liquidation proceedings on Nov. 18, 1884.
Second National Bank	May 14, 1884	Yes	National bank examiner announces that he is "satisfied that [the bank] is in a perfectly sound and solvent condition" (*New York Times*, May 15, 1884, 5).
Atlantic State Bank	May 14, 1884	No	The Atlantic State Bank was the Brooklyn correspondent of the Metropolitan National Bank. When the Metropolitan suspended payments, the Atlantic closed shortly after, on May 14 (*New York Times*, May 15, 1884, 1). State bank examiners completed an examination on May 16 (*New York Times*, May 17, 1884, 1). Bank does not open. May 21 state bank superintendent declares bank insolvent (*New York Times*, May 22, 1884, 8).

(*continued*)

TABLE 5.2. (continued)

	Date of examination	Clearinghouse member?	Some details
Panic of 1890			
North River Bank	Nov. 12, 1890	Yes	Bank forced to close by state bank examiner. State bank examiners begin their examination. Clearing House also examines bank and is "exceedingly doubtful" it will reopen (*New York Times*, Nov. 13, 1890, 1). On Nov. 13 the Clearing House refuses to issue loan certificates; regulators take possession of bank (*New York Times*, Nov. 14, 1980, 1).
Panic of 1893			
Canal Street Bank	June 6, 1893	No	State bank examiners start examination (*New York Times*, June 7, 1893, 9) and on June 8 announce that the bank would not be allowed "to continue or resume business" (*New York Times*, June 9, 1893, 8).
Panic of 1907			
Hamilton Bank; Twelfth Ward Bank	Oct. 24, 1907	No	Mercantile announces that it will no longer clear for these banks (Wicker 2000, 90). Oct. 19, bank examiners declare these banks solvent, but they remain suspended (*New York Times*, Oct. 25, 1907, 5).
Knickerbocker Trust	Oct. 21, 1907	No	National Bank of Commerce announces it will no longer clear for Knickerbocker (*New York Times*, Oct. 22, 1907, 1). Clearing House rejects Knickerbocker's request for a loan (Wicker 2000, 91).
Trust Company of America	Oct. 22–Nov. 1, 1907	No	Regulators name receivers to take over bank (*New York Times*, Nov. 1, 1907, 2). After experiencing runs, trust is examined several times, closes.

he knew" ("Condition of the New York Banks," *New York Times*, May 27, 1884, 1).

Clearing House Actions of Prompt Liquidity Provision

In the section "Special Bank Examinations during Suspensions of Convertibility" above, we discussed some instances of possible depositor losses being covered by the New York Clearing House (bailouts). Here we discuss the remaining cases that hint at explicit aid as opposed to temporary loans with repayment anticipated.

During the Panic of 1884, the Metropolitan National Bank, a New York Clearing House member, was in trouble. On May 14, 1884, the Metropolitan National Bank owed about $575,000 to the clearinghouse, which it was unable to pay. "The Clearing-house Committee have made an examination of the Metropolitan National Bank and find the assets justify them in recommending to the Loan Committee to advance the amount required to enable the bank to immediately resume business."[2] The *New York Times* estimated that the advance was $3 million. William Dowd, a member of the Clearing House Examination Committee and president of the Bank of North America, confirmed that the Metropolitan would reopen the next day. He stated that "Every bank that is sound will be assisted if it needs help," but that he did not think there would be any other failures (*New York Times*, May 15, 1884, 1).[3] The bank did not fail during the period of financial distress. The run by depositors of Metropolitan National Bank did not diminish, however. From May 17 to May 31, the net deposits at Metropolitan National went from $7.4 million to $1.7 million. By June 21, net deposits fell to $1.2 million. The bank voluntarily liquidated on November 18, 1884.

Wicker (2000) and Sprague (1910) reported that Metropolitan National had two-thirds of its deposits as correspondent balances. This large role as a correspondent bank suggests that other banks withdrew the majority of the Metropolitan National Bank deposits. What was most notable is that there was apparently no evidence of a contagion effect. We note that the Metropolitan National Bank was able to withstand the run with the aid of clearinghouse loan certificates in an amount approximately equal to their net deposit liabilities at the beginning of the financial distress ($7.54 million was its maximum indebtedness).

During the Panic of 1907, the New York Clearing House also examined the National Bank of North America and the New Amsterdam National Bank, concluding that the capital of the National Bank of North America was "unimpaired," and that the New Amsterdam National Bank "can, with proper management, be carried through safely" (Clearing House Committee *Minutes*, October 17, 1907, 339, handwritten). Later, "The Committee voted to aid the New Amsterdam National Bank in the sum of $335,000 — to be subscribed by individual banks, and in addition to the sum already advanced to the bank" (Clearing House Committee *Minutes*, October 17, 1907, 342, handwritten).

In the Panic of 1907, the New Amsterdam National Bank was assisted by the clearinghouse. According to the *New York Times*, October 21, 1907, the New York Clearing House issued a statement that

> A Committee of the Clearing House has examined the several banks of the association [National Bank of North America and the New Amsterdam National Bank] that have been under criticism, and, find them solvent, the Clearing House Committee has decided to render them such assistance to meet their deposits as the committee may think necessary.
>
> While no announcement of the course followed was made, it is believed that individual banks in the clearing house pledged themselves to provide specific amounts of money for use as needed, receiving for their advances collateral from the banks helped, as was done in the Mercantile's case. (1)

Despite the announcements of aid from the New York Clearing House, there was apparently a run on these institutions during the subsequent week. At the weekly publication of member bank balance sheet items for the week ending October 26, 1907, the cash-reserves-to-deposit ratio fell to 12 percent at New Amsterdam National Bank and to 7 percent at National Bank of North America. For each bank, the ratio was at or above 20 percent in the week ending October 19, 1907. Deposits at National Bank of North America fell from more than $13 million to a bit more than $8 million in one week. Deposits at New Amsterdam National Bank fell from $4.9 million to $3.4 million in one week.

On October 28, 1907, the *New York Times* reported that the "President of the New Amsterdam issues an announcement to depositors: '... The bank has been put through a vigorous and extraordinary examination by the NYCH, and has been found solvent, with capital unimpaired. This examination now places us in a singularly strong position'" (3). The bank was saved until the end of January. On January 29, 1908, the *New York Times* reported that the New Amsterdam National Bank decided to close (voluntarily liquidate) and was put in hands of the receiver. Resumption of convertibility occurred on January 4, 1908, and so the bank made it through the crisis (Wicker 2000, 9).

The National Bank of North America also received assistance. After its October 21, 1907, report quoted above, the *New York Times* commented that "Banking houses of international prominence were agreed last night in the belief that the Clearing House's measures will successfully meet the situation.

Several bankers in this group, including James Speyer and Jacob H. Schiff, expressed their views to this effect to The Times" (1).

Trust companies were not members of the New York Clearing House mainly for reasons associated with their business differences from banks.[4] This fact—the nonmembership of trust companies in the New York Clearing House—was a main justification for the New York Clearing House not coming to the aid of Knickerbocker Trust on Monday, October 21, at the request of the National Bank of Commerce. The clearinghouse did, however, financially assist trusts in other cases. Sprague (1910) and Wicker (2000) considered the denial of aid to Knickerbocker Trust an egregious error on the part of the New York Clearing House. If they are correct, J. P. Morgan committed the same error a day later.

According to the New York Times, October 22, 1907, the Trust Company of America experienced a run (1). The amount withdrawn was $500,000. A state bank examiner made an examination of all the loans of the Trust Company of America and found that no loans had been made to Charles Morse and that the loans to Charles Barney, the former president of Knickerbocker Trust Company, were only $175,000 and in sound condition.[5] Morgan and Company agreed to lend $1 million upon hearing the results of the examination of the Trust Company of America. That announcement, however, did not stop the run, and the next day $13 million was withdrawn (Wicker 2000, 92) and another $9 million again on October 24, 1907 (New York Times, October 25, 1907, 1).

Treasury actions in response to the Panic of 1907 were consequential and yet limited as a result of the minimal fiscal balances available to the US Treasury at that time. Muhleman (1908, 110) credits the US Treasury with adding approximately $46 million in gold to the balances of New York City banks.

Sprague (1910, 263–66) explained that the US Treasury deposited nearly $36 million in New York City national banks, $30 million of which was at the largest six banks. Wicker (2000, 98–100) emphasized that $24 million of US Treasury deposits in New York City banks was at three large banks (National City, First National, and Hanover Bank). The arrangement with these banks was for them to facilitate cash disbursements to trust companies.

The New York Times, October 24, 1907, reported that the secretary of the Treasury announced that "As evidence of the Treasury's disposition, I have directed deposits in this city to the extent of $25 million" (1). This amount increased to $35 million (Tallman and Moen 1990, 8; Wicker 2000, 93, 99). Most of this money was directed to assisting the trust companies that did not receive direct aid from the New York Clearing House Association. National City Bank and First National Bank loaned $2.5 million and a loose association of trust companies jointly provided $8.5 million. Hanover National, First National, National City, and Morgan's bank provided $1.5 million. On November 2, 1907, "Another examination of the trust reveals position to be 'less pessimistic than expected.' Trust companies agree to jointly provide another $15 million" (Wicker 2000, 97).

The runs on trust companies subsided on November 4 after a consortium of trust companies pooled sufficient resources ($25 millions) that then were allocated toward liquidity needs of those trust companies suffering depositor withdrawals. Still, without imposing a suspension of convertibility, New York City trust company deposits contracted sharply and never regained the size (especially the volume of deposits) that rivaled the New York City national banks.

Summary

It is notable that the New York Clearing House Association initiated special examinations of both member and nonmember banks and emergency loans to both members and nonmembers although they were not legally bound to do so. These actions were entirely voluntary, and the clearinghouse put in place proper procedures to ensure that such initiatives were orderly and responsible. An observation of a financial panic increased the likelihood that the clearinghouse would engage such activities, and the recurrent observation of panics suggested that member banks could expect the intervention of the New York Clearing House to combat the panics.

Why would some banks prop up other banks or make special examinations and then credibly announce the results to the public? These actions are consistent with the clearinghouse's management of the information environment. The New York Clearing House limited balance sheet information to reveal only the aggregates of the membership, and the special examinations signaled that the bank (or banks) that the public put in question was (were) not insolvent. The loans to specific banks and liquidity provision actions more generally combined with the information control to ensure that the banking system would not unravel as weaker banks faced runs. The reports required credibility, and there were examinations in which banks were deemed insufficiently strong and were closed (National Bank of Commonwealth and Marine National Bank).[6]

The goal of supporting illiquid banks involved screening out insolvent banks in order to prevent excessive losses to the New York Clearing House banks that were lending to the illiquid ones. New York Clearing House Association members would not lend to a weaker bank unless they thought that by doing so all the banks had a better chance of surviving. Smaller banks facing insolvency and that posed little risk to the system more generally would fail without assistance. Banks that were seen as solvent or whose failure was seen as a risk to the banking system more generally would be provided liquidity assistance.

"Too Big to Fail" before the Fed

The term "too big to fail" was coined by Congressman Stewart McKinney (of Connecticut; 1981–87) in reference to the 1984 rescue of Continental Illinois Bank.[1] Continental Illinois failed as a result of its exposure to a downstream bank, Penn Square, which had losses on oil-related speculations. The failure occurred in the larger context of the Latin American debt crisis (1983–89), and FDIC chairman William Isaac and Federal Reserve chairman Paul Volcker argued that the failure of Continental would have led to runs on other large US banks (see Kaufman 2004 for details). The failure of Continental was the largest bank failure in US history prior to the financial crisis of 2007–8. In fact, the failure of Continental involved a run by uninsured wholesale creditors—an omen for the events of 2007–8, which involved such creditors on a massive scale. In the years since the Continental Illinois failure, banks have allegedly engaged in taking risks greater than they otherwise would because of a belief that they would be bailed out by the government, possibly causing or contributing to the financial crisis of 2007–8, because large banks believe they are too big to fail. In this chapter we revisit this issue by studying the National Banking Era, a period in which large banks were considered too big to fail and hence were rescued by other large banks.

In the modern era it has been hard to find evidence that large banks are the beneficiaries of implicit too-big-to-fail government policies and become riskier as a result. Beck, Demirgüç-Kunt, and Levine (2006) studied sixty-nine countries from 1980 to 1997 and found that more concentrated banking systems are *less likely* to have financial crises, controlling for differences in bank regulations, national institutions affecting competition, and macroeconomic conditions (also see Evrensel 2008 on this point). Ahmed, Anderson, and Zarutskie (2015) have found that credit derivative spreads are no more sensitive to bank size than they are for nonfinancial firms. And it is hard to explain why the problem apparently was not present in the period between 1934 (when deposit insurance was adopted) and 2007. Nevertheless, the notion that some institutions are too big to fail remains an important topic of study.

The notion that some institutions are too big to fail has a long history, starting before Congressman McKinney coined the term. During the US National Banking Era, prior to the existence of the Federal Reserve System and deposit insurance, private bank clearinghouses provided emergency lending facilities to large member banks during financial crises and they assisted member banks when they needed help during systemic crises.[2] An editorial in the *Bankers' Magazine* of August 1901 explained the logic for doing so:

> If a bank possesses good assets and is merely temporarily embarrassed because of difficulty in immediate liquidation, the clearing-house association frequently comes to its assistance. In fact, it would usually do so, because it is good policy of the association to prevent the failure of any important member. Such a failure tries the weak points of all the banks. But if the clearing-house committee, on examination of the assets, finds no basis of security for the necessary assistance, and therefore refuses to grant it, it would be unwise for any individual to take the risk refused by the clearing-house. (vol. 63, no. 2, 162)

In this chapter we show that in its lender-of-last-resort role, the New York Clearing House adopted a too-big-to-fail policy during National Banking Era crises. The revealed preference of the clearinghouse was to help member banks to survive during crises. In this period, there was no central bank prepared to perform that role. Because a private-market coalition of banking institutions took these actions, it strongly suggests that a too-big-to-fail practice or policy per se (and the associated "moral hazard" problem of exacerbating bank risk taking) is not the problem causing crises. The banks had the incentive to prevent subsequent member bank risk taking, suggesting that there could be too-big-to-fail policies without the moral hazard of increasing risk. In the pre-Fed era, bailing out large, interconnected banks was a reasonable response to the vulnerability of short-term debt to runs that could unnecessarily threaten large banks and thereby the entire banking system.

Bank Failures and Clearing House Assistance

Twelve banks failed in New York City during the National Banking Era (*Annual Report* of the Comptroller of the Currency, 1920, vol. 2, 56–79). The number of failures is notably small. We examine the banks in table 6.1, which

TABLE 6.1. Banks that failed and banks that were aided or bailed out by the New York Clearing House Association during the National Banking Era

	Clearing-house member?	Date of data	Date of failure or assistance	Total assets			Due to + due from		Due to − due from	
				CH mean $ / distressed bank total assets	CH median $	CH SD	CH mean $ / distressed bank median	CH median $	CH mean $ / distressed bank median	CH median $
CH		10/1/1866		7,794,403	5,425,182	7,558,552	1,674,700	576,362	1,229,648	352,916
Croton N.B.	Yes	10/1/1866	10/1/1866	2,527,883			192,009		6,085	
CH		10/2/1871		8,377,293	4,994,797	8,122,750	2,263,636	681,584	1,544,753	205,632
Ocean N.B.	Yes	10/2/1871	12/13/1871	4,542,551			1,585,327		1,291,601	
Union Square N.B.	No	10/2/1871	12/15/1871	678,612			60,826		−55,612	
Eighth N.B.	Yes	10/2/1871	12/15/1871	1,074,773			4,433		−4,433	
CH		10/3/1872		8,370,216	5,748,511	7,362,133	1,947,783	649,259	1,254,767	181,015
Atlantic N.B.	Yes	10/3/1872	9/22/1873	1,191,230			162,371		32,960	
N.B. of Commonwealth	Yes	10/3/1872	9/22/1873	7,614,822			984,888		765,568	
CH		10/3/1883		9,284,117	6,069,928	8,326,248	3,178,363	1,218,725	2,293,712	365,400
Marine N.B.	Yes	5/13/1884	5/13/1884	6,072,313			837,519		363,089	
Metropolitan N.B.	Yes	5/15/1884	5/15/1884	17,652,227			8,067,882		5,496,866	
CH		10/2/1890		11,729,109	7,267,218	10,174,929	4,481,209	4,481,209	2,379,762	1,075,158
Bank of North America	Yes	10/2/1890	11/12/1890							
Mechanics' and Traders'	Yes	10/2/1890	11/12/1890	1,341,254			58,283		32,691	

	CH	Member	10/2/1890	11/12/1890							
North River Bank	CH	No	9/30/1892		12,892,959	8,520,158	10,907,902	5,215,760	2,781,476	3,720,372	1,652,404
National Bank of Deposit			3/6/1893[a]	5/22/1893[b]	1,742,211			519,864		227,600	
	CH		9/5/1900		24,271,097	10,901,817	33,077,232	7,629,665	1,389,722	6,353,220	778,331
Seventh N.B.		Yes	9/5/1900	6/27/1901	5,471,405			1,655,827		870,969	
	CH		9/9/1903		12,938,347	12,511,765	39,299,110	4,244,859	1,710,332	3,187,577	862,000
Equitable N.B.			9/9/1903	2/10/1904	511,366			31,913		765	
	CH		8/22/1907		40,489,030	24,093,411	54,453,221	13,048,241	1,796,310	5,843,367	174,518
First N.B. of City of New York			8/22/1907	10/25/1907	5,820,383			2,245,004		351,658	
Mercantile N.B.			8/22/1907	**10/19/1907**	24,093,411			7,898,580		4,016,170	
New Amsterdam N.B.		Yes	8/22/1907	6/30/1908	7,298,000			1,937,260		1,022,306	

Source: US Comptroller of the Currency, *Call Reports of Condition and Income.*

[a] Data added from the published balance sheet.

[b] Closure/failure date 6/9/1893 (receivership).

lists those that failed and those that were assisted by the clearinghouse (in bold). The rows show data on the banks and also summary statistics about the New York Clearing House (CH) for comparison. The data are from the *Call Reports of Condition and Income* of the US comptroller of the currency. For the clearinghouse measures, we aggregate the data for all member banks of the clearinghouse for that year.[3] The data in table 6.1 are from some time prior to the date shown in the third column. The failure date, shown in the fourth column, is the date a receiver was appointed. At the time of the bank's failure, it may look substantially different than, say, a year prior to its failure, so the dates in the two columns are usually different. The shaded rows indicate the major panics: 1873, 1893, and 1907.

For each failed bank, there is a row for clearinghouse data and just below is a row with the individual bank data. For the clearinghouse members, the columns show the mean, median, and standard deviation of clearinghouse members' total assets. We are also interested in measures of the interconnectedness of member banks as an indication of their systemic importance. We measure interconnectedness in two ways: (1) the amount due to other banks plus the amount due from other banks (a measure of the size of the bank in the interbank market) and (2) the amount due to other banks minus the amount due from other banks (a measure of the bank's risk as a counterparty). For "net due to" items, we are assuming that New York City correspondent banks hold a larger volume of interior bank deposits than they have in deposits at other banks. Note that for all the measures that we examine from the clearinghouse, the mean is consistently larger than the median, indicating positive skewness. This positive skewness reflects the fact that a few banks were significantly larger than their clearinghouse peers (as noted by Sprague 1910) and dominated financial activities of New York City as well as the rest of the country. This is indicated by the standard deviation as well. These banks (around six in number) held roughly 40 percent of total clearinghouse member assets.

Assistance during Noncrisis Times

In addition to the small number of bank failures, in the cases where banks failed in nonpanic times, the failing banks were typically much smaller and less interconnected than the average clearinghouse member bank. In the first failure in table 6.1, the failure of Croton National Bank occurred on October 1, 1867. Croton's total assets were $2.5 million, in comparison with the average clearinghouse member's total assets of $7.8 million. And Croton was not significantly interconnected with other banks, displaying very small measures of interbank activity relative to clearinghouse in table 6.1. The bank was effectively an isolated entity whose failure had little effect on the banking system.

Another example is that of the Seventh National Bank, which failed on June 27, 1901. As shown in table 6.1, the Seventh was small in total assets and had a smaller volume of interbank activity than the average clearinghouse member. The bank received no aid from the clearinghouse (see *New York Times*, June 28, 1901, 3).

The one example of a fairly large bank failure during nonpanic times is Ocean National Bank, which failed on December 13, 1871. When the Ocean Bank's troubles began, the clearinghouse advanced loans on the basis of their collateral, starting on Friday, December 8 (see *New York Times*, December 19, 1871, 2). The *New York Tribune*, December 13, 1871, reported that the Ocean National Bank "has been regarded with suspicion by the officers of the associate banks in the Clearing-House" (1) and when the Clearing House Committee examined the Ocean Bank, they found "the affairs of the bank in a very critical condition." The bank was expelled from the New York Clearing House Association, and the bank failed on December 13, 1871.

Even though there was no financial crisis at the time, the Ocean Bank failure occurred during a time of "bank excitement." The *New York Tribune*, December 15, 1871, reported, "Early in the morning there was a run on the Bank of the Commonwealth. . . . The officers of the different Clearing-House banks testify to the soundness and excellent management of the Commonwealth, which has thus proved its ability to meet all demands" (1). And according to the New York Clearing House Committee *Minutes* for December 14, 1871: "The National Bank of the Commonwealth having been drawn upon very heavily by its depositors in consequence of unfavorable rumors in circulation in regard to its condition and fearing a further run upon it—as many of the Clearing House Committee as could be immediately summoned, and the Chairman of the Clearing House met at the Bank and made an examination of its condition, the result of which was the publication in the city papers of the following morning of this notice." Appended was the official Clearing House endorsement: "The undersigned have this afternoon, at the close of business, made a thorough examination of the affairs and conditions of the National Bank of the Commonwealth, and find said bank to be perfectly solvent, and have entire confidence in the ability of the bank to pay all of its liabilities."

New York Clearing House Assistance during Crises

During a crisis, the New York Clearing House policy was to aid large, interconnected member banks, but to let small banks, whether they were members or not, fail. In other words, the policy was to rescue banks that were "too big to fail" or "too interconnected to fail," and the contemporary bankers' actions indicated that both characteristics were important to them.

During the Panic of 1873, as shown in table 6.1, two clearinghouse member banks failed, the Atlantic National Bank and the National Bank of the Commonwealth. While Atlantic was small, Commonwealth was not, with total assets of $7.6 million, in comparison with an average of $8.4 million for clearinghouse members.[4] The bank was larger than Ocean Bank, which failed just two years earlier. The Commonwealth, however, was no more significantly interconnected than Ocean Bank. Using our measure of total volume of interbank activity (due to plus due from), the Commonwealth Bank had a volume of $984,888 due to plus due from, in comparison with the Clearing House average of $2 million at the time. With respect to our net liquidity exposure to other banks (due to less due from), the Commonwealth had a net exposure of $765,568, in comparison with the Clearing House average of $1.2 million. According to the *New York Tribune* of September 22, 1873: "the Clearing-house Committee made a thorough examination of [the Commonwealth's] assets and liabilities, and at the conclusion of their investigations estimated the capital stock of the company to be worth about 109. . . . [George Ellis, its president] consulted with the presidents of other national banks, some of whom proffered assistance. . . . This assistance was not forthcoming" (2).

Subsequently, the receiver for the National Bank of the Commonwealth "announces . . . that he will pay the depositors in full" (*New York Times*, November 18, 1874, 8). But the provision of full payment of the depositors was not without doubts. The *New York Times* had published in July 1874 that "George Ellis, ex-president of the National Bank of the Commonwealth, was arrested yesterday . . . for embezzling $53,000 [that] belong[ed] to the bank" (*New York Times*, July 2, 1874, 8).

Perhaps the most illustrative example of too-big-to-fail policies of the New York Clearing House took place during the Panic of 1884. The Metropolitan National Bank was forced to close temporarily on May 14, 1884. The Metropolitan Bank was an important institution in New York City, playing a crucial role in facilitating the provision of liquidity during the Panic of 1857. Sprague (1910, 115) writes, "The Second National Bank [which failed] was a purely local institution, having no bankers' deposits whatever. On the other hand, about $7,000,000, nearly two-thirds of the total deposits of the Metropolitan National Bank, were due to other banks. Had the clearinghouse not acted with admirable promptness in coming to its assistance there is little question that out-of-town banks would have become alarmed for their deposits, not only in this bank but for those in the banks generally."

The New York Clearing House was acutely aware that the Metropolitan National Bank was the subject of rumored troubles and sent examiners to the bank immediately after it suspended payments. The Metropolitan Bank was examined by New York Clearing House examiners, "a committee of examination" (*Commercial and Financial Chronicle*, December 6, 1884, 634) and was deemed to have sufficient assets in good condition to warrant aid in the form of clearinghouse loan certificates. The committee appointed to examine the Metropolitan National Bank reported as follows: "The Capital of the Bank was found to be unimpaired. . . . [I]t was Resolved to extend aid to the bank to pay its debit balance in the sum of $400,000" (Clearing House Committee *Minutes*, vol. 1.1, March 11, 1854–December 10, 1894, 338, handwritten).[5]

The *New York Times* for May 16, 1884, reported, "The resumption of business, at noon, by the Metropolitan Bank helped restore confidence, and the practical guarantee, by the Clearing-house Association, of the stability of all banks, exercised very reassuring influence" (1). From the Clearing House Loan Committee records, we note that Metropolitan National Bank received the following amounts of clearinghouse loan certificates: $1.83 million by Thursday, May 15, another $2.5 million on Friday, May 16, and another $0.78 million on Saturday, May 17. With the addition of $1.19 million on Monday, May 19, Metropolitan National Bank held $6.3 million in clearinghouse loan certificates—more than 80 percent of its deposit total reported as of May 17. The liquidity provision to Metropolitan National Bank led to a moderation of panic conditions, and yet the fate of the bank was largely determined by the volume of withdrawals in the two weeks after the initial suspension. The level of deposits fell from $7.4 million on May 17 to $1.4 million on May 31, 1884.

The *New York Times* for May 15, 1884, noted: "The bank is the clearinghouse of a large number of country banks, whose funds are now locked up here, and unless the Metropolitan resumes at once there is no doubt that many of its correspondents will be forced to suspend, so that the effect of this failure will be widely and disastrously felt throughout the country" (1). Among the large New York City correspondent banks, Metropolitan held the sixth-highest concentration of banker balances.[6] Using our measure of interconnectedness, the Metropolitan National Bank had more than twice the total volume of interbank activity of the average New York Clearing House bank at that time and nearly twice the New York Clearing House average of net interbank exposure to bank deposits (as signaled also by the concentration of banker balances).

The interconnectedness reflected in the correspondent balances held by Metropolitan was clearly a key consideration of the examination committee drawn from New York Clearing House members. Below we present excerpts from a June 4, 1884, speech to the membership given by George S. Coe, president of American Exchange National Bank, a leading member of the New York Clearing House Association and a participant in the examination committee. The speech was later published in *Bankers' Magazine* in July of that year. By most accounts, the crisis became manageable by mid-June, and so the speech was composed promptly in response to the event.

The candor and clarity in this speech is impressive, but language from 1884 can be obscure. To ensure message clarity, we summarize Coe's key insights, which align closely to our view of proper responses to fight financial crises. First, Coe expresses the inability of the examination committee to determine whether the institution was solvent during the several hours prior to making the decision to aid Metropolitan, or not. Second, the most important aspect that the examination uncovered was that the Metropolitan National Bank held correspondent balances from interior banks that were substantial. Third, the decision to aid Metropolitan National Bank was made on the basis of its interconnected status and on the perceived negative repercussions of locking up interior correspondent balances if Metropolitan had remained closed. Finally, Coe's speech makes clear that the decision to aid Metropolitan was made with the recognition that the New York Clearing House could have taken losses totaling "one or two millions" as a result of the loans it made in the form of clearinghouse loan certificates.

In that speech, Coe expressed his view of the successful alleviation of the crisis in 1884:

> Under these circumstances, the Clearing House Committee were summoned together at midnight, to examine the condition of that institution, and to decide what action should be taken respecting it. A fearful responsibility was thus hastily thrown upon that committee. It was impossible in a few short hours, and in the apprehension of further possible events, to reach a definite conclusion upon the value of the large and diversified assets of that bank. When we examined its books, this most important fact at once appeared: that it owed some eight to nine millions of deposits, a large proportion of which consisted of reserves of interior banks, which could not be imperiled or locked up for another day without producing a further calamity of wide-spread dimension throughout the country. It was also evident that the consequent certain suspension of many banks in the interior cities would occur, and be followed by suspension of businessmen depending upon them, and by heavy drafts upon those banks here which held similar deposit reserves, and that the immediate danger to our city institutions was great just in proportion to the extent of such liabilities and to the amount that each bank was expanded relatively to

its immediate cash in hand. That, should the threatened wild excitement pervade the country, a general suspension of banks, bankers and merchants was inevitable, and in such case the magnitude of loss to every institution would be incalculable.

The Committee therefore came to the unanimous conclusion that it was better to confront the risk of losing one or two millions, if need be, by taking possession of the total assets of that bank, and by paying off its depositors, rather than by waiting to incur the hazard of an indefinite and greater loss, by a general financial and commercial derangement throughout the country; and that it was their manifest duty to promptly accept this grave responsibility, confidently relying upon their associates for approval and support. On behalf of the combined capital and surplus of the banks in this Association, amounting to about a hundred millions, and also to protect the property and assets held by them together, of more than three hundred millions, your Committee unhesitatingly acted, and thus saved the nation from immeasurable calamity. The Metropolitan [National] Bank was obviously the key to the whole situation. When this decision was announced the next morning, confidence was instantly restored, and business resumed its even tenor. Seven-eighths of the deposits of Metropolitan [National] Bank have already been paid off. Its many shareholders have been saved from threatened personal responsibility, and time is gained in which its large property may be more deliberately converted into money. The restoration of confidence was as sudden as was its loss; so sudden, indeed that the immensity of the danger can now hardly be appreciated.

This speech, delivered at the clearinghouse only three weeks after the initial suspension of Metropolitan on May 14, 1884, effectively captures all the key features of a banking panic. The reasoning to aid Metropolitan National Bank in 1884 was the same as we see with recent efforts to prevent the failure of systemically important institutions. The New York Clearing House examination committee had inadequate time to determine the true solvency condition of Metropolitan National Bank. Unlike Marine National Bank, which was allowed to fail, Metropolitan National Bank had systemic implications if it failed. The nearly $9 million in correspondent bank balances, much of which was reserves deposited at Metropolitan by interior banks, would be locked up if Metropolitan had remained in suspension. Further, Coe's expressed willingness for the clearinghouse members to take a loss of up to $2 million on its loans to Metropolitan. Admittedly, the New York Clearing House did not take such losses, largely because the New York Clearing House managed the orderly liquidation of Metropolitan National Bank.

Metropolitan National Bank was "too big to fail during a crisis." In effect, the description of clearinghouse actions within the Coe speech demonstrates unequivocally that the aid offered to Metropolitan National Bank on May 15, 1884, was an instance of "too big to fail" with additional conditions "in a disorderly fashion during a panic." The eventual liquidation of the bank was delayed for several months as a result of the clearinghouse loan certificates.

Newspaper reports as early as mid-June 1884 indicated that the clearing-house was recommending to Metropolitan National Bank that it consider voluntary liquidation. That event took place in November 1884. Most treat-ments of this event (e.g., Sprague 1910 and Wicker 2000) do not emphasize Coe's assessment that Metropolitan National Bank was aided despite not knowing its solvency status. Further, the *Annual Report* of the comptroller of the currency (1884, XLIII) describes the condition of the bank as reasonable and that the bank's failure was a result of rumor. Coe's description, though, suggests strongly that there was an awareness of the risk of Metropolitan's failure and a willingness of clearinghouse members to share that risk in order to prevent a major correspondent bank from failing during a banking panic. And recall that it was the sixth-largest correspondent bank in New York City, clearly interconnected and therefore systemically important. The Metro-politan National Bank voluntarily liquidated on November 18, 1884, and its failure was associated with no strife in the financial markets. From today's perspective, the liquidation might look like a model for an orderly resolution.

As described in chapter 5, the New York Clearing House examined three banks during the Panic of 1890. Of those banks, the North River State Bank was not a member of the clearinghouse. The New York superintendent of banking closed North River Bank on November 12, 1890, and it did not re-open. At that time, the clearinghouse formed a committee to engage in ex-aminations of the two member banks—the Bank of North America and the Mechanics' and Traders' National Bank. On November 14 and 15, the exami-nation committee expressed for each bank (first Bank of North America and then Mechanics' and Traders' Bank), the following statement: "capital is in-tact, it has a large surplus, and its means are ample to meet all its obligations." These banks were able to withstand temporary difficulties presented in this period.

Two notable factors distinguish the actions of the New York Clearing House during this panic. First, the approval of clearinghouse loan certifi-cates and a convening of the Clearing House Loan Committee that took place early in the panic on November 11, 1890. Second, the extension of aid through clearinghouse loan certificates was announced, but the amounts extended to banks was also made public, in contrast with the panics associated with suspensions of convertibility. The distinction of public announcements of the loans extended to the three troubled banks signaled that the New York

Clearing House treated the banking problems in 1890 as manageable. Isolating attention to the problems at these banks and making public the explicit loan amounts was perceived as a positive signal.

On May 22, 1893, the National Bank of Deposit was closed by order of the national bank examiner of the Office of the Comptroller of the Currency. The examiner considered the bank insolvent and the bank was placed in the hands of receiver on June 9, 1893. It is notable that National Bank of Deposit was not a member of the New York Clearing House Association and that it therefore had to clear its checks through a member bank. Seaboard National Bank served that role for the National Bank of Deposit. The failure involves some intrigue because the failure of its correspondent, the Columbia Bank of Chicago, was blamed for triggering the run.[7] Seaboard National Bank, which was its clearing agent at the New York Clearing House, announced that it would no longer clear for the National Bank of Deposit. Earlier, the clearinghouse had appointed a committee to examine the bank, a power that it had because banks that cleared through clearinghouse members had to submit to clearinghouse examinations. The New York Clearing House alerted the national bank examiner about the condition of the National Bank of Deposit. Its deposits had fallen from $1.5 million to $900 thousand rapidly.[8]

As we mentioned above in chapter 5, the New York Clearing House Association examined three large banks during the Panic of 1907. Of those three banks, the Mercantile National Bank was the most important. A committee selected from among clearinghouse members examined the bank after the close of business on October 17. Reports in the New York Times on October 17 and 18, 1907, stated that the clearinghouse examiners had a decision rule for the provision of aid—if the bank was deemed sound by the committee, then the clearinghouse would provide assistance to the bank to help it survive its troubles. The chairman of the clearinghouse released a statement at midnight that verified the bank's solvency, that it would be able to repay its debts, and that it would reopen the next day.

The Commercial and Financial Chronicle of October 19, 1907, stated that "after the Mercantile's debit balance of $745,000 had been paid at the Clearing House, the Clearing-House Committee also demanded the resignation of every director of the Mercantile Bank. As the result of such demand, all the directors of the bank at once resigned." The next day (October 20), the New York Times front-page story headline was "BANK HERE [New York City] IS SAFE IN HEINZE CRASH: Clearing House Committee Finds the Mercantile National in Sound Condition."

On October 21, 1907, the New York Times front-page headline was "BANKS SOUND; WILL BE BACKED; The Strength of the Clearing House Is Pledged to Give Needed Support. THE THOMASES OUT NOW Seth M. Milliken Heads Mercantile and W. F. Havemeyer the Bank of North America. UN-DESIRED CONTROLS END And Speyer, Schiff, and Other Leading Bankers Agree That the Situation Is Now Cleared Up." The clearinghouse had decided to extend as much aid as was needed. The total was $1.8 million with nine banks participating.[9] Subsequently, another $900,000 was advanced (Clearing House Committee *Minutes*, October 17, 1907, 337, handwritten). In the same article, the *Times* reported that the clearinghouse committee "agreed to make up any part of the Mercantile National Bank's debit balance of $1,137,000 which the bank might not itself be able to pay. This balance the Clearing House was called upon to provide the great bulk of this payment."

It was also announced in the *New York Times* (October 21, 1907, 1) that "the examination the Clearing House had made of the [other] banks under criticism [the National Bank of North America and the New Amsterdam National Bank] had shown them to be solvent and that the committee had decided to extend to them such aid as the committee might deem necessary to help meet the demands of their depositors."

> Thorough satisfaction was expressed everywhere at the action of the Clearing House in the matter of the Mercantile Bank. Brokers expressed the opinion that this prompt and vigorous action of the Clearing House showed that any weak spots in the banking situation would be promptly taken care of and showed further, according to their idea of the matter, that there were no real weak spots. The action of the Clearing House and the assurances with regard to this particular bank were accepted literally, and undoubtedly prevented much more serious demoralization in the stock market. (*New York Times*, October 19, 1907, 13)

The actions of the New York Clearing House to aid its members is clear. Where it came up short in 1907 was in aiding intermediaries outside its membership. The decision by the New York Clearing House to allow Knickerbocker Trust to go unaided was criticized by Sprague (1910), a contemporary observer, as well as by Goodhart (1969) and Wicker (2000). We concur with that sentiment and appeal to the justifications by George S. Coe as relevant in the case of Knickerbocker. Although there are reasonable arguments for the New York Clearing House not risking its assets to save a nonmember institution, the ensuing costs of not aiding Knickerbocker Trust and the failure of Knickerbocker Trust were huge. It led to the most severe period of the financial crisis in 1907, and likely the ramifications of that failure contributed largely to that distress. The clearinghouse likely would have aided Knickerbocker Trust if a coalition of trust companies had been arranged to share in the possible losses if Knickerbocker closed. If the complex governance issues could have been arranged quickly, it might have made 1907 more like 1884. But that did not happen.

Summary

The New York Clearing House Association constitution said nothing about bailing out member banks during crises. Nevertheless, the association did engage in bailouts of member banks that it could have allowed to fail. Clearinghouse member banks did so as an act of self-preservation. The banks recognized that, during a panic, members were "involuntarily compelled to make common cause with every other member in the risk attending any practical expedient for general relief" (Clearing House Special Committee of Five, June 16, 1884, Clearing House Committee *Minutes*, 1878–85, 158). And, consequently (speaking of the Panic of 1884), Bluedorn and Park (2015, 1) argue "that bailouts of [systemically important banks] by the New York Clearing House likely short-circuited a full-scale banking panic."

The speech by George S. Coe describes in detail the key issues that guided the examination committee to decide to issue loan certificates to Metropolitan National Bank in 1884. As a large and interconnected member bank, Metropolitan's possible failure risked a nationwide financial panic. The committee unanimously decided to aid Metropolitan National, whose solvency condition could not be conclusively determined. The decision in support of Metropolitan was made even though the actions might impose losses on the surviving members of the clearinghouse if Metropolitan National failed. Private-market participants were therefore acutely aware that their actions were effectively a bailout of the stricken bank. The benefit was the prevention of banking panic on a wider scale.

Privately orchestrated bailouts also occurred during the financial crisis of 2007–8. These bailouts were associated with forms of money and banklike institutions that were at the heart of that crisis. The forms of money and banks had changed by 2007–8. Short-term debt like repo, asset-backed commercial paper (a form of short-term debt), and money market funds all relied on privately produced collateral in the form of asset-backed and mortgage-backed bonds. Here too private bailouts occurred. For example, sponsors of money market funds bailed out their associated funds (see McCabe 2015). And, in the case of repo and asset-backed commercial paper, short-term debt backed by asset-backed and mortgage-backed securities, we saw sponsors of credit card securitizations bail out their special-purpose vehicles (see Robertson, forthcoming). In fact, investors in these credit-card-backed securitizations expected that such bailouts might occur. The evidence of Gorton and Souleles (2006) showed that the spreads of credit-card asset-backed securities at issuance incorporate into that spread both the risk of the sponsor and the underlying risk of the credit card receivables. All these bailouts were not required by the written contracts of the related firms and investment vehicles. These modern examples of private bailouts are modest initiatives in comparison to the private initiatives that aimed to alleviate financial crises during the National Banking Era.

7

Certified Checks and the Currency Premium

Information on the condition of banks was difficult to obtain in New York City during the early 1800s. In response to a perceived need for banking information, the New York superintendent of banking required that the New York Clearing House member banks—the most important banks for the financial system—publish weekly in a newspaper (the *New York Times*) a selection of balance sheet items to indicate whether banks were in reasonable financial conditions. In a financial crisis during the National Banking Era, the New York Clearing House Association would order member banks to stop publishing this bank-specific information in the newspapers. Information on specific banks was cut off, and only aggregate totals of the New York Clearing House were published. But some information was available, and a new financial market would open in response to the suppression of information and the suspension of convertibility, and the prices in this market revealed information about the likelihood of the New York Clearing House being bankrupt, and by extension, whether the whole banking system of the United States was insolvent. These prices can be thought of as representing the aggregated beliefs of people during the suspension period.

The Currency Famine

In normal times, the fractional reserve banking system allows a modest amount of cash to support a much larger volume of bank deposits that are a more convenient medium for engaging in large-denomination transactions. But when there is concern about the safety of deposits in some banks, or more general concern about the solvency of the banking system, the fractional reserve system of banking faces the risk of individual bank runs or, worse, system-wide banking runs, as in panics.

During a panic, depositors want cash, not deposits, but during a panic there is a shortage of cash. Because of the money multiplier, the cash that has been deposited into banks leads to the creation of many more demand deposits, so that banks cannot possibly honor the cash demands of all depositors. As a result, banks suspend convertibility of deposits into cash, and many households and firms hoard cash by keeping it outside the banking system. For example, the cash holdings of New York City banks dropped by $43 million between August 22, 1907, and December 3, 1907, which represented a contraction of more than 15 percent. Boies (1908, 82) described events in the Panic of 1907: "Never before in the history of this country has the mania to hoard money deprived the people of so vast a sum as that which has been withdrawn from circulation since the opening days of the October panic. . . . [I]t is safe to say that, taking the country as a whole, fully $100,000,000 in currency has been locked up by timid individuals, banks and corporations."

The cash that was hoarded was either cash that was not originally in the banks or cash that depositors were able to withdraw from their banks before the banks suspended convertibility. Where did the hoarded cash go? Boies (1908, 82): "As soon as the newspapers announced the cash settlements by the banks had been temporarily suspended the safe-deposit companies received applications from thousands for 'safe month boxes.' That meant that the hoarders wanted a safe place to store their money." And the same phenomenon was reported by Andrew (1908b, 294): "On October 26, the Astor Safe Deposit Company, at the request of Mr. J. P. Morgan, made a canvass of thirty-three of the principal safe deposit companies in that city, and found that from Tuesday to Friday of that panic week they had rented a total of 789 safes, or, as they estimated, about six times the usual number." *Dun's Review*, October 26, 1907, wrote, "Stringency in the money market has been the worst feature of the situation for some time, but it was aggravated by the withdrawal of millions of dollars from the banks, many frightened depositors putting their money in safe deposit boxes at the time when it is needed in circulation" (3). The same phenomenon occurred in other cities as well. Country banks also hoarded cash. Banks outside the reserve cities in the South, West, and Pacific states more than doubled their cash holdings.[1]

Cash hoarding is not frequently heard of in modern discourse, but there are instances where it still applies. The modern experience of cash hoarding happened after the failure of Lehman Brothers in 2008. In the subsequent few days, management at many financial firms gave explicit orders that no cash was to leave the firm, which were, in other words, orders to hoard cash. In a modern equivalent of cash hoarding, at least one firm sent employees to many commercial banks to open checking accounts at the deposit insurance limit (a practice that has subsequently been formalized with cash sweeps into insured accounts for firms). Excess demand for US Treasury bonds is another manifestation of a modern way to hoard cash. The recent negative yields on the government debt of Germany and Japan makes buying these bonds similar to a safe-deposit box. Bond holders are willing to pay to have their cash stored in the form of these bonds.

Hoarded cash during the National Banking Era panics was often left in safe-deposit boxes, which meant that the cash did not circulate. In the modern theme of this book, cash hoarding led to a substantial shortage of safe debt. Because of widespread cash hoarding during banking panics, those events were often described as "hoarding panics" or "money-hoarding panics." Another term that was used was "currency famine." John De Witt Warner (1895, 3) wrote, "Our people found themselves not merely drained of currency but forbidden by most carefully drawn statutes to utilize the expedients which would have been most natural and effective. No civilized nation has ever experienced such a currency famine. None has ever found itself so fettered by positive law in its efforts to rescue itself. None ever so promptly arose to the emergency." Warner is referring to the fact that private bank money (banknotes, like those that banks issued prior to the US Civil War) was essentially outlawed by a prohibitive tax. Bradstreet's, August 12, 1893, wrote that "The irrational but widespread hoarding of currency has compelled jobbers and manufacturers in many instances to do business more nearly than ever on a cash basis, which has resulted in further restriction of trade throughout the country" (511). Nevertheless, private money of some kind was issued during panics in the form of clearinghouse loan certificates (discussed in chapter 4) and certified checks, discussed in this chapter.

To stave off the drain of cash from banks, banks restricted the convertibility of deposits into cash, also known as partial suspension, whereby banks provided depositors with only small amounts of cash. When bank depositors sought to withdraw larger amounts of money from the bank during a panic, they were not given cash but instead they would be given certified checks (or loan certificates in the Panic of 1907). Certified checks stamped "Payable through the Clearing House" were handed out as cash during panics (see Andrew 1908a and Kniffin 1916). Stamping the checks "Payable through the Clearing House" meant that accounts could be credited and debited on the basis of these checks. The certified checks were bearer instruments used to

buy merchandise or stock and sometimes to meet payrolls. In effect, these issues were temporary fiat currency that would be acceptable within local areas,
but not exchangeable into cash at full value during the panic.

In England there were clearinghouses but there was also the Bank of England. Nevertheless there was hoarding during panics and England too resorted to using checks: During the Panic of 1866 in England,

> For the daily balances of the clearings of each bank, bank notes are no longer
> required, as these are paid by cheques on the Bank of England, where they
> pass from one account to the other without the exhibition of a single bank
> note. The enormous amount of this circulating medium in London may how-
> ever be imagined, although it is impossible to ascertain its extent, by the fact
> that during the past year 1,489,137 cheques were presented through the clear-
> ing house, on one bank, of which 9,552 were passed on one day. Even for du-
> ties daily received at the Custom House, bank notes are no longer necessary,
> as in order to facilitate the transaction of business in this department of the
> State, these duties can be paid by cheques of Bankers on the Bank of England.
> All that is required by the receiver, is for the merchant to obtain a cheque for
> the amount of the duty from his banker, and thus no longer to incur the risk
> of drawing, from the banker's till, notes which might be lost or stolen in their
> transit to the Custom House. (Gassiot 1867, 16)

In the United States, a certified check for $10 was not the same as a $10 national banknote or $10 in coins. National banknotes were backed by the gov-
ernment (US Treasury bonds had to be deposited with the US Treasury for
a national bank to be able to issue its notes), and coins were "backed" by
their metallic content. Certified checks were the joint liabilities of the clearinghouse member banks. Because these checks were privately backed, there
was the risk that the clearinghouse would default and the checks could suffer
a loss. As a result of this difference between cash and certified checks, a new
market opened during the suspension period, a market for buying and selling cash in terms of certified checks. For example, to buy $1.00 of currency
might have required $1.05 of certified checks, leading to a 5 percent currency
premium. And one could think that the premium was also a reflection of the
total volume outstanding, which increased the likelihood that the clearinghouse would face insolvency. But those amounts were not tracked carefully,
and so there is little data to test the intuition.

Certified checks traded against cash at a price—the "currency premium."
This premium was the outcome of this newly opened market for cash money
and can be thought of as a measure of the beliefs of households, firms, and
banks about the solvency of the New York Clearing House, and effectively the
US banking system. In other words, while the clearinghouse cut off the pub-

lication of bank-specific information, the new market revealed information about the expected duration of the suspension period as well as the solvency of the entire banking system. Concerns about the length of a suspension period indicate liquidity issues—how long the US financial system would have to make do without a fully functional system. Previous experiences of panic could be a guide for duration, and there were known mechanisms in place to adjust to the circumstances. Concerns about the solvency of the financial system also had precedents in previous panics, and likely comprised the largest proportion of the currency premium. This combination of a lack of bank-specific information and an informative currency premium embedding beliefs about the solvency of the system focused the attention of firms and households on the overall solvency issue.

Certified Checks

As a form of money during crises, certified checks were introduced and began trading during the Panic of 1873. Sprague (1910, 54, 56), referring to the Panic of 1873, wrote that:

> the following momentous resolution was adopted [by the New York Clearing House]:
> That all checks when certified by any bank shall first be stamped or written "Payable through the Clearing House."
> The adoption of this resolution involved the partial suspension of cash payments by the banks. It did not signify that no money whatever would be paid out to depositors, but it placed the dwindling supply of currency more absolutely within the control of the clearing-house committee. . . .
> . . . The first and most immediate consequence of partial suspension by the New York banks was the appearance of a premium upon currency in terms of certified checks.

Timberlake (1984, 5) points out that the resolution "put certified checks on a par with clearinghouse loan certificates. The banks accepted them as settlement media by common consent through their clearinghouse association, but did not have to redeem them with legal tender." In other words, certified checks were the joint liability of the clearinghouse.

Certified checks helped alleviate the shortage of a transactions medium due to currency hoarding. *Bradstreet's*, August 12, 1893, wrote: "The scarcity of currency under the pressure of the present stringency has led to the suggestion of the use of certified checks in making up pay-rolls, and in other ways to take the place of currency to a limited effect" (501). Certified checks looked like money.

Identical with these [loan] certificates in character and function, tho [sic] dif-
fering in form, were the clearing-house checks issued in a number of cities.
Like the certificates, they were issued by the associations to member banks
upon the deposit of approved securities. Like them, they were accepted for
deposit in any of the banks, but were payable only through the clearing house.
They were also in currency denominations, and were often quite as elabo-
rately engraved, so as to resemble currency. The one peculiarity which distinguished them from certificates was that, instead of merely certifying indebtedness on the part of the clearing-house association, they took the form
of checks drawn upon particular banks, and signed by the manager of the
clearing house. (Andrew 1908a, 509)

Certified checks were "payable to bearer" or "payable only through the clearinghouse." Sometimes the checks were made payable to "John Smith, or
bearer," or similarly.

Clearinghouse member banks accepted certified checks as cash in the
clearing process. This put every bank at risk to the possible failure of the
certifying bank and created an incentive to monitor each other. But, unlike
clearinghouse loan certificate issues, the checks were not explicitly guaranteed. Still, certified checks were used as a form of hand-to-hand currency. An
editorial in *Bankers' Magazine* put it this way: "The issue of 'clearing-house
checks' has shown that here is a form of currency that may be used to great
advantage in times of panic. . . . There is, perhaps, not much danger of loss
to the holders of any of this form of currency, since the banks constituting
the various clearing-houses will no doubt see to it that there is ample security
for all the notes put out" ("The Central Bank Scheme," *Bankers' Magazine* 76
[January 1908]: 7–8, quote on 8). How much was issued? Noyes (1894, 29n1)
stated,

> For obvious reasons, it is very hard to arrive at any trustworthy estimate of the
> amount of money thus brought into the market. The Wall Street firm which
> did the largest proportion of the business estimates the amount of money
> which changed hands during the currency premium at $15,000,000; but this,
> though based on personal experience, is largely guesswork. Some up-town
> retail stores sold their daily receipts of currency, a fact pretty publicly proved
> by the vigor with which other retail houses, in their advertisements at the
> time, boasted that they had regularly deposited their cash receipts in the bank.

The use of money substitutes during panics, including clearinghouse loan
certificates and certified checks, was widespread nationally. Andrew (1908b)
reported that during the Panic of 1907, of the 145 largest cities, 71 made use of
these money substitutes, and in 20 other cities depositors were asked to mark
their checks "payable only through the clearinghouse."

In the United States, the issue arose of whether the certified checks legally counted as a form of money. An 1864 law had levied a tax on private banknotes, effectively to eliminate their issuance by state banks, which predominated prior to the US Civil War. If they were money, then an enormous tax would have to be paid by the issuing banks. But certified checks were unofficially deemed not to be money and so were not subject to the tax. This, however, was essentially a selective fiction. The National Bank Act had a provision that prohibited a national bank from issuing "any other notes to circulate as money than are authorized by the provisions of this title." And further, there was a 10 percent tax on any notes issued by state banks. Nevertheless, "a large number of national banks issued what were for all practical purposes circulating notes in the form of cashier's checks in convenient denominations. . . . These checks usually purported to be 'payable to bearer,' but they were 'payable only through the clearing house,' or 'in exchange,' or, as the phrase sometimes went, 'in clearing-house funds'" (Andrew 1908a, 510). Further, by making the certified checks payable to bearer or a fictitious person, smaller banks thought they were avoiding the law. It seems that the legality of certified checks was never challenged in a court. There was simply widespread forbearance because of the need for the additional supply of a circulating medium. Essentially, during times of crisis, the stipulations of the law were overlooked.

Aside from the question of whether certified checks were money, there was another problem with how certified checks circulated as cash substitutes. Under the law, checks presented or deposited had to be paid in legal tender, unless otherwise agreed. Angert (1908, 26) gives the following example: "Suppose a country bank presents its check to a city depository and is refused currency, and in a subsequent [law]suit it is shown that the amount of currency demanded would have prevented a run on the bank and its suspension; would not the court say that the injury to the country bank's business was such a loss as under the rules of damages should be compensated for?" *The Financier* (October 4, 1873, 182) argues that there is no issue as far as the loan certificates are concerned; the comptroller of the currency can take no official action as it does not violate the law. Section 50 of the National Bank Act says "that on becoming satisfied, as specified in this act, that any association has refused to pay its circulating notes as aforesaid and is in default, the comptroller of the currency may forthwith appoint a receiver." Further, *The Financier* notes, the act of March 3, 1869, prohibits the certification of checks except when there are actual deposits being made at the same time and provides that any violation of this restriction is subject to the same penalty as specified in Section 50. If a bank does not redeem its (national bank) notes in legal tender, and if its reserves have fallen below the legal rate, then "*after notification from the comptroller,* it fails for thirty days to make good the deficiency; when its officers certify checks beyond the actual amount of deposits of the maker of the check at that time" (*The Financier*, 182; emphasis in original), then the comptroller can take action. There then follows a rather cumbersome procedure for possibly closing the bank.

But with regard to demand deposits: "The law does not undertake to protect depositors, except by the reserve requirement, the personal liability imposed upon stockholders, and the various restrictions intended to secure a bank against failure" (*The Financier*, October 4, 1873, 183). *The Financier* concludes that "It thus appears that the power of the comptroller to close up banks is less than is commonly supposed, and that there is no authority granted him by law to take possession of a bank which has gotten into trouble, as was done with the Ocean [Bank], the First National of Washington, and the Bank of the Commonwealth" (182).

Angert (1908) notes that no such case was made. Instead, the country bank would suspend convertibility, as would the city bank. Again, it appears that there was never a court case to test the law. *Bradstreet's*, August 12, 1893, reported that "The question of the legality of this practice was submitted to the Comptroller of the Currency . . . and he has rendered an opinion to the effect that he sees no legal objection to the plan" (501). Noyes (1894, 26) notes, "it was alleged, in the daily press and on the floor of the United States Senate, that New York City banks were refusing to redeem checks of their own depositors in legal tender money. This accusation was made with bitterness, and it was not denied. The popular sentiment was, however, strongly against the proposed senatorial investigation. No bank depositor to whom cash payment was refused ever gave public utterance to complaint. No legal process was invoked."

The Market for Money

The money market opened because, in a crisis, certified checks are not perfect substitutes for national banknotes, greenbacks, silver and gold certificates or coins (these constitute "cash"; see appendix D). In the money market, cash was traded for certified checks. During a panic, there is an excess demand for cash. For some purposes, cash historically has been the only acceptable form of money. For example, meeting payrolls usually required cash and, in some instances, like customs tax payments, only gold coin would suffice. But cash hoarding leaves a low supply of cash. Noyes (1894, 28) described what happened during the Panic of 1893:

Currency . . . went to a premium [over certified checks]. Two or three active Wall Street money brokers at once inserted newspaper advertisements offering a premium for gold or silver coin, or for paper legal tender currency. This premium was at first one and one-half and two per cent; it rose once to four per cent. In quick response to these advertisements, the hoarded money of New York and its vicinity poured into the Wall Street offices. The brokers paid for this currency, in turn, by certified checks on their own bankers. They sold the currency at an average advance of one-half of one per cent. Two classes of buyers chiefly furnished the demand. First, and most naturally, there were employers of labor with large weekly or monthly pay-rolls, whose deposits lay in banks which flatly refused to pay them cash for checks. Second, and more numerous than might have been supposed, there were banks which were unwilling to refuse cash payments, but which were not averse to paying a premium to replenish their cash reserves.

And the *New York Times*, August 12, 1893, wrote,

Trading in cash was still carried on in a heavy scale, however, in spite of the generally easier feeling in the Street. . . . In the money brokers' offices the story of the day before was repeated. There were crowds eager to sell notes or coin, and other crowds anxious to buy. The sellers outnumbered the buyers, for the reason that the wide publicity given to the premium on currency served to bring out scores of hoarders of amounts running from the tens into the thousands of dollars. . . . Some of the brokers said that their largest customers were up-town merchants, who needed money to make customs payments. (9)

The money brokers referred to were apparently nonbank financial firms. People would go to these firms to trade certified checks for money and vice versa. "In the office of the money brokers was a crowd limited only by the size of the rooms, while dozens of would-be buyers or sellers waited near the doors for a chance to get up to the counters and do business" (*New York Times*, August 11, 1893, 6). The two sides of the market for money were sellers of cash, typically selling cash that had been hoarded, who were motivated to sell by the existence of the premium, and buyers of cash, which included companies in need of cash to meet payrolls, as well as others who wanted to hoard the cash. For example, the *New York Times*, November 8, 1907, in an article headlined "Premium Brings Out Hoarded Currency," reported that

The Wall Street money brokers who have been buying and selling currency during the present flurry, estimated yesterday that they had succeeded, by the offer of premiums, in drawing out of strong boxes this week $5,000,000 to $8,000,000 of hoarded money. One firm placed the amount at $10,000,000. . . . The demand yesterday came largely from manufacturers and large commercial houses who have to meet heavy payrolls tomorrow, and who could not obtain the full amount of cash from their banks. One concern, a large smelting works in New Jersey, bought $100,000, paying 3¼per cent premium. (3)

While the Clearing House cut off the public revelation of member bank-specific information, the currency premium in the market for certified checks was revealing information. Beliefs about the solvency of the banking system were reflected in the value of currency premium. The currency premium reflected beliefs conditional on all the Clearing House's actions: issuing clearinghouse loan certificates, special examinations of member and nonmembers, and increases in the aggregate reserves of the Clearing House. Depositors' beliefs about the solvency of the New York Clearing House, essentially the solvency of the US banking system, can be measured in terms of the currency premium over certified checks.

The Currency Premium

Figures 7.1A, B, and C show the currency premiums for the panics of 1873, 1893, and 1907, respectively. The currency premiums are near or at zero by the end of the panic (dating the end by a zero currency premium), but, notably, the currency premiums do not always monotonically decline during the suspension period in any of these panics. The premiums reached a high of five percent in all three cases. A premium of five percent means that you receive $9.50 in cash for a $10 certified check. The currency premiums were highest at the beginning of a panic when it was not yet clear that the New York Clearing House actions would be effective or were going to be effective. In 1893, the currency premium arose following the suspension of convertibility, which took place August 3, nearly six weeks after the first issues of clearinghouse loan certificates. As a result, the currency premium was not as closely associated with the degree of uncertainty in financial markets in 1893 as in 1873 or 1907. We explore the relationship of the currency premium and the importation of gold during the crises of 1893 and 1907 further in the next chapter.

In the Panic of 1893, suspension occurred in early August, but the currency premium, at least as reported by the press, appeared later. In the Panic of 1907, the currency premium was high for a long period of time and did not really go down until there was enough gold in the country (discussed subsequently) for the New York Clearing House to rescind suspension and restore full convertibility of deposits into cash. That pattern could indicate why the Panic of 1907 led to the creation of the Federal Reserve System. The situation was becoming beyond the control of the New York Clearing House.

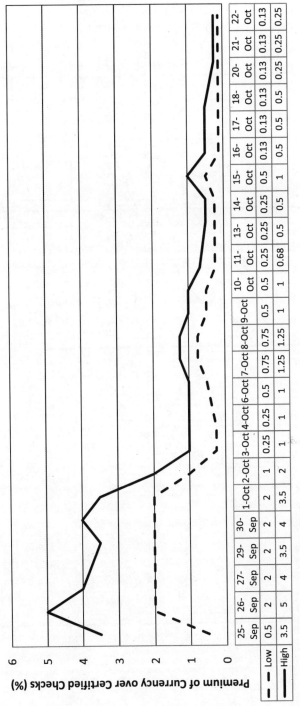

	25-Sep	26-Sep	27-Sep	29-Sep	30-Sep	1-Oct	2-Oct	3-Oct	4-Oct	6-Oct	7-Oct	8-Oct	9-Oct	10-Oct	11-Oct	13-Oct	14-Oct	15-Oct	16-Oct	17-Oct	18-Oct	20-Oct	21-Oct	22-Oct
Low	0.5	2	2	2	2	2	1	0.25	0.25	0.5	0.75	0.75	0.5	0.5	0.25	0.25	0.25	0.5	0.13	0.13	0.13	0.13	0.13	0.13
High	3.5	5	4	3.5	4	3.5	2	1	1	1	1.25	1.25	1	1	0.68	0.5	0.5	1	0.5	0.5	0.5	0.25	0.25	0.25

FIGURE 7.1A. Currency premium for Panic of 1873

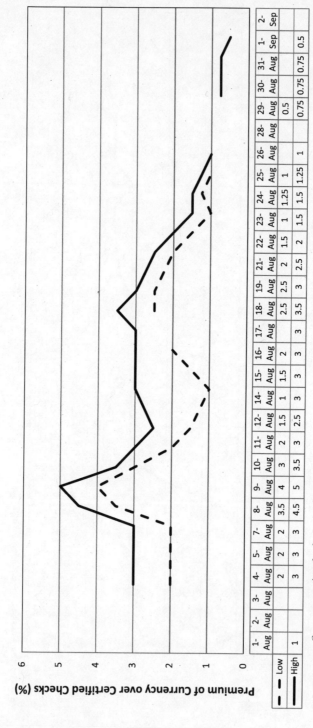

FIGURE 7.1B. Currency premium for the Panic of 1893

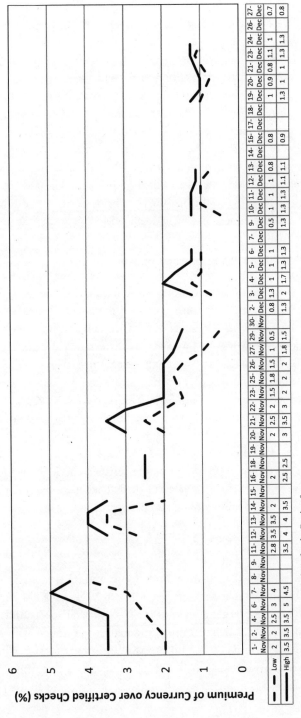

FIGURE 7.1C. Currency premium for the Panic of 1907

Source: Data from *New York Tribune* and *New York Times* (various dates), Sprague (1910, 56, 186, 280).

What do the currency premiums mean? What is implied about the solvency of the New York Clearing House Association? To get a sense of the meaning of the premium, we can calculate the implied (risk-neutral) probability of default. Though it will be a very rough measure, it can provide some sense of what market participants believed about the solvency of the New York Clearing House during a panic. To make this calculation, first note that a certified check is a pure discount bond (selling at a discount because of the currency premium). That is, a one dollar check, worth less than one dollar in currency today, is a claim on one dollar of cash when returned to the bank at some future date after resumption of convertibility has occurred. However, this future date—the maturity date of the bond—is not known.

The discount reflects two factors: the time value of money and the probability that the clearinghouse itself will default.[2] We can get a sense of the implied probability of default as follows. To calculate the probability of default as implied by the currency premiums, we need to know (1) the maturity of the pure discount certified check, (2) the recovery rate (per dollar of certified check) if the New York Clearing House were to fail, and (3) a risk-free rate (think of a US Treasury rate) consistent with the assumed maturity. These three factors are unknown. The maturity is uncertain and time-varying. The maturity is not set and will be longer to the extent that the crisis goes on. And for any particular maturity that might be assumed, there are no US government bonds with that (short) maturity. And, since no clearinghouse ever failed, we have no historical examples of recovery rates. Nevertheless, over a reasonable range of parameter values, the implied probability of clearinghouse default is high. And that is the point.

The basic calculation is as follows. Let the currency premium be c. Then the price of a zero coupon bond, that is, the certified check, is $100/(100 + c)$ $\equiv P$. From the price we can calculate the yield. Then a good approximation for the risk-neutral probability of default per year is

$$\frac{y-r}{1-RR}$$

where y is the yield, r is the risk-free interest rate, and RR is the recovery rate (the amount the holder of a certified check expects to get back if the clearinghouse fails). Then we can get a sense of the (risk-neutral) probability of default of the New York Clearing House as implied by the currency premiums. Figure 7.2 plots these implied default probabilities assuming the maturity is 180 days. There are two cases for the risk-free rate: 0 and 1 percent. Nothing is earned if the cash is hoarded and that is the only risk-free alternative; the

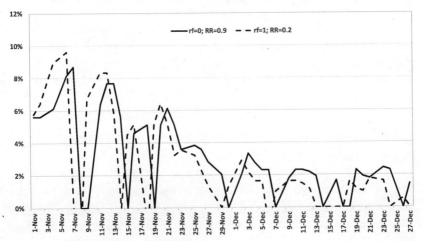

FIGURE 7.2. Panic of 1907 implied default probability

Source: Data from *New York Tribune* and *New York Times* (various dates), Sprague (1910) for currency premium, authors' calculations of probability of default.

Note: Maturity = 180 days

other case assumes $r = 1$ percent. Two recovery rates are used: $RR = 0.9$ and $RR = 0.2$.

In the figure the (risk-neutral) default probabilities reach a high of almost 9 percent and then trend down to zero. A probability of 2 percent that the New York Clearing House will default is a very high number. But the figure is only suggestive because in reality the maturity was not known with certainty, and we do not know the other parameters for sure. The point is that although the plots of the currency premiums may seem low, the implied default probabilities from these premiums can be quite high.

The implied probability of default seems to have been high, indicating that at the height of the panic people thought that there was about a one in ten chance that the New York Clearing House was insolvent. That probability assessment arose because these panics were systemic events in which the entire financial system was on the verge of failure. Similarly, the Panic of 2007–8 also threatened the solvency of the entire financial system. Recall that the chairman of the Federal Reserve Board of Governors, Ben Bernanke (2010), stated in his testimony before the Financial Crisis Inquiry Commission that "out of . . . the 13 most important financial institutions in the United States, 12 were at risk of failure within a period of a week or two." In the modern crisis of 2007–8, a different financial instrument was revealing about the probability of system-wide bank failures. A derivative contract, the credit default swap, is a kind of insurance contract on losses due to default of a single bank. But the prices of these instruments as a group were informative about the risk of system-wide bank failure. (See, e.g., Giglio 2011 and Eichengreen et al. 2012.)

The Importance of the Currency Premium

The currency premium publicly summarized the public's assessment of the probability of banking system solvency. As in other financial markets, the premium (or price) embedded the beliefs and information of the public. And the premiums were published in newspapers for all to see. So, everyone knew that everyone else was thinking in the same way, and this was summarized by the currency premium. What was particularly interesting, though, is the brief duration of the highest currency premiums during panics. In each instance, the premium on currency hit its highest levels immediately after suspension and then declined to levels that were still elevated but never again reached the peak levels. The decline to a zero currency premium took place over several weeks and was nonmonotonic. From a historical perspective, it seems that the public's perception of the actions of the clearinghouse and the outcomes measured in the aggregate banking statistics were helping to settle down the financial market. The next chapter investigates some particular signals that were central elements in how depositors resolved their uncertainties about the condition of the banking system.

8

The Change in Depositors' Beliefs during Suspension

When panics start, depositors rush to their banks to withdraw their deposits as cash. That sounds like a bank run, but banking panics are different—in panics, depositors effectively run from the banking *system*, not just from their bank. Taking cash out of the banking system is more serious than a run on one bank because panic withdrawals from the banking system can cause a magnified contraction in credit. In these systemic events, banks have to scramble for cash reserves (or substitutes) to support their loans and investments. We have described the set of actions—clearinghouse loan certificates, certificated check issues, information suppression, special examinations, and public announcements—employed by the New York Clearing House Association banks in order to combat the panic, but no one action was sufficient to settle financial markets. In each panic, several weeks passed after the clearinghouse took its actions before relative stability of the financial market was restored. From the beginning of a panic until the return of deposits to banks, depositors (both individual households and interior banks) must have changed their beliefs about the solvency of the banking system in order for them to choose to redeposit their funds in New York Clearing House banks after having previously removed them or tried to withdraw them. Somehow their beliefs changed from panic to no panic. Having a perspective from the previous chapters, we are now in a position to investigate how the beliefs of depositors changed. Suspension of convertibility of deposits into currency and the subsequent gold imports are both important elements among a number of actions and outcomes that set the conditions for the change in beliefs that was necessary for recovery from the crisis.

Summary of the Timing of Crisis Events

We can learn a lot from the timing of events. Table 8.1 summarizes the timing of events in New York. The table presents an overview of the five panics
during the US National Banking Era. In appendix A we provide the details of
the sources for the information in table 8.1. The table contains the important
dates that are central to what follows. The columns in table 8.1 are in chrono-
logical order for the severe panics. This is important, as we will see below.

Columns 1–5 of the table concern the start of the panic. Column 1 of the
table shows the date that is often popularly cited as the start date of the panic,
although, as we say above, the early events were chaotic. Column 2 lists the
last date on which the New York Clearing House published bank-specific information in each panic. Column 3 shows the date when clearinghouse loan
certificates were first issued. Column 4 shows the date that convertibility was
suspended. Column 5 shows the date on which the currency premium on
certified checks first became positive. When the panic starts, columns 2 and 3
are the clearinghouse policy responses. The panic is ongoing, as the currency
premium indicates.

As noted above, in the severe panics of 1873, 1893, and 1907, the *first* action
of the clearinghouse is to suppress bank-specific information. Then clearinghouse loan certificates are issued, followed by suspension of convertibility, though this is not an action of the clearinghouse, but, rather, happens
spontaneously. (As described in chapter 4, the suspension of convertibility
takes hold as banks struggle with deteriorating cash liquidity.) After these
actions, the currency premium becomes positive. In the more severe panics,
we observe a timing sequence that is for the most part consistent. Two things
distinguish 1884—first, it was the only case in which clearinghouse loan certificates were issued only in New York City (no other city's clearinghouse issued loan certificates); second, it was a panic in which the main concern was
preventing runs on a few banks from affecting the financial system in general,
and it was successful in avoiding an episode of currency hoarding.

Table 8.1 shows that, except for 1884 and 1890, in all the other panics the
clearinghouse stopped the release and publication of bank-specific information after a given date as the first action the clearinghouse took. What all five
events have in common is the suppression of bank-specific information and
the issuance of loan certificates. The dates of loan certificate issuance are also
notable, as the issuance depends on the information that the clearinghouse
member banks have. In a few cases, the clearinghouse could see the panic
coming, but in all cases, the clearinghouse took prompt actions to combat
panic conditions. Clearinghouse loan certificates were issued two days prior

TABLE 8.1. Event dates for National Banking Era panics in New York City

		Start of the Panic					End of the Panic		
	2	*3*	*4*	*5*	*6*	*7*	*8*	*9*	*10*
1	Date CH stopped publishing bank-specific information	Date of first CH loan certificates	Date of suspension of convertibility	First date at which currency premium was positive	Date at which currency premium was zero	Date of resumption of convertibility	Date of last CH loan certificate issue	Date that individual bank info resumed	Date of final cancellation of loan certificates
Panic of	Panic start date								
1873	Sept. 18	Sept. 20	Sept. 20	Sept. 22	Sept. 25	Oct. 23	Nov. 1	Nov. 20	Dec. 6	Jan. 14, 1874
1884	May 14	May 24ª	May 14	No suspension	NA	NA	No suspension	June 6	June 7	Sept. 23, 1886
1890	Nov. 11	Nov. 15	Nov. 12	No suspension	NA	NA	No suspension	Dec. 22	Mar. 7, 1891	Feb. 7, 1891
1893	June 16	June 17	June 21	Aug. 3	Aug. 5	Sept. 2	Sept. 2	Sept. 6	Nov. 4	Nov. 1
1907	Oct. 21	Oct. 26	Oct. 26	Oct. 26	Oct. 31	Dec. 28	Jan. 1, 1908	Jan. 30, 1908	Feb. 8, 1908	Mar. 28, 1908

Note: Appendix A contains the sources for the dates in the table. "NA" means "not applicable" because it did not happen in that panic.
ª The *Commercial and Financial Chronicle* published a balance sheet on May 31, but the numbers were the same as for the May 24 balance sheet.

to suspension of convertibility in 1873 and one month prior in 1893; in 1907 suspension of convertibility and the first issue of loan certificates were co-incident. There was no suspension in 1884 and 1890, but loan certificates were issued in significant amounts. Still, even in 1884 and 1890 the New York Clearing House Association did not publish bank-specific information, though only for two weeks in 1884. In the severe panics, the currency premium arises following a suspension of convertibility when there is also an issuance of clearinghouse loan certificates and certified checks. In these instances, there was an aggregate shortage of cash reserves in the New York City financial system.

What about the ending of the crisis? Columns 6–10 are about the ending of the panic. Column 6 shows the date at which the currency premium became zero. The date of resumption of convertibility is in column 7. The date of resumption is difficult to pin down because resumption was never officially or publicly announced. Column 8 shows the last date that clearinghouse loan certificates were issued. The date that clearinghouse members' bank-specific information is again published is in column 9. Notably, the publication of bank-specific information takes place one or two months after the apparent date of resumption. The final cancellation date of the loan certificates is in column 10.

The currency premium movements, and in particular when it hit zero, was discussed in the press. In 1873, for example, *The Financier* on November 1, 1873, wrote, "The general financial situation has continued to steadily improve. The banks have been gaining in legal-tender strength at the rate of over three-quarters of a million per day. They have resumed currency payments without any formal announcement, and the premium on currency is entirely a thing of the past" (234).

And with regard to the Panic of 1907, *Dun's Review* on November 30, 1907, wrote, "Several suspended banks resumed, and on the opening days it was noticed that deposits usually exceeded withdrawals. These indications of restored confidence and the return of hoarded money to circulation greatly improves the outlook. Another favorable feature was the announcement by several currency brokers that no more premium business would be transacted" (6). And later *Dun's Review* on December 7, 1907, reported that "Hoarding money is disappearing, the premium on currency and returning confidence having brought much cash into circulation" (6). Yet *Dun's Review* on December 14, 1907, wrote, "A premium was still commanded for currency [last week]" (9). These conflicting observations in the quotations reveal explicitly the idea that the currency premium was not monotonic—it could fall close to zero and then increase again.

How did panics end? The sequence of events for the severe panics is notable. The currency premium hit zero *before* resumption and *before* individual bank information starts being published again. In other words, the market price of systemic risk goes to zero before there is any return to normalcy. By that point, market participants can see the light at the end of the tunnel, so to speak. These expectations are embedded in the currency premium. Individual bank information is published again a month or two only after convertibility is resumed, probably because there are still some interbank exchanges that are not in balance. If bank-specific information indicated shortages of cash at some banks, those banks would still be able to make interbank exchanges with clearinghouse loan certificates. The release of information on banks then would provide depositors a (noisy) signal about the identity of banks with outstanding clearinghouse loan certificates. As a result, the publication of bank-specific information took place after the stock of outstanding clearinghouse loan certificates was relatively small. And resumption of convertibility was never announced by the clearinghouse. The banks appear to ease into it, without any widespread coverage in the press and without the clearinghouse making any announcement. See appendix A.

After New York City, the next most important financial center was Philadelphia. Table 8.2 shows the same information for Philadelphia. There was no panic in Philadelphia in 1884. The Philadelphia Clearing House Association also stopped the publication of individual bank-specific information and issued loan certificates in the other four panics. As in New York City, the currency premium became zero to signal the end of the suspension period. Resumption then occurred and only later was individual bank-specific information published again.

The Importation of Gold

The New York Clearing House took actions to signal to their depositors that the banking system was solvent and liquid. The actions taken were fundamental to liquidity and solvency of the banking system, and these actions were publicly observed, having been reported in the press. For the panics of 1893 and 1907, the evidence presented below describes the mechanism that allowed the New York Clearing House banks and other intermediaries to import gold from abroad. The mechanism relies on an existing institutional structure that enabled large New York City national banks, as well as international gold arbitrageurs, to contract for gold importation from financial centers overseas.

A large volume of gold imports flowing into New York City was a key

TABLE 8.2. Event dates for National Banking Era panics in Philadelphia

		Start of the Panic				End of the Panic			
	1	2	3	4	5	6	7	8	9	10
Panic of	Panic start date	Date CH stopped publishing bank-specific information	Date of first CH loan certificates	Date of suspension of convertibility	First date at which currency premium was positive	Date at which currency premium was zero	Date of resumption of convertibility	Date of last CH loan certificate issue	Date that individual bank info resumed	Date of final cancellation of loan certificates
1873	Sept. 18	Sept. 30	Sept. 24	Sept. 21	Sept. 25	Oct. 24	Nov. 17		Dec. 1	
1890	Nov. 11	Nov. 18	Nov. 19	No suspension	NA	NA	No suspension		Feb. 16, 1891	May 22, 1891
1893	June 4	June 20	June 16	Aug. 7	Aug. 9	Sept. 5	Sept. 5	Nov. 20	Nov. 20	Dec. 9, 1894
1907	Oct. 21	Nov. 5	Oct. 28	Oct. 28	Nov. 4	Jan. 7, 1908	Jan. 7, 1908	Feb. 8, 1908	Feb. 10, 1908	Feb. 10, 1908

Note: Appendix A contains the sources for the dates in the table. "NA" means "not applicable" because this did not happen in that panic.

signal of solvency (and impending liquidity) that the New York Clearing House banks could convey to the public. And the press followed gold imports closely. For example, *Dun's Review* on November 16, 1907, wrote, "Liberal importations of gold have greatly strengthened the financial situation, and cargoes are en route that will arrive next week. The movement has exceeded expectations" (6).

Laughlin (1912, 262) expresses a similar idea with a practical and operational motivation: "Here is the fatal deficiency of bank-note issues as a means of curing a panic. In 1907 the one thing needed was lawful money which could be used as reserves. We must face facts, and not be led away by theories. The New York banks got this lawful money in two ways: (1) by importing gold and (2) by deposits from the [US] treasury."

The Panic of 1873 took place before the United States returned to the gold standard, and so gold flows may have played a part in the recovery from that crisis, but the role that gold played in 1873 differs from the role it played in 1893 and 1907. Gold inflows in 1873 indicate increasing assets but not cash liquidity. We discuss the Panic of 1873 separately, after the discussions of 1893 and 1907.

Gold imports were important for bank depositors because the gold was coming into the banks in the United States, signaling the confidence of foreign investors in the solvency of the New York Clearing House banks. Further, it was a response to the liquidity shortage, during which the New York Clearing House banks imposed restrictions on the convertibility of deposits into cash. For correspondent banks that had deposits in New York City banks, the gold imports were also an important factor in changing their beliefs about the severity of the crisis. Interior banks held substantial deposit balances in their New York City correspondent banks. When panics took hold, the interior correspondent banks often withdrew large portion of their balances from their New York City correspondent bank. Local depositors in New York City could hoard their cash in safe-deposit boxes temporarily and then redeposit that cash quickly. Interior depositors had to ship their cash, which would take time to arrive back in New York City. But they were also a large component of New York Clearing House deposits. We show that both the gold imports and a net increase in deposits from interior banks were important conditions for the New York Clearing House banks before they chose to restore deposit convertibility, our indicator of the end of a panic.

Evidence below is consistent with the claim that depositor beliefs changed when the liquidity of the New York Clearing House banks, as a group, was apparently restored and that such information was widely available to the public and embedded in the currency premium. The change in beliefs among depositors must have taken place prior to the removal of payment restrictions because net deposit inflows from the interior to New York Clearing House banks had to become positive prior to the lifting of payment restrictions.

In 1893 and 1907, gold imports from abroad after the suspension of convertibility comprised the most publicized and effective actions taken by clearinghouse banks during both panics. We highlight key observations and public announcements at specific dates to indicate a change in beliefs—a change that signaled an increase in deposits from the interior correspondent banks. We propose that actions taken by the New York Clearing House banks to increase reserve balances, the publication of those actions, and the resulting increases in reserve balances helped change depositor beliefs. *Dun's Review* on January 11, 1907, wrote, "Culminating as it did in the most tremendous inpour of foreign gold upon a panic stricken market that the world has ever seen, the movement of international exchange can certainly claim a place of first dramatic interest in the epoch-making financial history of 1907" (31).

New York Clearing House Aggregates

The aggregate balance sheet of the clearinghouse members was published during the period of suspension, and so it could be observed. In this subsection, we look at data on the New York Clearing House's aggregate liquidity position during the panics. We examine data on the issues of clearinghouse loan certificates and the net reserve surplus (or deficit) relative to required reserves.

Using data from Andrew (1910) and from Moen and Tallman (2015), we examine how the New York Clearing House banks fared during the panics. The New York Clearing House mandated a 25 percent reserve for each member bank, and so the periods in which the aggregate reserve balance fell below required reserves should signal distress. Figures 8.2, 8.3, and 8.4 below show the New York Clearing House reserve surplus, the outstanding level of clearinghouse loan certificates, and the currency premium. In the figures, we observe a pattern between the clearinghouse loan certificate volume and the reserve deficit of New York Clearing House banks. They are mirror images of each other, with a correlation of −0.68 in 1893 and −0.75 in 1907 (based on weekly data). Essentially, as currency is drained from the banks, clearinghouse loan certificates are issued. And, as the reserve surplus increases, the level of outstanding loan certificates falls. The figures also include the currency premium. The currency premium is also negatively correlated with the reserve surplus: −0.47 in 1893 and −0.74 in 1907.

Bradstreet's on July 33, 1893, wrote, "Last Saturday's weekly bank statement was essentially a negative showing. The only change of importance was the decrease of $812,925 in the deficiency in legal reserves" (463).

The Panic of 1893

Wicker (2000) makes clear that the Panic of 1893 was centered in the interior of the country; it did not greatly affect New York City or the New York Clearing House in its initial stages. The reserve surplus of New York Clearing House banks diminished after the beginning of the panic in June, but the first instance of a reserve deficit in this episode was in early July, and it hovered at around $5 million. For perspective, the level of net deposits in the New York Clearing House banks ranged between $375 and $400 million, and so the deficit was not much more than 1 percent of net deposits (or about 4 percent of reserve levels). The provision of clearinghouse loan certificates in late June apparently attenuated panic conditions, but it did not change the direction of the reserve balance. For the Panic of 1893, the date of the suspension of payments (August 3) initiates the period of increased severity of the panic.

Statements in the *New York Tribune* on July 21, 1893, indicate that New York Clearing House bankers were concerned that the Chicago Clearing House had not yet agreed to issue clearinghouse loan certificates (in fact, they did not issue any during the Panic of 1893). Further, the newspapers described New York City banking and financial interests as expressing widespread dissatisfaction with the Sherman Silver Purchase Act of 1893 (part of the dissatisfaction was political, because it was far less distortionary than the Bland Allison Act that it replaced). Still, the news about the US Treasury's gold supply expressed fears that the US maintenance of the gold standard was likely under threat. And discord among the central reserve cities indicated disarray in the midst of a financial crisis. On page 2, the article with the headline "Money Leaving the City?" emphasized the renewed drain of cash from New York City banks with shipments toward the interior. The article also mentioned that bankers had already assumed that net cash shipments out of New York City would exceed inflows. A key comment noted that bankers were considering imports of gold, but only if it could be done at a reasonable profit. In the July 22 *New York Sun*, an article reported that bankers bemoaned "feeble gold imports" and suggested that necessary gold imports were not feasible at existing exchange rates.

The front-page article in the *New York Sun* on August 4, 1893, stated that a currency premium arose from the unwillingness of certain banks to respond to demands for currency, which we interpret as effectively a suspension of convertibility announcement. The article was sympathetic to New York City banks, noting that the cash drains from New York City had been protracted throughout the summer and threatened the reserve balances of the New York Clearing House banks. News of cash drains from New York City and bank unwillingness to pay cash caused distress among the depositors of New York City banks and added a speculative motive (get cash while you can) to withdraw cash from clearinghouse banks. Further, the same issue of the *New York Tribune* had an article with the following headline:

Almost a Currency Famine
The Scramble for Small Bills Puts Them at a Premium
Hoarding of Money One Cause of the Trouble

The suspension of convertibility was initiated on August 3, 1893, and a currency premium arose by the weekend. The liquidity scramble after the suspension of convertibility was mainly observable in the New York Clearing House banking aggregates and in the related currency premium. The currency premium was highest (between 4 and 5 percent) on August 8 and 9. By August 11, the reserve deficit among New York Clearing House banks was the deepest weekly reserve deficit of this panic at $16 million. In terms of the percentage of "lawful reserves," this figure was about 16 percent.

The currency premium in New York City and elsewhere generated large-scale gold inflows from overseas because the cash premium made gold imports highly profitable during such crises. The effective gold standard in 1893 operated with the "mint parity" US dollar–UK pound exchange rate at $4.86656 (US dollars per British pound). In normal circumstances, the gold import (export) point was $4.835 ($4.899) approximately −0.655 percent below (above) the mint parity exchange rate. Exchange rate price differentials outside the range were sufficient to motivate shipments of gold.

An exchange rate below the normal gold import point ($4.835) would typically motivate an inflow of gold into the United States. The mechanism required the purchase (or borrowing) of British pounds at the lower exchange rate (say $4.81). One would then take the pound proceeds and buy gold at the gold parity rate ($4.86656 from official sources supporting the gold standard), and then ship the gold to the United States. The value of the gold in the United States dollars (at mint parity) is higher than the price ($4.81) that was originally paid for pounds, so that the importer makes a profit in excess of shipping costs. In the example, $4.86656 − $4.81 = .05656, a 1.162 percent gross return (about 0.5 percent net of gold shipping expenses). The gain may seem small, yet it was a lucrative activity for large-market participants. The activity requires two to three weeks to mature and generates an 8 to 9 percent net annual return with relatively low risk.

When the currency premium was about 4.0 percent, the value of the gold in the United States would be 4.86656*1.04 or 5.0612, which then made it extremely profitable to import gold to the United States even when the exchange rate was above the normal gold export point ($4.899).[1] Hence, the suspension of convertibility, which generated the currency premium, comes prior to the observation of substantial accumulations of gold inflows. Appendix C describes the mechanism using example transactions.

We lack frequent observations of the subcomponents of aggregate liquidity measures as they were officially produced by the New York Clearing House. New York City daily newspapers, however, include numerous relevant component measures of reserves. In the summary of newspaper articles below, the key quantitative contributions are the running totals of clearinghouse loan certificates outstanding and the accumulation of gold imports in New York City banks.

Financial market reporting turns upbeat on August 11, 1893, when the newspaper articles report that imports of gold have been negotiated. In the *New York Tribune*, the disturbing headline was "Banks Won't Pay Out Cash," and the text indicates that currency brokers were able to get as much as a 4 percent premium for it. However, in the same article it was stated that the currency premium was not expected to persist for long because it had already motivated the importation of gold from overseas that was anticipated to be about $23 million.[2] On Sunday, August 13, 1893, the *New York Tribune* describes how imports of gold for the week totaled nearly $14 million (4) (a report the following day stated $13.2 million with $7.477 million in US coin).

By August 18, 1893, the *New York Tribune* reported that there was still a 3 percent premium on currency in spite of "heavy arrivals of gold." The article indicates the daily increase in clearinghouse loan certificates of $365,000, which then increased the volume of clearinghouse loan certificates outstanding to $37.38 million (as of August 17, 1893, which matches exactly the total outstanding calculated by Moen and Tallman [2015] from the individual clearinghouse loan certificate requests). On August 19, 1893, the *New York Tribune* reported that net gold imports were approximately $17.3 million in the prior four weeks (three of which had a currency premium) and noted the persistence of the currency premium. The article reported that more gold shipments were on the way. By Monday, August 21, 1893, the accumulated gold inflow was measured to be $24.46 million, but there was no sense of cheer. Rather, the newspaper article noted that the stock market was still in decline.

In the aggregate, the reserve balances among New York Clearing House member banks increased consistently each week after the low point observed in the week ending August 11. The weekly reserve balance numbers improved after that observation, largely from gold imports. The imports increased because of the profitability of gold imports arising from the large currency premium.

There was a notable change in tone in the article in the *New York Tribune* on Saturday, August 26, 1893. It noted that the currency premium was fast disappearing (it had fallen to about 1 percent the previous two days), that there was good indication that the Sherman Silver Purchase Act would be repealed, and that there were inflows in the form of increases in deposits that were restoring the reserves of the New York Clearing House banks.

> Four prominent Clearing House managers compared notes yesterday and their estimates of the gain in reserves were respectively $4 million, $5 million, $6 million, and $7 million. The net gain of the banks through the operations of the Sub-Treasury this week was over $3.7 million and unless the shipments to the interior were heavier than is generally supposed there will be several millions of imported gold to be added, to this amount. Should another heavy reduction in the deficit in reserve be reflected to-day it is argued that the foreign gold due to-day and next week will cling largely to the hands of the commercial banks. (3)

As gold inflows helped to restore reserve levels after suspension of convertibility on August 3, reports of redeposit of funds in New York Clearing House banks (presumably by interior correspondents) all contributed to an improvement in the financial setting. The key indicators for the banking system—the reserve deficit and the currency premium—became noticeably benign in newspaper articles. By August 31, the currency premium was less than 1 percent (0.625 percent in the *New York Tribune*, 3).

We find evidence from both the stock and bond markets that is consistent with the hypothesis. Figure 8.1 displays weekly stock price and bond price index measures from May 20, 1893, through November 4, 1893. These two series illustrate "return correlation" and display strong comovement from June 4 through July 29; each index falls notably and consistently over this period. The bond price index bottoms out on August 5, 1893, just after the suspension of convertibility, and the stock price index on that date displays a slight rebound from its local trough during the previous week. For the period of suspension—August 3 to September 2—the two indexes display a modest upward trend.

We find corroboration in our view from a notable contemporary observer. Noyes (1909, 196) highlights the "unusual sum of forty-one millions gold imported during August," which was the largest gold inflow in any month up to that time in US history. "With this relief, the acute spasm of 1893 ended."

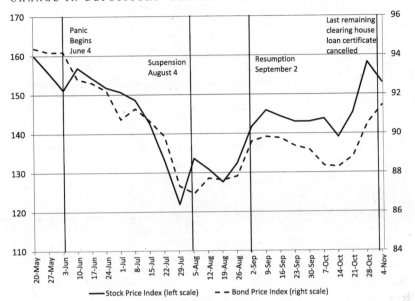

FIGURE 8.1. Panic of 1893 period: weekly stock price and bond price indexes
Source: Data from Kemmerer (1910) and Schwert (1990).

The Panic of 1907

The sequence of events during the Panic of 1907 bears some similarity to the event sequence for the 1893 episode. There are, however, notable differences in the timing of actions by the New York Clearing House—in 1907, the suspension of convertibility took place at the same time that clearinghouse loan certificates were announced; see table 8.1. The timing difference apparently did not change the perceived relationship between the currency premium and the subsequent gold inflows into New York City. The relationship between the gold inflows and the measures of financial distress, however, were clearly different. In 1907, the currency premium arose at the onset of the panic and the palliative effects of gold inflows took longer to moderate the crisis conditions. One reason for this difference was that depositor runs on trust companies continued even as the gold imports arrived, whereas in 1893, the panic was mainly among interior banks.

During this panic, there were weekly figures for imports of gold; see table 8.3. The currency premium hovered around 2–3 percent for most of the first two weeks of November. The inflows of gold are associated with a decline in the premium, but it is not monotonic. The correlation between the high currency premium and the accumulated gold for the period November 2, 1907, through January 4, 1908, is −0.89. In the week of November 29,

TABLE 8.3. New York financial market indicators of distress and monetary quantities

Week	Week ending	Currency premium		Call money rate		Net gold imports	NYCH loan certificates	Reserve deficit
		Low	High	Low	High	Accumulated	Net outstanding	Includes gold
42	Oct. 19, 1907	0	0	2.25	10	0.018	1.3	11.175
43	Oct. 26, 1907	0	0	5	125	−1.285	16.61	−1.225
44	Nov. 2, 1907	1	3	3	75	−1.765	57.235	−38.825
45	Nov. 9, 1907	1	4	4	25	5.508	72.095	−52
46	Nov. 16, 1907	2.5	4	5	15	26.619	80.185	−53.725
47	Nov. 23, 1907	1.5	3.5	3.5	15	39.032	84.885	−54.15
48	Nov. 30, 1907	0.75	1.75	3	12	55.578	84.595	−53
49	Dec. 7, 1907	0.5	2	3	13	69.389	86.97	−46.2
50	Dec. 14, 1907	0.5	1.5	2	25	78.856	87.32	−40.1
51	Dec. 21, 1907	0.5	1.25	6	17	84.560	87.865	−31.75
52	Dec. 28, 1907	0.25	1.25	6	25	88.675	86.495	−20.225
1	Jan. 4, 1908	0.125	0.375	5	20	97.763	80.815	−11.6
2	Jan. 11, 1908	0	0	2	9	101.390	68.345	6
3	Jan. 18, 1908	0	0	2.5	6	101.938	24.12	22.6
4	Jan. 25, 1908	0	0	1.5	3	102.313	6.65	37.1
5	Feb. 1, 1908	0	0	1.5	2	103.095	5.555	40.5

Source: Tallman and Moen 2012, 285, table 2.

Note: Numbers in bold denote observations indicating substantial financial distress. Net gold imports, New York Clearing House loan certificates, and reserve deficit are calculated in millions of US dollars.

1907, the reserve deficit shrank slightly and the gold imports continued. By that week, the accumulated gold imports exceeded $55 million. The currency premium remained below 2 percent in the early part of December as the reserve deficit diminished and the gold continued to accumulate. The gold imports into the United States continued to accumulate throughout the year and through most of January, although the import amounts dwindled after January 4.[3]

The change in reserves chart displayed in figure 8.2 shows how the currency premium declined as reserve inflows became consistently positive, as observed in 1893. Like in 1893, the currency premium in 1907 (figure 8.3) fell to zero when the New York Clearing House bank reserve balances were nearly positive, which occurred in January 1908.

The Panic of 1873

The Panic of 1873, the first panic of the National Banking Era, is different from those of 1893 and 1907 for a number of reasons. First, the Panic of 1873 occurred when the United States was off the gold standard, having suspended

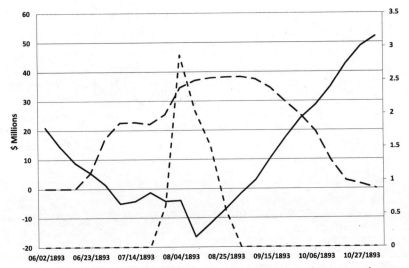

FIGURE 8.2. Panic of 1893 period: biweekly reserve surplus, clearinghouse loan costs, and currency premium

Source: Data from Kemmerer (1910), Clearing House Loan Committee minutes (various dates), and currency premiums from the *New York Times* and *New York Tribune* (various dates).

Note: Solid line = reserve surplus (left scale); *long dashes* = clearinghouse loan costs outstanding (left scale); *short dashes* = currency premium (%) (right scale)

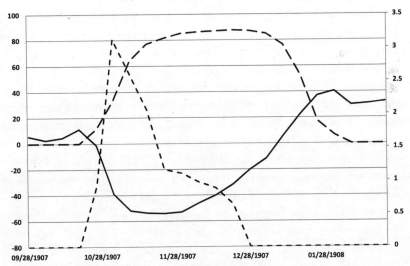

FIGURE 8.3. Panic of 1907: monthly reserve surplus, clearinghouse loan costs, and currency premium

Source: Data from Kemmerer (1910), Clearing House Loan Committee minutes (various dates), and currency premiums from the *New York Times* and *New York Tribune* (various dates).

Note: Solid line = reserve surplus (left scale); *long dashes* = clearinghouse loan costs outstanding (left scale); *short dashes* = currency premium (%) (right scale)

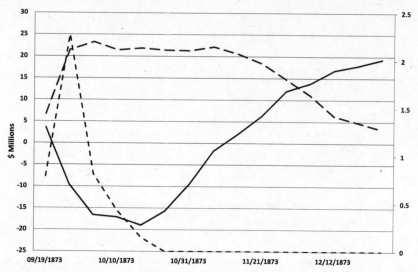

FIGURE 8.4. Panic of 1873: triweekly reserve surplus, clearinghouse loan costs, and currency premium
Source: Data from Kemmerer (1910), Clearing House Loan Committee minutes (various dates), and currency premiums from the *New York Times* and *New York Tribune* (various dates).
Note: Solid line = reserve surplus (left scale); *long dashes* = clearinghouse loan costs outstanding (left scale); *short dashes* = currency premium (%) (right scale)

it during the Civil War. Second, unlike the events of later panics, the New York Clearing House member banks agreed to formally pool their reserves. And, finally, the New York Stock Exchange closed for ten days.

Despite these differences, figure 8.4 displays patterns similar to those in figures 8.2 and 8.3 for the panics of 1893 and 1907. The correlation between the outstanding clearinghouse loan certificates and the reserve surplus was −0.85, and the correlation between the currency premium and the reserve surplus was −0.36. Figure 8.4 shows that the currency premium started to decline before the reserve surplus became positive, but it did not hit zero until the reserve surplus started to trend upward. The currency premium declined as the change in reserves became less negative, that is, the reserves were still contracting, but at a slower rate than the sharp decline from September 19 to 6, 1873.

Because the United States was not on the gold standard in 1873, the mechanism discussed above whereby the currency premium created an incentive for gold to be shipped to the United States was not active in 1873. Despite not being on the gold standard, gold was still necessary for payment in international trade transactions, and net trade surpluses led to greater gold inflows. Sprague (1910, 58–59) reports that gold did flow into the United States:

"on Friday, September 25, $2,500,000 was taken from the Bank of England for export to the United States. This was the beginning of a considerable movement which continued until the end of October, a total of $15,000,000 being sent to the United States from Europe."[4] And the *New York Times* on September 29, 1873, reported that "[t]he first shipments of English Gold from London to New York to arrive here next week are believed to be in good part on account of recent large loans for American Railroads and the Canadian Government" (2). Still, it does not seem as though this channel was as important as in the later panics.

The New York Clearing House actions, which were more dramatic than in the later panics, are likely to have played a large role in the resolution of the crisis. On September 20, 1873, the day that the clearinghouse stopped publishing bank-specific information, the association adopted a resolution reading in part: "in order to accomplish the purposes set forth in this agreement the legal tender belonging to the associated banks shall be considered and treated as a common fund, held for mutual aid and protection, and the committee appointed shall have the power to equalize the same assessment or otherwise, at their discretion" (*Commercial and Financial Chronicle*, September 27, 1873, 411). The provision to "equalize the reserves" had also been used in 1860, at the outbreak of the Civil War. As Sprague (1910, 48–49) explains, since the banks were not equally strong in reserves, "the arrangement for equalizing reserves . . . diminished the likelihood of the banks working at cross purposes—a danger which the use of clearing-house certificates alone can not [*sic*] entirely remove." Sprague attributes the pooling of reserves and the use of loan certificates as the chief factors ameliorating the panic. Yet inflows of capital from abroad can be taken as an important signal of confidence in the solvency of the financial system in the United States.

On September 20, 1873, the New York Clearing House Association voted to form a committee to oversee the issuance of clearinghouse loan certificates, by a unanimous vote. It was determined to issue up to $10,000,000 of certificates (*New York Times*, September 21, 1873, 1). And the *New York Times* on September 25, 1873, summarized the actions of the association:

> The action of the Associated Banks of New York in the Clearing-house this morning settled the following important points as to their course through the recent panic:
>
> *First*—That having already provided $10,000,000 Clearing Certificates of their own, which were all issued up to last night, the further sum of $10,000,000 was authorized today, and when these are exhausted, another $10,000,000 will be issued. . . .

Second—The Banks resolve to stand by each other, for common defense against a common panic or emergency. They agree to certify checks *payable only through the Clearing-house,* which means that the debtor Bank, next morning, can settle its balances either in Certificates of the Association or in Greenbacks. . . . These Greenbacks and all other Greenbacks and Treasury Certificates calling for Greenback Notes held in the Banks, are pooled or stocked for equal division, according to the capital of all the Associates.

Thirdly—The Banks resolve that any Bank in the Association "declining to participate fully in the arrangement" above noticed, for the purpose of attempting to make a factitious reputation or credit by departure from the letter or spirit of these measures of relief and mutual defense, shall, on report to the Manager of the Clearing-house, *be expelled from the Association.* (2, italics in the original)

These actions had a calming effect; the *New York Times,* on September 23, 1873, commented as follows:

When the Associated Banks convened in the Clearing-house, and the real condition of the Banks said to be involved in trouble were made known, the turn in confidence was immediate, the Clearing-house Association forthwith proceeded to the issue of any part of $10,000,000 Clearing Certificates. . . . To add the better turn of affairs, it was found that the clearances of Saturday's business was [*sic*] decidedly easier than was apprehended. Only two banks were in arrears, and these availed at once of the Clearing Certificates agreed to be issued on Saturday.

When it was generally known on the Street that the Associated Banks were all right, and amply prepared to make common cause in the course of business, without the drawback of a single failure of their number, there was a sense of relief. (2)

A few days later, the *New York Times* wrote again:

There is further very decided relief in Money affairs to-day, the result mainly of the sweeping action of the Associated Banks to issue their Clearing Certificates, bearing 7 per cent. interest on the pledge of the public funds at par and of general securities at 75 per cent. of their lowest market value, including, of course, Bills Receivable or Notes Discounted, *to any amount required,* to relieve the difficulties growing out of their general suspension early in the week. . . . The effect of this action was to satisfy the public mind that all possible mercantile embarrassment is to be averted. (September 29, 1873, 2; emphasis in original)

The New York Stock Exchange closed on September 20 and reopened ten days later. The problem with the stock exchange was that stocks were cleared by brokers using certified checks. The transactions involved large overdrafts from banks (see *New York Tribune*, September 24, 1873, 6, for details). The Stock Exchange Committee sent a letter to the Clearing House Committee, explaining that "The great obstacle we have to deal with in resuming the operations of the Stock Exchange is . . . the mode of settling our transactions. As long as the banks on whom checks are drawn are distrustful of each other, so long will a condition of unreasoning panic continue. . . . To reopen the Stock Exchange under this condition of affairs would simply . . . be the inauguration of a run upon the banks" (*New York Tribune*, September 25, 1873, 5).

The closing of the stock exchange allowed potential buyers of distressed stocks to organize resources to buy at the low prices, which were apparently viewed as profit opportunities:

> A still better feeling prevailed in Wall street [*sic*] yesterday at the close of business on Saturday. . . . Hundreds of thousands of dollars have been brought to New York by out-of-town parties, who are anxious to buy good securities at low figures. . . . The opening of the Stock Exchange will probably tend to set this money in motion and again restore it to the banks. . . . [A]s the opening of the Exchange will tend to restore confidence and render securities marketable, the banks cannot fail to again come into general use, and as a natural consequence swell their volume of deposits. (*New York Times*, September 30, 1873, 1)

The Stock Exchange reopened on September 30, 1873. The *New York Tribune* of October 1, 1873, reported that "The Stock Exchange was reopened yesterday without any renewal of the panic; before the session closed the official announcement was made that no one had failed, and that there was not a single delinquent member on earlier transactions. This virtually marks the close of the panic; public confidence has been restored in great measure, and trade and commerce are flowing back in their natural channels" (1). Indeed, September 26, 1873, is the date of highest currency premium, which generally declines after that date; see figure 7.1A for 1873, figure 7.1B for 1893, and figure 7.1C for 1907.

The reopening of the stock exchange aided the banks in being able to sell collateral they had seized when borrowers using the call loan market had defaulted. As the *New York Times* wrote on October 6, 1873:

> The reduction in the Clearing Certificates is no doubt due to the recovery in Stock values after the reopening of the Exchange. This enabled some of the Wall Street Banks that held demand loans on Stocks, which they could not collect while the Exchange remained closed, and had to be repledged in the extremity of the panic to the Clearing-house at 75 per cent. of their lowest market value, to retire their Certificates. . . . The relief of the Clearing-house

by the liquidation of loans to Brokers, some of which were forced loans . . .
will enable the Clearing-house committee to carry through certain large
Banks whose failure would not only add fuel to the crisis, but greatly distress
mercantile interests. (2)

During the crisis there was a great deal of discussion about what the government could and could not legally do (see *Commercial and Financial Chronicle*, September 27, 1873, 406). The US Treasury was limited in the actions that
it could legally undertake. The government did redeem some bonds, paying
out $13,000,000 in currency. *New York Times* on September 23, 1873, wrote
as follows: "The Treasury Office to-day was enabled to buy about $3,500,000
United States 5-20s at the rate of 110.72 cent." And wrote again on September
29, 1873: "The Treasury in the last week has paid out, at all points, $35,000,000
Greenback Notes. Of this sum $22,000,000 Notes were exchanged for the
$5,000 and $10,000 Certificates (heretofore used for clearings in the great
cities) and pay for United States 5-20s. The Treasury has also supplied since
the panic set in about $3,000,000 Circulating Notes to the new National
Banks of the South and West" (2). Sprague (1910, 42) argues that this was of
little consequence in relieving the panic because almost all the bonds were
purchased from savings banks, and they were unwilling to deposit the money
with commercial banks.

Summary

Depositors' beliefs about the solvency of the New York City financial system took time and reassuring events to change. Partly, those beliefs began to
stabilize when key components of bank balance sheets—reserve balances—
were fortified with infusions of gold from abroad. Beliefs changed further
when the reserve balances moved in the positive direction even though the
net "required" reserve balance among New York Clearing House banks was
still in deficit. Stability in the financial market was virtually reestablished
when depositor beliefs—including those of the correspondent bankers of
the interior of the country—were confident that the solvency and liquidity
of the New York Clearing House was restored. We can summarize this statement with regression results that relate our proxy for beliefs, the currency
premium, to the level of clearinghouse reserves.

We estimate a simple regression to highlight the contemporaneous relationship between the changes in the level of reserves held at the New York
Clearing House member banks and the changes in the currency premium
over the three National Banking Era panics in which there was a suspension

of the convertibility of deposits into currency. Equation 1 provides a description of the relationship:

$$(1) \qquad \Delta CP_t = \alpha + \beta_1 \, \Delta \, RSD_t + u_t$$

where CP = currency premium (average for the week) and RSD = reserves at the end of the week held by New York Clearing House member banks.

Tables 8.4A and B display the results. The estimated coefficient on the change in reserves is negative in each of the subsample periods (each panic), as well as for the pooled estimate. We note that there are only 22 observations for the pooled sample and 6, 6, and 10, respectively, for the three subsamples. The limited number of observations is why we focus on a simple estimation strategy. Still, we estimate the standard errors using a heteroskedastic consistent estimator and find that the coefficient estimates for change in reserves to be negative and statistically different from zero for each of the periods 1893 and 1907 and the pooled sample. The results emphasize how the currency premium spikes up as the reserves decline and flow out of the banking system and vice versa, the currency premium falls as reserves come back into the New York Clearing House banks, signaling the change in depositor beliefs about the prospects for the financial system.[5] Empirical results are similar for all regressions if we use as the explanatory variable the change in the reserve surplus or deficit (relative to required reserves).

TABLE 8.4A. Regression results for change in the currency premium measure

| | Dependent variable: change in currency premium | | | |
	1873	1893	1907	Pooled sample
Constant	−0.36 (0.35)	0.12 (0.43)	−0.03 (0.23)	−0.08 (0.19)
Change in reserves				
1873	−0.09 (0.06)			
1893		−0.14*** (0.05)		
1907			−0.07*** (0.01)	
Pooled sample				−0.08*** (0.017)
Adjusted R^2	0.22	0.33	0.44	0.37
D-W statistic	1.76	1.54	1.53	1.58
Number of				
observations	6	6	10	22

Note: Standard errors (in parentheses) are estimated with the Eicker-White heteroskedastic consistent estimator.

*** Denotes significance at the 1 percent confidence level.

TABLE 8.4B. Regression results for change in the currency premium measure using the change in the reserve surplus or deficit relative to required reserves as regressor

	Dependent variable: change in currency premium			
	1873	1893	1907	Pooled sample
Constant	−0.27 (.37)	0.15 (0.46)	−0.06 (0.20)	−0.05 (0.20)
Change in reserves in surplus or deficit of required reserves				
1873	−0.13 (0.08)			
1893		−0.12*** (0.04)		
1907			−0.07*** (0.01)	
Pooled sample				−0.07*** (0.013)
Adjusted R^2	0.22	0.18	0.56	0.35
D-W statistic	1.65	1.34	1.39	1.52
Number of observations	6	6	10	22

Note: Standard errors (in parentheses) are estimated with the Eicker-White heteroskedastic consistent estimator.

*** Denotes significance at the 1 percent confidence level.

9

Aftermath

It often has been repeated by the popular press as well as in numerous postmortems of the recent financial crisis that the central bank interventions during 2007–8 "averted another Great Depression," and that is perhaps so. It is very hard to evaluate central bank or clearinghouse responses to crises. Obviously, we have no counterfactuals. To evaluate the New York Clearing House Association's actions during a panic, we look at rather narrow metrics: Did clearinghouse member banks fail? Were there losses on clearinghouse loan certificates, and if so, how much were the losses? These questions also address the nature of fighting crises. In financial crises, almost all banks survive, although during the crisis there are fears that the entire system might go down. If panics essentially arise from an information issue about which banks were insolvent, then it should be the case that very few clearinghouse member banks actually failed. Further, there should be relatively small losses to the clearinghouse from defaults on clearinghouse loan certificates. The alternative hypothesis is that the banks took on too much risk and that many banks were effectively insolvent.

New York Clearing House Member Bank Failures

How well did the New York Clearing House do in avoiding bank failures and losses? We saw in table 1.1 that few national banks actually failed during recessions with panics. Did New York Clearing House members fail during the panics or shortly after? We address this question in several ways.

First, the 1920 *Annual Report* of the comptroller of the currency (56–73) lists all the national bank failures and the reason for the failure up until that date. There are thirty-three possible causes of failure, and each bank failure is assigned one cause. One reason for failure is "closed by run." There are seven cases of banks closed for this reason. None of these cases was a bank in New York City.

Second, Dudley (1890, 6) lists the New York Clearing House members that left the clearinghouse for some reason, up to 1890. He lists twenty-four members that left. Of these, the following occurred during or just after a panic:

- National Bank of the Commonwealth, September 22, 1873, in hands of receivers
- Metropolitan National Bank, voluntarily liquidated November 18, 1884
- Marine National Bank, failed May 6, 1884

The first day of suspension in the Panic of 1873 was September 22. And the Panic of 1884 started in May. The comptroller's *Annual Report* has the National Bank of the Commonwealth listed as failing as a result of "Injudicious banking and depreciation of securities," and the failure occurred at the start of the panic. The Metropolitan National Bank is not listed in the 1920 *Annual Report* of the comptroller of the currency. But in the comptroller's *Annual Report* of 1901, the Metropolitan is listed as having been voluntarily liquidated.[1] The Marine National Bank is listed as closed as a result of "Fraudulent management, excessive loans to officers and directors, and excessive loans to others."

Finally, another way to answer this question is by checking clearinghouse membership before the panic and comparing it with the membership list eight months later to see whether banks failed (or merged) in the aftermath. That is, a bank may have been propped up by the clearinghouse during the period of suspension but then allowed to fail afterward.

PANIC OF 1873

The New York Clearing House issued loan certificates on September 20, 1873. Just before the panic, on September 13, 1873, the *Commercial and Financial Chronicle* listed sixty clearinghouse member banks. Convertibility was resumed on November 1, 1873. On June 6, 1874, *Commercial and Financial Chronicle* listed the same sixty clearinghouse member banks. No clearinghouse members had disappeared.

PANIC OF 1884

The New York Clearing House issued loan certificates on May 15, 1884. Before the panic, on February 23, 1884, the *Commercial and Financial Chronicle* listed sixty-three clearinghouse member banks. By September 1, 1884, the only clearinghouse loan certificates outstanding were those issued to the Metropolitan National Bank; clearinghouse loan certificates are entirely canceled on September 23, 1886. On October 11, 1884, the *Commercial and Financial Chronicle* listed sixty-one clearinghouse member banks. The two banks missing are the Wall Street Bank and Marine National Bank of New York. Otherwise the two lists are the same.

The *Annual Report* of the comptroller of the currency of 1884 states that the Marine National Bank failed on May 6, 1884 (XXXIII), and lists the bank as in *voluntary* liquidation (CLXXVIII). The Wall Street Bank was chartered by New York State. In the *Annual Report of the Superintendent of the Bank Department of the State of New York*, 1885, the Wall Street Bank is listed as failed, as of April 11, 1884 (viii). The narrative suggests that Metropolitan National Bank was aided so that it would not fail during the crisis period in May. In its situation (losing so large a volume of deposits), failure or liquidation seemed inevitable. It voluntarily liquidated on November 18, 1884, months after the panic subsided. Metropolitan National Bank still had more than $5 million in clearinghouse loan certificates when it voluntarily liquidated in November 1884; their clearinghouse loan certificates were the last canceled, as described above.[2]

Although Dudley (1890) and the comptroller's *Annual Report* do not mention the Wall Street Bank, Clews (1888, 521) lists it has having failed in August 1884. According to Bayles (1917, 273), there was a posted notice saying that the bank had failed "owing to irregularities on the part of the cashier." Bayles says that the "Wall Street National Bank . . . changed on the 19th day of October, 1883 [*sic*?], to a State bank. . . . It failed in less than a year from that time" (274).

PANIC OF 1890

Clearinghouse loan certificates were issued on November 12, 1890, and were all finally canceled on February 7, 1891. Comparing the list of New York Clearing House members on November 1, 1890, to that of May 16, 1891, shows that of the sixty-four members prior to the crisis, there was only one failure, North River Bank. North River was a state bank; it was liquidated in 1891.

PANIC OF 1893

Clearinghouse loan certificates were issued on June 21, 1893, and were finally canceled on November 1, 1893. Comparing the list of New York Clearing

House members on May 27, 1893, to that of December 23, 1893, shows that of the sixty-four members prior to the crisis, none failed. This finding is consistent with Wicker (2000), who argues that the Panic of 1893 was not focused in New York City, but rather among interior locations.

PANIC OF 1907

Clearinghouse loan certificates were issued on October 26, 1907, and finally canceled on March 28, 1908. Comparing the list of New York Clearing House members on October 19, 1907, to that of August 1, 1907, shows that of the fifty-three banks in the New York Clearing House prior to the crisis, five failed during the crisis. The banks not on the March 28, 1908, list were the Mechanics' and Traders' Bank, the Oriental Bank, the First National Bank of Brooklyn, the National Bank of North America, and New Amsterdam National Bank. The *Annual Report* of the attorney general of the State of New York, for the year ending December 31, 1908, said, however, that the Mechanics' and Traders' Bank did reopen as the Union Bank of Brooklyn. The report said that only one bank did not resume business (31), and so it seems that of the state banks, only the Oriental Bank failed. The same report shows that the Oriental Bank's assets were turned over to the Metropolitan Trust Company. Neither of these banks is listed as closed or liquidated by the superintendent of banks of New York (*Annual Report*, 1908). The *Annual Report* of the US comptroller of the currency for 1907 lists the First National Bank of Brooklyn as insolvent and closed on October 25, 1907, the day before loan certificates were issued.

The National Bank of North America was liquidated during the crisis, but without losses to creditors. "That the National Bank of North America was not insolvent when it was closed was fully demonstrated by the rapid liquidation of its affairs under the receivership. Its creditors were paid in full with interest from the date of closing. . . . The receivership was finally closed October 31, 1908" (Kane 1922, 272). In the case of the liquidation of New Amsterdam National Bank, the bank was put into receivership on January 30, 1908, also without losses to creditors. "Its depositors were paid in full with interest from the date of closing, and the receivership was finally terminated April 14, 1909, after turning over to an agent of the stockholders cash and assets amounting to $1,027,612" (Kane 1922, 272).

The *Wall Street Journal* on October 16, 1908, noted that "there were fifteen institutions in New York and Brooklyn altogether which closed their doors, either at the height of the panic in October or subsequently as a result of the bank run. Of these fifteen three were national banks, eight were state banks and four were trust companies. . . . But far more interesting . . . is the fact that the depositors of these suspended institutions have not or will not, lose a dollar of their money" (8).

Excluding the one case of voluntary liquidation (Metropolitan National) and cases where there was liquidation but no apparent depositor losses, the final tally of failures of New York Clearing House members appears to be three banks in 1884 (the Wall Street Bank, Metropolitan National, and the Marine National Bank of New York), one in 1890 (the North River Bank), and two in 1907 (the Mechanics' and Traders' Bank and the Oriental Bank). There were no bank failures during the panics of 1873 and 1893 in New York City. There are a few ambiguous cases as well, but, overall, there were few failures.

Losses on Clearinghouse Loan Certificates

There were no losses on clearinghouse loan certificates. Gilpin and Wallace (1904, 18) wrote that "Since 1860, a total of $168,774,000 in loan certificates have been issued at various periods, and all were duly redeemed without the loss of a dollar." Similarly, the Federal Reserve did not incur losses on any loans made through an emergency lending program during the recent financial crisis.

Summary

At the time of a financial crisis, it appears that the entire financial system might collapse, and without action it likely would collapse. But ultimately there is action and collapse is avoided, and in the aftermath of the crisis there are few bank failures and no losses to emergency lending programs. These two statements seem hard to reconcile, but that is the essence of the information problem at the root of panics.

What Ends a Financial Crisis?
Historical Reminders

A central theme in our book is that studying financial history provides insights into how and why financial crises still arise in a modern economy and, in particular, into how to end them. So, what do we learn from the National Banking Era crises under study?

For one thing, Bagehot's (1873) rule for fighting crises is not enough to end a panic; on its own it is insufficient to restore confidence in the financial system. During the crises of the National Banking Era much more was involved to restore confidence than just opening emergency lending facilities. Restoring confidence is a process that takes time and requires delicate information management. And the information management is designed to convey confidence in the *banking system*. This management process involves suppressing some information and providing other information. This is the essence of fighting crises, and that follows naturally from the concept of a crisis as an information event. Indeed, any concept of a financial crisis should imply how that crisis should be fought and ultimately end. That is the key overarching point shown by studying the panics of the National Banking Era.

Key authorities must control the information about financial institutions. From our study of the National Banking Era crises, the suppression of bank-specific information, the production of aggregate information, and occasional bank examinations and "stress test"–like announcements are crucial inputs into restoring confidence. The issuance of clearinghouse loan certificates essentially securitized the banking system by pooling all member bank assets to back the loan certificates. The relevant information then is about the entire clearinghouse (effectively the banking system in the case of the New York Clearing House), rather than information about a single bank, which becomes irrelevant to depositors. Overall, these actions eliminate the incen-

tive for depositors to spend the resources to acquire bank-specific information. These actions all fall under the rubric of "managing the information
environment" during a crisis. At times, *less* information is desirable.

Proper responses to financial crises may require the abrogation of standard rules of behavior or even violation of laws. The suspension of convertibility of deposits into cash was a violation of law and yet such laws were not
enforced. In the cases drawn before the courts, enforcement of such laws was
viewed as likely to produce a worse outcome for the wider financial market
and economy. Bailing out member banks was not part of the New York Clearing House agreement, and yet a committee of clearinghouse members agreed
to help member banks of uncertain financial condition. And unlike modern
crises, the private-market bankers who decided to bail out a member bank
would have shared directly in the losses had the bailed-out bank failed and
had the ultimate liquidation of the bank lost money.

In the next few pages, we summarize the key points from our investigation of this period in US banking history. The repeated implementation of
standard actions during National Banking Era panics may not always have
directly analogous initiatives available for use in modern panics. But in some
cases, the historically analogous actions are not so different from those of
today, so that they remain relevant for understanding the sources of panics as
well as effective activities to fight financial crises in modern economies. The
principles for fighting crises are the same.

To guide the discussion of responding to a National Banking Era financial
panic, think of applying first aid to a bleeding wound. First, find out the location of the wound (from where the blood flows)—comparable to determining the form and the location of short-term debt. Next clean the wound and
find ways to stop the bleeding—the first advice is to apply sterile bandages.
Application of a tourniquet for a limb wound is akin to suspension of convertibility, if possible, and should only be applied in an informed way. The
provision of liquidity is ensuring that there is sufficient blood flowing in the
system—elevation of the wound above the heart slows the outflow; this is like
clearinghouse loan certificates, which really reallocates liquidity among banks
but only temporarily adds to the supply of payment media. A bleeding patient
is likely frantic—calming the patient is important for allowing the other alleviation actions to work. Managing the information in a financial crisis is
analogous to calming the patient. The other actions—bending or breaking
laws and preventing a major failure of an interconnected institution—have
less clear analogues but they illustrate extraordinary steps to alleviate the crisis situation. In an emergency bleeding event, it is advisable to add gauze atop
bloody bandages, which is not advisable in normal situations. Neither was

suspension of convertibility nor bailing out large and interconnected banks. We would also note that when confronted with a frantic, bleeding patient, it is not the moment to complain and lecture about possible risky actions taken by the patient earlier that resulted in the patient needing attention.

Short-Term Bank Debt and Crises

In each of the panics we study, the key trigger of panic is when doubts arise about the value of short-term bank debt. We refer to those instances as short-term debt becoming information-sensitive, that is, when its value fluctuates and is uncertain and no one wants to hold it because of doubts about its value. When public information arrives that raises rational concerns about the value of the assets backing the bank debt, short-term debt holders panic; they want their cash. That is because holders of the short-term debt cannot identify specifically which banks are in trouble or whether any of them is in fact in trouble. The transition of bank debt from information-insensitive to information-sensitive debt is the point at which a panic begins.

Doubts about the value of short-term debt is the root cause of financial crises, which have occurred in the history of all market economies. The commonality of this trait makes studying history useful for clarifying the key role of short-term debt in financial panics.

The major issuers and primary holders of short-term debt have changed over time and the form of the short-term debt has evolved as well. For instance, the key form of short-term debt in the Panic of 1873 was bank deposits, in contrast to, for example, the Panic of 1837 or the Panic of 1857 when the banknote (bank-issued currency) was the short-term debt that was run. The issuers of bank deposits in 1873 were mainly national banks and state banks. In New York City, the banks stricken with deposit withdrawals from bank runs were members of the New York Clearing House and were systemically important as key correspondents for interior banks.

In 1884, the bank runs were more localized and affected only New York City banks. Again, the New York Clearing House members were the main targets of bank runs, and the Metropolitan National Bank was subject to the most severe contraction of deposits in that crisis. The short-term debt was therefore deposit accounts at banks, and the interior banks were the key holders of the short-term debt. The large proportion of deposits at Metropolitan were deposits of interior banks, and so the bank was susceptible to runs by that group. Similarly, the short-term debt in 1890 was also deposit accounts at New York Clearing House banks, but not only national banks. Two of the banks most heavily stricken were state-chartered clearinghouse member banks.

In 1893, the financial distress arose from outside the New York City financial market. Still, the New York Clearing House banks faced drains of gold by foreign investors worried about the US adherence to the gold standard, as well as drains of funds from New York City by their interior correspondents in need of their reserve deposits. Short-term debt was mainly in New York Clearing House member correspondent balances—banker deposits at central reserve city banks—held as certified reserves that satisfied reserve requirements, as was typical for interior banks. The volatility of these deposit balances increased during panics and led to funding shortages on the New York Stock Exchange call loan market. When financial signals in New York City indicated doubts about whether the New York banks could deliver cash in exchange for interior deposits, the interior banks effectively ran on their deposit accounts.

Identifying the short-term debt at risk becomes more important for any discussion of the Panic of 1907. In that panic, the short-term debt that became questionable was held by trust companies, none of which were members of the New York Clearing House. With the failure of Knickerbocker Trust on October 22, 1907, the panic withdrawals of deposits from trust companies in New York City began. Deposits at national banks that were members of the New York Clearing House actually increased, but the financial market in New York City was certainly in crisis. Trust companies provided a key intermediation step in the liquidity available at the New York Stock Exchange. Prior to a call loan from a bank, a broker would have to have stock collateral in his possession to deliver it to the bank for a call loan. Trust companies provided the initial credit—an uncollateralized "daylight loan"—that enabled the purchase of the stock. After a broker provided the collateral to a bank for a call loan, the broker would take the proceeds of that loan and repay the trust company loan. The runs on trust companies after the Knickerbocker Trust failure shut down this credit provision as well as any new call loan funding by other trusts. Without full recognition of how Knickerbocker's failure would affect this liquidity provision by trusts, the clearinghouse members likely underestimated the severity of the crisis that the Knickerbocker Trust failure sparked.

Restoring Confidence—Liquidity, Information Control, and Bending Existing Rules

Identifying the form of short-term debt at risk, the identity of the institutions that hold it, and what information influences the valuation of the assets that back the debt being run on are all important for determining the appropriate response to a financial crisis. But these key characteristics are only setting the stage for combating a financial crisis. We highlight the actions taken to alleviate the core problem in a panic—the loss of confidence—because we think that there are analogous actions that can be implemented in future crises.

Information control and management are key inputs to ending banking panics. Bank debt serves as a transactions medium as well as a short-term store of value. An effective transactions medium should have a price that does not vary, and such a stable price helps bank debt perform the role of a short-term store of value. Then the efficient bank debt is information-insensitive. To envision efficient bank debt as information-insensitive deviates from standard price theory, very different from how we think about the price system generally. *But bank debt is different; it is the exception to the price system rule.*

A financial crisis is an information event. And, paradoxically, in a financial crisis *even less* information is best. One way to think of a financial crisis is that the price system is suddenly working when in normal times it does not need to operate. That is, bank debt prices suddenly reflect "information"—a crisis—but these prices would not be meaningful. In normal times no information is conveyed about banks through their debt because the prices do not change, by design. In a financial crisis, short-term debt holders suddenly run to the bank to get cash because the value or price of cash is known, and so debt holders prefer to have that. But the information that they interpret as relevant does not really clarify the value of the assets backing the debt. In essence, the bank debt as "information-sensitive" leads to bad outcomes.

How can confidence be restored? The application of Bagehot's rule—from 1873—reflects some well-known practical applications. Central banks should lend against good (in normal times) collateral at a high (but not astronomical) interest rate relative to market rates. In each of the National Banking Era crises that we studied, the New York Clearing House emergency lending took the form of loan certificates issued against good collateral at a high rate. Didn't Bagehot's rule work?

Application of Bagehot's rule alone did not restore confidence. Indeed, it is not clear how the rule is supposed to end crises without some other actions. The basic idea seems to be that the central bank, by lending cash against collateral, allows banks to get enough cash to hand out to depositors or other short-term debt holders so that they would eventually realize that they could get their cash back. But what would cause them to later deposit the cash back into the banks? From an operational standpoint, Bagehot's rule as applied during the National Banking Era was to get as much cash into circulation in order to convince depositors that they could get their cash from their bank if they wanted it. Surely, the depositors realized that the additional liquidity came from the clearinghouse in the form of a temporary loan against the collateral. In that setting, emergency lending programs cannot by themselves re-create confidence. Returning to the first-aid analogy, it fails to stop the bleeding. Something else must happen in the meantime to settle down market participants.

During the National Banking Era, banks suspended convertibility so that they did not give out all their cash. Suspension of convertibility might "slow the bleeding," but suspension along with clearinghouse loan certificates did not per se restore confidence. Further, with suspension of convertibility depositors really could not get all their deposits out of banks as cash. In fact, few instances of panic really led to more than 10 percent of deposits leaving the banking system in cash-hoarding episodes. Suspending convertibility went in the opposite direction of Bagehot's rule, which was meant to quell depositor demands for cash. Suspension of convertibility sometimes magnified cash demands in the opinion of Wicker (2000).

For the clearinghouse, we know that an effective response to financial panic requires more than Bagehot's rule. Bagehot's rule often overlooks the importance of secrecy in successful lending programs, specifically the anonymity of borrower identity and suppression of bank-specific information are critical to the response.[1] In the most severe National Banking Era crises, as in the crisis of 2007–8, emergency lending programs were announced publicly, but the identities of the borrowing to banks were kept secret. This secrecy limited the ability of short-term debt holders to isolate weak banks and instead forced them to focus on the general solvency of banking system as a whole. Specifically, the clearinghouse prohibited the publication of bank-specific information, which kept weak banks from being identified. Further, the clearinghouse kept both the amounts of individual bank borrowing and their identities secret for the member banks that participated in their lending program, clearinghouse loan certificates. During crises, saving the financial system meant not letting weaker banks get picked off one by one.

In the case of the clearinghouse, there was, first, the suspension of the publication of individual bank information and then restrictions on deposit convertibility (into cash), which prevented the financial system from being liquidated in runs. In the first-aid analogy, this amounts to calming the patient and slowing the bleeding. Issuing loan certificates legally bound the clearinghouse member banks together. Jointly, these actions forced depositors to focus on the solvency of the clearinghouse rather than individual banks. By joining together via the issuance of loan certificates, all the assets of the member banks effectively became one big portfolio. Depositors now needed to have a view on the solvency of banking system itself and not individual banks. The opening of the market for certified checks allowed the currency premium to reflect depositor beliefs about the solvency of the clearinghouse.

The clearinghouse reduced information to the public because during a panic the clearinghouse did not actually know which banks were insolvent. In real time, no entity can credibly assess the value of the opaque bank assets. That fact is the main reason for a bank panic in the first place. The New York Clearing House thought it better to keep the financial system from unraveling sequentially by withholding bank-specific information on balance sheets as well as on lending programs.

The New York Clearing House convinced depositors of its solvency only by combining individual bank portfolios into a single portfolio. The net total of the financial resources of these banks was a powerful balancing force that went a long way toward convincing people that the banking system was solvent. But, in the National Banking Era, even the combined resources of the largest banks was not enough to convince depositors of the solvency of the banking system. The currency premium was positive—there was still a perceived probability that the system would not survive.

The New York Clearing House had to take other actions to convince depositors that the banking system was solvent and prepared for business, even if it was not "normal" business. But these additional actions made a compelling signal to depositors that the banking system was solvent and liquid.

Here is where we veer into the actions that were either illegal or verge on that margin of the law. Suspension of convertibility during a gold standard period and the appearance of the currency premium led to a profit opportunity from importing gold. In the panics of 1893 and 1907, the key public signal was the large-scale infusion of gold (net inflows) into the banking system from abroad. Newspaper accounts of the imports highlight the increase in available liquidity in the New York financial market along with reliable accounts of contracts for gold imports that would arrive in the weeks to follow. These inflows also convey a more subtle signal arising from the fact that foreign holders/investors (sources of gold) were willing to send gold to the United States, and foreign lenders were willing to lend to the US banks to facilitate the gold shipments. The shipments and the credit extensions were signals of confidence in the solvency and liquidity of the US financial market from a credible source, the foreign investor.

Restoring confidence in the 1893 and 1907 panics was aided by the proper functioning of a gold standard in the presence of a currency premium. This was not the case in the Panic of 1873, when some gold was imported and the US Treasury did repurchase some US government bonds. And, once the stock market reopened, banks could sell the stock they had seized as collateral for defaulted call loans. So there was no single mechanism that effectively built up bank reserves. It was necessary to take actions of various forms in order to accumulate sufficient liquid resources that would convince depositors that the value of their deposits was safe. Using the first-aid analogy, these infusions of liquidity were akin to a transfusion—an outside infusion of needed liquidity. Although somewhat different from capital infusions, the additional gold liquidity into the banking market was a durable reserve asset on the banks' books. The inflow of gold is the closest analogue to the Troubled Asset Relief Program (TARP) capital infusions to respond to the recent 2007–8 financial crisis.

During the suspension periods of the National Banking Era, the New York Clearing House sometimes conducted special bank examinations as a means of introducing information that would settle markets. The actions were associated with information management, and yet they conflict with our comments about the credibility of information on bank solvency during a crisis. Even with a brief period of information suppression as in 1884, the New York Clearing House actions signaled that Metropolitan National Bank would not fail during the financial crisis. Its examination report suggested that Metropolitan's assets were in good condition and that the New York Clearing House would issue to Metropolitan clearinghouse loan certificates in a volume sufficient for it to reopen for business. The speech by George S. Coe delivered to the clearinghouse a few weeks after that decision indicated that the examination group could not evaluate sufficiently the condition of Metropolitan's assets prior to making its decision to aid the bank. So, was the announcement by the New York Clearing House misinformation? Not if one considers that the New York Clearing House was putting its capital at risk by aiding Metropolitan. In essence, the decision to lend to the bank was equivalent to saying that it was not going to fail because of a lack of liquid assets. And if Metropolitan had failed with losses, the New York Clearing House had established procedures to allocate the losses accordingly among New York Clearing House members.

The Metropolitan National Bank instance in 1884 provides another takeaway for the modern reader—do not let a large, interconnected institution fail *during* a crisis. The outcome of the crisis of 1884 is a benign one in comparison with the Panic of 1907, when the interconnectedness of Knickerbocker Trust and trust companies more generally was underestimated. Suffice it to say that 1884 is considered a successful prevention of a minor banking panic from worsening to a financial crisis, and the success reflects largely the decision to prevent a large, interconnected bank from failure during the crisis. The eventual liquidation of Metropolitan took place long after the financial markets settled down.

We can learn about the benefits of preventing the failure of a large institution during a crisis by investigating the case of Knickerbocker's failure. The holders of short-term debt wanted their cash back, and when Knickerbocker ran out of cash, the only alternative to failure (suspension) was to sell assets. Instead, Knickerbocker suspended its activities and closed its doors rather than liquidate assets in a fire sale. In a fire sale, intermediaries struck with depositor runs would sell their best assets first because those assets tend to hold their value even amid financial distress. If many banks took the same actions at the same time—creating an excess supply of assets for sale and pushing down market values—then a rush to sell assets that spread across banks and other financial intermediaries would result in massive problems among the very institutions that required cash. The very event that suspension of convertibility was designed to prevent—namely asset fire sales—happened partially during the Panic of 1907 because trust companies in New York City never implemented the suspension of convertibility that the clearinghouse member banks employed. The drainage of liquidity out of trust companies jeopardized the entire financial system but it did not cause a market-wide financial collapse, as a result of specific actions taken by the US Treasury and private bankers, led by J. P. Morgan, to provide liquidity. In the case of trust companies, the liquidity came through the purchase of trust assets by other commercial entities during the panic.

Avoiding fire sales of assets during crises is a fairly common tactic among financial market participants and has been known since the eighteenth century. When speaking of a panic in England in 1797, Poor (1877, 196) noted that "With the announcement of suspension the panic instantly subsided." But the working knowledge of the history of suspension of convertibility and of not enforcing debt contracts was lost in the twentieth and twenty-first centuries. That knowledge was lost because financial crises were not supposed to happen in advanced economies.

Summary of Restoring Confidence during the National Banking Era Panics

This chapter's goal is to identify central unifying themes in the actions taken by the New York Clearing House to combat financial crises and from those themes draw conclusions about what worked and what might still work in fighting modern financial crises. We highlight how all the panics centered on short-term bank debt and the shock of when there arise concerns about its value. As a result, it is crucial to know where that short-term debt resides, what intermediaries issue it, who holds it, and in what form it is being held. In the antebellum United States, most short-term bank debt was in the form of private banknotes. After the Civil War, the bank debt was mainly in the form of bank deposits, but also in the deposits of other intermediaries, like trust companies in 1907. For most of the National Banking Era panics, the interior correspondent banks were the key intermediaries that held a large proportion of deposits in New York Clearing House banks, and so it was important to instill confidence in those short-term debt holders to end a panic.

The production of confidence during a financial crisis is a challenging feat, and yet it was just what was necessary from the New York Clearing House to fight crises. The leaders of the clearinghouse realized the importance of managing the information available to the public during a crisis, and they limited the amount and form of information that was released to be aggregate and not bank specific. Further, they made crucial announcements of bank conditions during crises and backed up announcements indicating the soundness of banks with extensions of liquidity loans to signal their commitment their success.

Financial crises are uncommon occurrences even if there were five in the United States during the fifty years of the National Banking Era (1863–1913). In the three most severe panics, the New York Clearing House banks stretched their power and suspended or restricted the convertibility of deposits into cash, an action that was strictly prohibited by law. The action slowed the liquidation of deposits and allowed the clearinghouse members to assemble their coordinated responses to the crises. Suspension also gave rise to a currency premium, which led to the importation of gold—a needed infusion of persistent and durable liquidity into the banking system. Without suspension as in the early part of the Panic of 1893, it was challenging to get gold into the United States, but once suspension was imposed and the currency premium arose, gold flowed rapidly in.

The case of Metropolitan National Bank in 1884 is central to the discussion of preventing a large, interconnected bank from failure during a crisis. Largely as a result of the intervention by the New York Clearing House, Metropolitan National Bank survived the panic sufficiently to limp along for a few months until it voluntarily liquidated about six months after the panic struck. When we contrast this outcome with the results from the Panic of 1907 after the failure of Knickerbocker Trust, the wisdom of preventing a failure during the panic—not necessarily preventing failure altogether—appears clear.

In the next two chapters, we show how the key inferences drawn from the National Banking Era about how to fight financial crises bear resemblance to the modern actions taken to combat financial crises regardless of the differences in institutional structure or of the technology of financial market transactions.

Modern Crises: Perspectives from History

In any time period, a financial crisis starts in a chaotic way, and modern-era crises (when central banks are present) create even greater confusion than the panics of the National Banking Era. When discussing the Panic of 2007–8, former Treasury secretary Tim Geithner (2014, 119) wrote, "At the start of any crisis, there's an inevitable fog of diagnosis." This fog is thicker and more widespread in the modern era.

In modern crises, the timing of key events differs from the typical sequence observed during the US National Banking Era, when there was no central bank. Modern-era financial crises invariably involve expectations that the central bank or the government will intervene in markets in some way, and, as a result, runs on short-term debt do not necessarily start right away. Firms and households wait to see what will happen. At the beginning, short-term debt holders suspect that one or more financial institutions may be insolvent. Some financial institutions may in fact be bankrupt, closing their doors. Banks have liquidity problems because there are usually slower large withdrawals (a silent run) but not sudden mass runs. There is no suspension of convertibility by banks. Some banks cannot get loans in interbank markets. But it's not clear that the events are a systemic crisis.

Without an explicit run, the central bank and other public authorities are not sure the events are a crisis, and so policy makers wait to see what develops. Households and firms wait too. When events finally begin to spiral out of control (e.g., Lehman), there is a mass run prompting the government to act. No one is sure what to do. Some counsel that (any) proposed responses will foster "moral hazard" and authorities advocate standard responses to address those problems that might make sense long before a crisis hits but are not appropriate during a crisis.[1]

At some point in this scenario, the government considers issuing a partial or blanket guarantee of bank debt, or the banking system is nationalized. At a minimum, emergency lending facilities open. And this scenario may be accompanied by political instability. Economic activity is usually devastated. (See, e.g., Reinhart and Rogoff 2009.)

As a result of the confusion about what to do, when to do it, and who should do it, most measures to fight a crisis are taken ad hoc, piecemeal, usually delayed or dragged out with much political maneuvering and finger-pointing. To some extent, the chaotic nature of the crisis determines the outcome, but the chaos also arises from a failure to recognize a crisis when it is a crisis. There may be no data or relevant measures and so there is no real picture of the financial system. There may be a failure to know which firms are really "banks" or what debt is really money-like—that is, the form of the short-term debt at risk is not clear. A major problem is that the authorities have no *concept* of a crisis. The last crisis prior to the one at hand was too far in the past for active policy makers to recall, and all the relevant crisis-fighting experience and knowledge has been lost, and so everything must be learned again. These chaotic events lead to the view that each crisis is unique, but although each crisis has unique elements, the core elements are not unique. We have shown how the panics of the National Banking Era were unusual opportunities to investigate the essential elements of a crisis without the complication of central bank interventions. Those panics make clear that a financial crisis centers on short-term debt. Information-insensitive debt can become information-sensitive, especially after a credit boom. This switch from information-insensitive to information-sensitive is the onset of the crisis. This fact gets lost on observers of modern crises.

This transition from the benign information-insensitive state to the information-sensitive crisis state does not happen instantaneously, but it does happen quickly. We can see an example of this transition in the case of Sweden in the early 1990s. After a credit boom in Sweden, the tipping point came when real estate (especially commercial real estate) prices fell. At the end of 1990, Swedish real estate prices had fallen by 52 percent from their peak. This led to a run on a finance company called Nyckeln ("The Key"), which had a large real estate exposure. Nyckeln found that it could not roll over maturing *marknadsbevis*, a kind of commercial paper (short-term debt). As with repo (repurchase agreements) in 2007–8, the run in Sweden did not consist of depositors demanding to withdraw, but rather holders of *marknadsbevis* were unwilling to renew their funding. In short order, the crisis spread to the entire *marknadsbevis* market, which dried up in a few days. The crisis then spread to banks and other markets. But it was not until September 1992—

two years later—that the systemic nature of the events was recognized (see Englund 2015, 42).

Why did it take so long to realize that it was a systemic banking crisis? Like the United States in 2007–8, this event was the first systemic crisis in Sweden since the 1930s. By the 1990s, the financial world was different. In Sweden, reliance on the international money market for funds had become the norm, so much so that lending was not dependent on banks' deposit base. Demand deposits had shrunk in importance. According to Englund (2015, 42):

> Instead of coming from depositors fearing to be last in line, liquidity risk now was stemming from investors fearing to be unable to get out before the market dried up. Arguably, Swedish depositors in the early 1990s felt their deposits to be safe, in spite of the absence of deposit insurance. Hence, the risk of a depositor run was small, and even in a very critical situation deposit withdrawals could be expected to be limited. Access to short market funding, on the other hand, turned out to be very volatile which played a crucial role in the crisis.

The form of bank debt had changed, as had the firms that were "banks," and analogous changes in bank debt took place in the National Banking Era. The inability to see the changes in the form of bank money and in the nature of banking arise because the changes take place over a fairly long time. During the National Banking Era, a similar change took place when it was conceptually difficult to understand demand deposits. Were demand deposits "money"? How extensively were demand deposits used? Bray Hammond ([1957] 1991, 80), in his Pulitzer Prize–winning book *Banks and Politics in America*, wrote, "the importance of deposits was not realized by most American economists . . . till after 1900." And Wicker (1966, 21) quotes Russell C. Leffingwell, the assistant secretary of the Treasury, who wrote as late as 1919, "All of these people who believe in the quantity theory of money . . . choose to call bank deposits money, but bank deposits are not money." The form of bank debt—and who was holding it—had also changed at Continental Illinois, the large US bank that faced a run in May 1984. Continental Illinois was heavily dependent on short-term, largely foreign, wholesale funding, and it was these lenders who ran on that debt. (See Carlson and Rose 2016.) The bank regulators guaranteed all of Continental's debt (including bondholders), worrying that Continental's failure might lead to widespread runs in the context of the Latin American debt crisis, to which large US banks were exposed. Continental was the canary in the coal mine that US banking was changing, but the change went unnoticed.

The same was true twenty-four years later in the United Kingdom when Northern Rock suffered a bank run. Northern Rock's reliance on demand

deposits from households had fallen to 23 percent of total liabilities. Northern Rock was mostly reliant on wholesale funding. And Northern Rock was
not an outlier among British banks in this regard (see Shin 2009). Northern
Rock was nationalized in 2008. Like the Swedish regulators, the British regulators were late in seeing the crisis and in recognizing the systemic nature of
the events. In September 2007, Northern Rock secretly requested assistance
from the Bank of England. But this request was leaked and became public,
causing the England's first bank run in 150 years.

One conclusion we can draw from the panics of US history and from
these selected modern crises is clear: Bank debt is not just demand deposits.
All short-term debt is vulnerable to runs, and that simple insight is crucial to
having an informed perspective on these unusual events.

Understanding the systemic events requires having a *concept* of what a
crisis is. Without a coherent concept of a crisis, it becomes challenging to
initiate decisive action until things get bad enough that the crisis is obvious.
But if bank authorities do not wait, and instead act decisively as in the case
of Continental Illinois, then the policy makers are accused of acting without
need. They are accused of creating "moral hazard." And, in the case of Continental Illinois, the rescue ultimately started the too-big-to-fail imbroglio that
continues today. But since crises do not typically happen repeatedly in the
same generation, the public also lacks a concept of a crisis.

The examples of Sweden, Northern Rock, and Continental Illinois are instances of events that most resemble those of the National Banking Era. These
instances were runs on uninsured wholesale debt. The dangers of wholesale
funding were underestimated and not fully investigated before these events,
and so it was not expected that there would be runs by wholesale funding
sources. Goodhart, in the *Financial Times* of September 19, 2008, wrote, "virtually no one, whether practitioner, regulator or academic, ever expected
that wholesale financial markets would dry up for so long." In retrospect,
the evidence suggests that because wholesale funding was perceived to be
without the risk of a run, there appear to have been no confounding effects
arising from market participants' expectations that the central bank would
intervene. This same absence of confounding effects of expectations was also
the case in 2007–8, when the crisis was centered on US dealer banks relying
heavily on short-term sale and repurchase agreements (repos).

Below we discuss several modern crises. We do not provide all the details
of each crisis. We focus on crisis management rather than on the origins of
the crisis. The key inferences taken from what we characterize as appropriate actions to fight crises during the National Banking Era in the previous
chapter will be used to uncover similar inferences about the best actions to

take in order to combat modern crises. Despite their chaotic nature and the various modern institutions that respond to crises, the historical antecedents remain informative about the proper actions to take to quell crises. Government and central banks respond to modern crises, and here we list how some of those responses line up with the responses by the New York Clearing House Association.

Overview of Financial Crises since 1970

Laeven and Valencia (2012) identify 147 banking crises, of which 13 are borderline events, over the period 1970–2011. Crises took place in developed economies as well as in emerging market economies and in countries with deposit insurance as well as in those without it. As a practical matter, Laeven and Valencia define a banking crisis as systemic if two conditions are met:

1. Significant signs of financial distress in the banking system (as indicated by significant bank runs, losses in the banking system, and/or bank liquidations)
2. Significant banking policy intervention measures in response to significant losses in the banking system[2]

The first year of the crisis corresponds to the year that both these criteria are met. Because of the initial chaos, it takes some time for a government or central bank response, and so the date given as the start of the crisis is late. This problem is discussed by Boyd, De Nicolò, and Loukoianova (2009), who show that the dating that academics apply to crises is systematically late.

How do governments respond to contain the crisis? Laeven and Valencia (2012) collected detailed information on 65 of the events in their sample of 147. Of those 65, in 85 percent of the cases, emergency lending facilities were offered to the banks. In just over half of the events, the government issued a blanket guarantee of the bank debt, making information about the banks irrelevant. In 9 percent of the cases there was a deposit freeze. The actions taken to quell modern banking crises have analogues in the National Banking Era. As mentioned throughout the book, Bagehot's rule of providing liquidity on good collateral at a high rate is the one historical theme repeated in modern crises. That rule likely operates in the 85 percent of the examples with liquidity facilities provided to banks. In the 50 percent of cases in which there is a blanket guarantee of bank debt, an action that makes the question of the quality of banks' backing assets (the bank loans) irrelevant (assuming the guarantee is credible). The government assumes the risk that the bank loans have deteriorated. The same is true for nationalization of the banking system. As long as the government has the fiscal firepower, this alleviates depositors' concerns. The blanket guarantee effectively removes the incentive for depositors to attempt to exchange the debt for cash because the debt value is supported. It also removes the incentive for depositors to seek information on specific banks because there is no distinction between the debt of healthy banks and that of insolvent banks. In the historic episodes that we study, the blanket guarantee of all deposits was infeasible and so the private clearinghouse response—to issue clearinghouse loan certificates, suspend publication of bank-specific information, and in extreme cases suspend convertibility of deposits into cash—reflected the best available options at their disposal. In the (admittedly rare) case of a deposit freeze, there is a clear analogy to the suspension of convertibility. A freeze halts the outflow of money from the banks, like a suspension of convertibility or bank holiday. In the modern era, the freeze must be accompanied by some other public policy that convinces depositors that the banking system and their bank are solvent. Banks need to be examined and possibly restructured. Capital may need to be injected. Otherwise it just delays the outflow from deposit accounts.

Emerging Market Financial Crises

Most of the crises described in the summary so far occurred in emerging market economics. One category of financial crisis that occurs in emerging markets is called a "sudden stop." A sudden stop is a situation in which private capital inflows into an emerging market economy quickly reverse and flow out to a significant extent. Such sharp reversals lead to large declines in output and a collapsing banking system. (The inflows must be significantly below their mean to qualify as a sudden stop; see Calvo, Izquierdo, and Talvi 2006.) Emerging markets have sometimes experienced sudden stops as shown in table 11.1. The right-hand column shows the size of the outflow of capital relative to the country's GDP. Note that in the table there are no sudden stops in advanced countries, but we discuss the case of Spain below. Prior to the sudden stop, large capital inflows increase the likelihood of a banking crisis. Caballero (2016, 309) argued that the "windfall of international capital amplifies financial risks because the greater availability of capital increases the funds intermediated by the banking sector, fuelling excessive growth in lending, hence increasing the likelihood of a crisis."

These "sudden stop" crises are about short-term debt and runs on this debt. Rodrik and Velasco (1999, 1) wrote, "Almost all of the countries affected by the financial turmoil of the last few years had one thing in common: large

TABLE 11.1. Sudden stops

Country, episode	Sudden stop percentage of GDP
Argentina, 1982–83	20
Argentina, 1994–95	4
Chile, 1981–83	7
Chile,[a] 1990–91	8
Ecuador, 1995–96	19
Hungary, 1995–96	7
Indonesia, 1996–97	5
Korea, 1996–97	11
Malaysia,[a] 1993–94	15
Mexico, 1981–83	12
Mexico, 1993–95	6
Philippines, 1996–97	7
Thailand, 1996–97	26
Turkey, 1993–94	10
Venezuela, 1992–94	9

Source: Calvo (2003), who cites Calvo and Reinhart (2000), based on data from the *World Bank Debt Tables* and Institute for International Economics, *Comparative Statistics for Emerging Market Economies*, 1998.

[a] Sudden stop due to the introduction of controls on capital flows.

ratios of short-term foreign debt, whether public or private, to international reserves. In Mexico in 1995, Russia in 1998, and Brazil in 1999, the debt was the government debt;[3] in Indonesia, Korea, and Thailand in 1997, the debt was primarily owed by private banks and firms. But in each case the combination of large short-term liabilities and relatively scarce internationally liquid assets resulted in extreme vulnerability to a confidence crisis and a reversal of capital flows."

The Asian crisis started in Thailand in summer 1997 and was a complete surprise. It quickly spread to the neighboring countries of Indonesia, Malaysia, and South Korea. It came as a shock because the countries affected had experienced high growth rates and balanced government budgets. Radelet and Sachs (1998a, 25), wrote as follows:

[A] rising share of foreign borrowing was in the form of short-term debt. . . . [B]y the end of 1996 short-term debts to offshore banks in Korea, Thailand, and Indonesia had reached $68 billion, $46 billion, and $34 billion, respectively. Indeed, these numbers understate total short-term liabilities, since nonbank finance (for example, bonds) is not included. The ratio of short-term debt to foreign exchange reserves in each of these three countries exceeded one after 1994. A ratio greater than one is not by itself sufficient to spark a crisis, as long as foreign creditors are willing to roll over their loans. However, it does indicate vulnerability to a crisis.

So, as Chang and Velasco (1998, 1) argued, the East Asian "crash is not a new and frightening creature . . . but a *classic financial crisis*, the likes of which we have seen before in so-called emerging markets. Chile in 1982 and Mexico in 1994 provide the clearest, but by no means the only, precedents" (emphasis in original).

Indonesia, 1997–98

The Indonesian financial crisis of 1997–98, part of the Asian crisis generally, was one of the most devastating, maybe the most devastating crisis since the economic contractions associated with the transition economies of Eastern Europe. The crisis came in the context of astounding economic success. The East Asian economies had experienced high growth rates for a generation before the crisis. Radelet and Sachs (1998a, 18) wrote, "[I]n Indonesia, Korea, Malaysia, and Thailand average life expectancy at birth rose from fifty-seven years in 1970 to sixty-eight years in 1995, and the adult literacy rate jumped from 73 percent to 91 percent. Notably, the benefits of economic growth were widely shared throughout the population. Incomes of the poorest fifth of the population grew just as fast as average incomes, and poverty rates fell substantially in each country." Indonesia's economic performance for the three decades leading up the crisis was among the best in the world; real GDP growth averaged about 7 percent annually since 1970, resulting in a quadrupling of average income in a single generation (Harvie 1999). Stephen Grenville (2004, 3), the author of the Independent Evaluation Office report on Indonesia for the International Monetary Fund (IMF), wrote,

> The Indonesian crisis was surprising during the event and puzzling afterwards. This was a country that had experienced three decades of 7 percent annual growth, had coped successfully with a series of setbacks, had one of the longest serving and most experienced teams of economic policy makers, had no serious macroeconomic imbalances, and had adequate foreign exchange reserves. Why did it experience a crisis far more serious than its Asian neighbors—in terms of the fall in the exchange rate, the damage to the banking system, the fall in GDP and the tardiness of the recovery (and, it might be added, the move away from good economic policy)?

And the crisis was unanticipated.[4] And it was truly horrible. The key exposure in Indonesia was to dollar-denominated debt issued by the nonbank private sector and the government in amounts that far exceeded foreign exchange reserves at Bank Indonesia (Batunanggar 2002, 7). In response to the sinking of the Thai bhat, the central bank, Bank Indonesia, gave up on intervening to keep the currency in a band and let it float. The Indonesian currency, the rupiah, fell 75 percent between July 1997 and January 1998, magnifying the cost of dollar-denominated debt. There was a deep and prolonged recession accompanied by a massive banking crisis. Output dropped by 14 percent, millions lost their jobs, and poverty increased significantly (Harvie 1999). The Jakarta Stock Exchange dropped by 50 percent. There was political uncertainty because of Presidential elections coming in March 1998. Because of rising prices and unemployment there were violent riots, partly directed at the Chinese minority. This led to the end of the 32 year reign of Suharto. In the end, the fiscal costs of crisis resolution were over 50 percent of annual GDP (see Batunanggar 2002, 3).

The Indonesian government asked the IMF for assistance on October 8, 1997. Indeed, the collapse of the Indonesian banking system was a surprise because the banking system itself was not directly exposed to the dollar-denominated debt. The first IMF Letter of Intent essentially saw the banking problems as relatively minor.[5] It was thought that closing a few of the worst banks, privatizing government-owned banks, and strengthening legal and regulatory structures would avoid future problems. In response to an IMF recommendation, on November 1, 1997, sixteen small banks (out of more than 200 banks in total) were closed. The closure plan included protection for deposits up to 20 million rupiah (about $6,000). This was for small investors who accounted for 90 percent of the deposit accounts (by number) in the banking system. The closure plan included banks owned by Suharto's family and associates. (The one owned by President Suharto's son reopened under a different name.)

The closing of the sixteen banks was a disaster. Instead of calming the situation, it had the opposite effect. It overlooked the importance of recognizing that verifying the solvency of an institution is nearly impossible in a crisis. It was not clear whether the closures of those banks would lead to further closures. The information environment was not controlled. "Anonymous lists of 'good banks' and 'bad banks' began circulating around Jakarta" (Blustein 2001, 107). From just those lists, it seems that a reasonable expectation was that other banks would soon be closed. Also, large depositors who made up most of the deposits by value were not covered by the guarantee. The result was a mass bank run. Bank Indonesia provided emergency liquidity support. Still, domestic credit dried up. After much confusion, the authorities realized that they had made a mistake and Bank Indonesia made the partial guarantee of deposits into a blanket deposit guarantee (on January 27, 1998), which was expected to remove the incentive to acquire bank-specific information "The moral-hazard zealots at the Fund [IMF] had been fighting this proposal since late 1997, but by this stage, the bank runs were so ruinous as to leave little room for debate" (Blustein 2001, 219). According to Batunanggar (2002, 21–22), who was a senior analyst at Bank Indonesia (the central bank) at the time, "a very limited deposit insurance scheme was not effective in preventing runs during the 1997 crisis. . . . [I]f a blanket guarantee had been introduced earlier at the outset of the crisis, the systemic runs might have been reduced. That said, the introduction of the blanket guarantee did not instantly stop bank runs. . . . [There was] a lack of trust that the government would stick to their commitment." McLeod (2004) traces the IMF's Letters of Intent and shows that the government and IMF consistently lagged behind events in recognizing the severity of the banking sector problem. During the period November 1997–2000, there would be six major rounds of intervention into the banking system to try to quell the banking crisis (see Batunanggar 2002). In April, seven of the largest fourteen banks were taken over by the Indonesian Bank Restructuring Agency, which had been set up in January 1998. In March 1999, thirty-eight banks were closed, although politics delayed the closure and some politically connected banks were not closed (see Batunanggar 2002, 13).

Among many explanations for the severity of the Indonesian banking crisis, controversy has focused, in particular, on the closing of the sixteen banks and the resulting disastrous bank runs. In fall 1997, IMF officials rejected the idea of a blanket guarantee of deposits, on the basis that it could create "moral hazard." The IMF had the view that restoring confidence required tough action on closing financial institutions, tightening regulatory standards, and requiring financial institutions to strengthen their capital base, as well as other structural reforms (see Radelet and Sachs 1998a, 62–63). Referring to the closing of the sixteen small banks, Radelet and Sachs note: "The IMF's actions in Indonesia were particularly egregious." "Most of the [IMF's] structural reforms . . . simply distract attention from the financial crisis" (67). The IMF initially defended itself; Enoch (2000, 5), for example, writes, "it is not clear what counterfactual policy prescription at the time would have led to fewer problems."

It is true that the problems in a crisis are hard to address and the situation itself is complicated. The IMF had the correct goal—to restore confidence—but pursued the wrong strategy to create it. Indeed, there may well be insolvent banks, fraud, and asset stripping, and so on. But the issue of the banking and financial crisis and the costs of not quelling a crisis are larger than these problems. In a banking crisis, depositors need to be convinced that the banking *system* is not going to collapse. They cannot be credibly convinced that the regulators know for sure that only a certain number of banks are the problem. And, as it turned out, they were right. The IMF policy was ineffective. The IMF believed that it could contain the banking crisis by closing the sixteen small banks.[6] But it backfired. Closing the sixteen banks contributed evidence to the rational view that more banks were going to be closed.

Enoch, Baldwin, Frécaut, and Kovanen (2001, 44) wrote, "The announcement of the [blanket] guarantee did not of itself generate credibility that the government would indeed stand behind all depositors and creditors. Depositors continued to withdraw their funds, leading to continuing needs for [central bank] liquidity support. Only after the bank closures of April 1998 had been succeeded by the prompt transfer of deposits from the closed banks to a designated state bank was credibility in the guarantee achieved among the public." The blanket deposit guarantee, though late, eliminated the need for market participants to acquire bank-specific information. It took time before the policy took hold because after numerous initiatives that did not work, there was some doubt about whether the policy was going to be credible. But the blanket guarantee worked. In fact, without the blanket deposit guarantee, the banking system would unravel as more and more banks were sequentially run on and then closed. Without the blanket guarantee, short-term debt would have remained information-sensitive.

This problem of acting late, not recognizing the extent of the crisis, will appear over and over again. In a bank run or a situation where there is a latent run due to expectations, the extent of possible problems in the banking system cannot be credibly determined. The blanket guarantee was not introduced earlier, say in October 1997 because "the extent of the banking sector's difficulties was not apparent at the time" (Enoch et al. 2001, 41). The issue is whether the systemic event can be seen if one knows what to look for. And from history and recent events, it is always about short-term debt—where it is, who holds it, how much it is, and what must be done to stop the run on it.

Argentina, 2001–2

Like Indonesia before its crisis, Argentina had been doing remarkably well. It was the star performer in Latin America in the 1990s.[7] Then, Argentina went into a recession starting in 1999 when the Brazilian currency, the real, was devalued in the wake of the Asian crisis, with further turmoil due to the Russian crisis in late 1998. Brazil was important because of the Mercosur free-trade arrangement, which involved Argentina, Brazil, Paraguay, Uruguay, and Venezuela. Capital flows into Argentina reversed in a sudden stop. Then

Argentina's recession of 1999–2001 morphed into a devastating financial crisis "after months of creeping financial uneasiness" (Bortot 2003, 169). The trigger for the crisis was a series of bank runs in late 2001. There was also the huge sovereign debt default ($155 billion). Argentinian GDP growth was 8.1 percent in 1997 and early 1998 but was −3.4 percent in the second half of 1998. Real GDP fell 28 percent from the 1998 peak to the 2002 trough. Unemployment peaked at 23.6 percent in 2002. These are comparable to the real output contraction and the unemployment rates experienced in the United States during the Great Depression.

How did Argentina get into such a financial and economic collapse? After a period of hyperinflation, in 1991 Argentina had adopted a currency board arrangement linking the peso to the dollar at a legal conversion rate of 1:1. Just prior to the crisis, almost 100 percent of Argentine public debt, domestic and foreign, was denominated in US dollars (see Calvo and Talvi 2005). Bank deposits were in both dollars and pesos. The deteriorating economic situation—capital outflows (a sudden stop), declining growth, exchange-rate overvaluation, and a large sovereign debt burden—raised the specter of exiting from the currency board arrangement. Breaking the dollar-peso one-to-one exchange rate would significantly reduce the real debt service of dollar-denominated debtors. And it would have allowed the exchange rate to adjust, but at the large cost of bankrupting many firms—and the government.

Depositors were likely fearful of a freeze on deposits and "pesification." "Pesification" refers to the forcible legal redenomination of dollar-denominated debt contracts into peso-denominated contracts at a government announced exchange rate. Such a redenomination would substantially reduce the real debt service of dollar-denominated debtors.

In November, depositors withdrew more peso deposits than dollar deposits. Dollar currency was at a premium. Like the currency premium during National Banking Era panics, the premium arose because the perceived value of peso deposits was considered to be less than the value of dollar deposits. Figure 11.1 shows the offshore currency premium in trades between pesos and dollars. The currency premium spikes in July 2001 and largely stays positive until jumping when the regulatory restriction on withdrawals of dollar-denominated deposits (the "corralito," explained below) is introduced.[8] The premium means losses for depositors converting peso-denominated deposits into dollar-denominated deposits. This series shows that depositors feared a devaluation. And it shows that the market participants knew that a break from the one-to-one convertibility arrangement would be disastrous for the banking system. From February to December 2001, Argentine banks lost 50 percent of their deposits (Calvo and Talvi 2005).

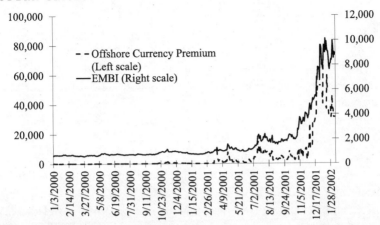

FIGURE 11.1. Argentina: country risk and currency risk
Source: De la Torre, Yeyati, and Schmukler (2003a) from EMBI from JP Morgan. Reprinted with permission.
Note: The offshore currency premiums as measured by Schmukler and Servén (2002) were calculated with the one-month nondeliverable forward (NDF) discount, the forward exchange rate minus the spot exchange rate from Deutsche Bank and Bloomberg.

What was the biggest fear of depositors? Was it the fear of a devaluation of the peso or was it a fear of bank insolvencies? De la Torre, Yeyati, and Schmukler (2003a, 2003b) examined this issue by analyzing a panel of bank-level deposits that distinguished between peso-denominated accounts and dollar-denominated accounts. Included in the sample were the fifty largest banks, accounting for 98 percent of total private deposits in December 2000. The analysis shows that the increasing fear of the currency risk generated a run on the currency; there is a shift from peso to dollar accounts between February 2001 and July–August 2001. This then evolves into a run on all bank deposits, possibly out of fears "that a major devaluation could lead to bank failures and some form of deposit confiscation" (de la Torre et al. 2003b, 64). In fact, during the subsequent period of December 2000–November 2001, the deposit withdrawal that was focused on a few banks and on certain types of banks spread to all banks. In this period, deposit withdrawals were substantial.

Is it a crisis? To address this question, de la Torre, et al. (2003b) regress the change in monthly deposits on various bank-specific characteristics in order to determine the effects of bank fundamentals. They proceed as follows: "If depositors distinguished between banks with different risks, bank fundamentals would appear as statistically significant in the regression. We run the same regressions for different types of deposits and for different periods, namely, a 'precrisis' period (1997–1999) and a 'crisis' period (2000–

2001). Bank fundamentals are chosen based on standard measures of bank risk characteristics" (13). They found that during the precrisis period the variables associated with individual bank risk are significant. But during the crisis period, these variables are insignificant (except for cash divided by total assets). "In other words, the importance of systemic effects (relative to bank fundamentals) rose sharply during the crisis period, suggesting that whatever the influence bank-specific fundamentals had on depositors' behavior in the preceding period, it was dwarfed by systemic factors during the 2001 run" (13–14). The evidence supports the idea that systemic aspects of the crisis dominated individual bank information, clearly indicating that banking system solvency was under scrutiny.

During the crisis, the solvency of the banking system was the issue. Despite this fact, the bank runs came late. The recession was well under way when increasing fears of devaluation and the possible confiscation of deposits triggered a silent run. By November 2001, peso deposits had declined by more than one-third and dollar deposits had fallen 10 percent (see IMF 2003, 5). At the end of November, the government imposed a partial freeze on US dollar deposits—called the "corralito" (little fence)—to prevent capital flight. Bank and foreign exchange trading holidays were declared. Under the corralito, dollar-denominated withdrawals were forbidden, and weekly withdrawals in pesos were initially restricted to a limit of Arg$250.

The corralito was a response to a massive bank run during which private-sector bank deposits had fallen by more than 6 percent during November 20–28. There were riots in the streets. And the peso lost 40 percent of its value. The political situation deteriorated. There was a partial default on Argentine public debt. There ensued a terrible depression during which industrial production fell 18 percent and unemployment rose to around 25 percent. *The Economist* wrote, "The economy has ground almost to a halt, as the chain of payments between consumers, businesses and suppliers has broken down. Cash is at a premium" (March 2, 2002, 26).

Because of the corralito restriction on withdrawals, there were long lines at banks of people opening new accounts, with an estimated 600,000 new accounts opened to evade the corralito limits (see Bortot 2003, 170). In the next three months, there was a 66 percent devaluation against the dollar. In December, there were more mass runs and food riots. Political turmoil saw three presidents come and go until President Duhalde was sworn in on January 3, 2002. On the same day the president abandoned the currency board.

Having abandoned the currency board, the government introduced pesification, turning dollar-denominated debt into peso-denominated debt. The pesification was asymmetric: debts to banks were converted 1:1, while deposits got a boost at 1:1.4. In other words, there was asymmetric pesification of bank assets and liabilities. As a result, banks were stuck with subsidizing their debtors and their depositors to the tune of forty cents on the dollar. During the last year before default, banks had suffered a series of runs and had become deeply undercapitalized. Bank owners complained bitterly about the asymmetric pesification and threatened to walk away from their banks.

Like the suspension periods that took hold during the US National Banking Era, in Argentina during the financial crisis there was a shortage of cash—a currency famine. As a result, provinces issued their own currencies, quasi monies. Between 2001 and 2002, fifteen out of twenty-three provinces issued their own currencies to deal with provincial budget deficits and to provide a transaction currency. So, during 2001 and 2002, there was a large increase in the emission of provincial bonds in the form of low-denomination quasi money, which was used to pay wages and other inputs. This operation was started by several provinces, most notably Buenos Aires, and it was followed by a similar attempt of the national government, which, to comply with the requirements of the various fiscal pacts, started issuing a "federal" bond (Letras de Canelación de Obligaciones Provinciales [LECOPs]) of national circulation.

The currency premium and the shortage of a transactions medium in Argentina in 2001–2 is analogous to characteristics in historical crises. In the National Banking Era, such circumstances led to certified checks being used for transactions. In Argentina, new currencies also arose to meet this need. The fifteen provincial currencies issued between 2001 and 2002. The central government also issued LECOP "bonds," which were used as money. By the end of the first quarter of 2002, these quasi monies amounted to 45 percent of the stock of currency in circulation. (See Argüero 2013 and de la Torre et al. 2003b.)

The banking system of Argentina lost more than 50 percent of its deposits—this is a clear example of a systemic banking crisis. Failure to prevent the extraordinary extent of the deposit contraction magnified the costs of the financial crisis. The corralito was insufficient to prevent the extensive collapse of banking in Argentina—it was an ineffective attempt to suspend convertibility of deposits into cash. It was too little and too late.

Spain, 2008–17(?)

On June 7, 2017, the European Commission approved the first use of the European Union bank resolution procedures on Banco Popular Español, the fifth-largest banking group in Spain with more than $100 billion in loans.

Banco Popular suffered a run and a shortage of liquidity that drove it under. The *Financial Times*, June 8, 2017, reported that Banco Popular lost €3.6 billion in deposits in the two days before the rescue. Banco Santander, Spain's largest bank, bought Banco Popular for one euro. This is the latest news in the Spanish banking crisis that began in 2008. According to Garicano (2012a, 79):

> For a financial crisis of such a magnitude that it threatens both the solvency of the Spanish state and effectively destroyed the credibility of the Spanish supervisors, it is surprising how slowly it has developed. With a similar combination of a large real estate bubble and a complicated financial crisis the Irish bank recapitalisation (and the nationalisation of Anglo Irish) in January 2009 took place a full three years before the entire Spanish financial system had to confront the reality of its losses with the collapse of Bankia in May 2012.

The fact that the crisis dragged on for almost nine years is in part due to some unique features of the Spanish banking system. First, an important part of the financial system, savings banks called "cajas," had a flawed governance structure that gave entrenched political interests substantial influence over them. Second, Spain did not have a real lender of last resort. (Liquidity provision was vested in the European Central Bank.) Basically, it is not clear—as of this writing, whether the crisis is over.

In 2008 the Spanish financial system consisted of three types of intermediaries. There were the cajas, which constituted 50 percent of the Spanish credit market just prior to the start of the crisis. There were the large international banks: Santander and BBVA. Finally, there were other banks, some fairly large, like Banco Popular. As of year-end 2009, there were 353 credit institutions consisting primarily of commercial banks, cajas, and cooperatives. The total assets of those institutions were about €3.7 trillion (351 percent of Spain's GDP), of which 61 percent and 35 percent were held by commercial banks and cajas, respectively.

The cajas are rather different in that they were operated under an unusual governance structure, according to which regional and municipal authorities were legally assured of representation in the governance structure. The cajas were owned by foundations and had no real publicly traded equity-like claims. The share-like claims were "cuota participative," but these instruments had no control rights and there was no secondary market. One result of this was that the cajas were poorly governed, often by unqualified political appointees. (See Santos 2017a, 2017b.)

During 1999–2008, Spain had a housing and construction boom that was financed in large part by foreign lenders, wholesale funding. This was new for banks and cajas. Santos (2017b) wrote, "Spanish banks and cajas changed their funding patterns, increased their reliance on wholesale funding and made heavy use of securitization vehicles to finance the real estate boom" (abstract). Lenders to Spanish banks included German Landesbanks, Barclays, Deutsche Bank, ING, and others. Spain developed a large current account deficit. This made Spain vulnerable to a sudden stop, which occurs as part of the crisis. Here was the short-term debt, and like Argentina, the vulnerability set up the eventual experience of the sudden stop.

So, the story of the crisis in Spain starting in 2008 is long and sad. After the collapse of Lehman Brothers in September 2008, the financial crisis erupted in all advanced economies. Governments in all these countries stepped in to provide support for financial institutions, including standalone actions for certain specific institutions as well as system-wide programs. (See Bank for International Settlements 2009.) In the case of Spain, the government introduced a €100 billion debt guarantee program for 2008, and another €100 billion if needed in 2009. On December 23, 2008, the European Commission approved the Spanish government's debt guarantee program under which new debt issuance of all credit institutions (promissory notes, bonds, debentures) were covered until December 31, 2009. The authorization for the guarantee was later extended until 2012. The Spanish debt guarantee plan was part of the larger plan that the fifteen countries in the eurozone hoped would unfreeze credit markets. The debt guarantee program reduced the incentive to acquire bank-specific information, but managing the information environment required more than just that action.

At that time the prevailing view was that Spain did not really need such a debt guarantee plan because the Spanish banks had so far withstood the effects of the crisis because of conservative regulation such as strict lending rules. The *New York Times*, June 26, 2012, under the headline "Spanish Officials Hailed Banks as Crisis Built," wrote that "Spanish financial leaders in influential positions mostly played down concerns that something might go terribly wrong." But, there was the feeling that if Spain entered a period of economic slowdown after the decade of the property boom, then there would be problems. In an interview in the daily newspaper *El Mundo*, the economy minister Pedro Solbes said that the rate at which bad debt had risen in Spain was "worrying."

In the third quarter of 2008, the Spanish economy entered a recession as the decadelong property boom ended. In that quarter, Spain's GDP contracted for the first time in fifteen years and, in February 2009, Spain and other European economies officially entered recessions. The Spanish economy contracted 3.7 percent in 2009 and 0.1 percent again in 2010. By June 2011, unemployment stood at more than 4.8 million unemployed, amounting to 21 percent of the working population. And the unemployment rate for younger workers was 46 percent. The recession ended when GDP grew by 0.7 percent in 2011, but there was a double-dip: in the first quarter of 2012, Spain was officially in recession once again.

In the financial sector, the first real difficulties began in March 2009 at the time when the Bank of Spain (the central bank) rescued the first caja, Caja de Castilla-La Mancha (CCM), the country's first bank rescue in many years. At this point, financial authorities realized that this case was not an isolated event. There would be more problems with some other institutions with nonperforming loans and low capital-to-assets ratios. In June 2009, a bailout fund was created, the FROB (Fondo de reestructuración orenada bancaria), and funded with €99 billion. One of the goals of the FROB was to implement mergers of weak cajas. Mergers were the strategy undertaken to deal with the weak cajas because, as a result of their governance structure, cajas could not be bought or sold. Cajas could, however, sell assets or consolidate by merging with other savings banks within the same region under Spanish law of that time. In 2010 there were four big merging operations and three outright purchases of small entities by larger entities.

There were silent bank runs, that is, there were no long lines in front of banks, in general, but still there were deposit drains moving funds out of the banking system. Santos (2017b, 36): "As always with banks, deposit withdrawals were accelerating events. . . . Assessing the extent of *retail* deposit withdrawal is difficult as the financial statements don't itemize the different entries that are reported under the heading 'client deposits'" (emphasis in original). Not so with wholesale funding. In the case of Caja Madrid, for example, wholesale financing went from essentially zero in 1992 to 30 percent in 2008 on the eve of the crisis. (See Santos 2017b, 24.)

Meanwhile, macroeconomic conditions were deteriorating, worsening the financial positions of the majority of the cajas. The proportion of nonperforming assets and loan defaults in their balance sheets rose. In May 2010 a second caja was bailed out (CajaSur). And at the same time, the European Supervisory Authority undertook the first of a series of stress tests to examine the financial strength of the Spanish banking system. It was subsequently announced that the stress tests showed that banks were in a solid financial situation to absorb potential losses in an adverse macroeconomic scenario. The results also revealed, however, that five big savings banks were in fragile positions, with very low solvency ratios. They urgently needed recapitalization. The information environment was getting out of policy makers' control, and stress tests normally used to enhance confidence in the banking system were not achieving that goal.

The year 2011 saw the FROB use an enormous amount of resources to rescue financial institutions. Also, there were nationalizations of institutions and the Bank of Spain increased required capital ratios. Still, the lack of confidence in Spain's economy and in Spain's banks closed the international market for new issues, generating serious liquidity problems. Santos (2017b, 22) wrote, "The crisis intensified when the financial liabilities of the banking sector dropped dramatically" as foreign short-term debt holders backed away. The panic was under way, largely in the form a sudden stop in the wholesale funding market.

A new stress test was conducted by the consulting firm of Oliver Wyman to determine the fragility of institutions in the financial sector. According to Garicano (2012b):

> The Oliver Wyman report, the fourth evaluation of the solvency of the financial system in three years, makes very clear that the problematic *cajas* were busy reclassifying, refinancing, and extending loans to cover up their losses in the previous four years. Indeed, the evidence of a cover up on the part of the worst *cajas'* management during 2008, 2009, and 2010 was overwhelming. And yet, the Banco de España [Bank of Spain] did not confront it. In fact, it kept being surprised when in each *caja* that failed the holes uncovered were larger than expected. Already the first entity that was intervened (CCM) as far back as March 2009, showed that the real NPL [nonperforming loan] levels post intervention (17.6%) were more than twice as large as the reported ones. This should have been the point for the Banco de España to get ahead of the curve by ordering an audit of the whole sector (which eventually did happen, three and a half years later). Instead, no one went back to the other *cajas* to try to correct the numbers. Each further intervention (CajaSur, CAM) resulted in similar jumps, and each time the reaction was circumscribed to the fallen entity.

In May 2012 there was the spectacular collapse of Bankia, which was the fourth-largest bank and had been created in December 2010 by merging seven cajas. The nationalization of Bankia subsequently triggered a bailout by the European Stability Mechanism with €41 billion. Bankia was headed by Rodrigo Rato, a former head of the IMF and the economy minister. There was a criminal fraud investigation and Rato was later convicted.[9] The headlines of the *Financial Post* on May 20, 2012, were "Investors flee Spain as banking fears deepen, Greeks warned of catastrophe: European Commission throws Spain a lifeline as fresh fears over its banking sector sent shock waves through markets around the world." The credibility of the banking authorities was now at risk, and restoring confidence became that much more important as well as that much more difficult.

It was now clear that saving the overall financial system, including the cajas, required massive support from the Spanish government, so much that the government requested external assistance from the European Financial Stability Facility (EFSF). In July a memorandum of understanding was signed between the EFSF and the government of Spain by which the latter was to receive €100 billion to cover losses and to recapitalize failing institutions. Martin-Aceña (2014, 85) wrote, "By December 2012 the funds channeled to the banking sector amounted to the staggering figure of €61.2 billion, or about a 5.8% of GDP; 36.5% of these funds has come from the FROB, the rest, 63.5%, from the EFSF. The amount of help received by the Spanish banks in terms of GDP was the second largest of the European Union and the United States, and only after the assistance received by the Irish financial system." By 2017 there had been three years of growth in Spain and the level of GDP was just below the precrisis level. So why did Banco Popular fail in June 2017? And is the crisis over? The slow bleed continued because nonperforming loans do not just disappear. And it is not clear that confidence in the banking system was ever reestablished.

The Bank of Spain's *Financial Stability Report* of May 2016 dryly noted that "The NPL ratio for loans at consolidated level of Spanish deposit institutions declined in 2015 to 6.3% (from 8% in December 2014). In the case of loans to the private sector, the NPL ratio fell from 8.8% in 2014 to 7.1% in 2015" (25). The problem is that a high rate of nonperforming loans persists and can reduce credit growth and growth of the economy, which in turn can make it harder to decrease nonperforming loans. And if the economy goes into a recession, there will be more nonperforming loans. It's not over yet. *The Telegraph*, June 24, 2017, wrote as follows:

> Italian and Spanish banks suffered the largest outflows of depositors' money last year [2016] as customer fears over the safety of money held at Southern European lenders escalated. More than €100bn (£83bn) of deposits were withdrawn in the 11 months to the end of November last year, with €61bn taken out of Italian banks, the largest overall outflow of money from any Eurozone banking system, according to Credit Suisse. Spanish banks suffered the second largest withdrawals at €48bn, equal to just under 3pc of total Spanish bank deposits, while Greek banks recorded the largest percentage fall in deposits with €42bn withdrawn, equal to a fifth of the country's total deposit base. Together Greek, Portuguese, Irish, Spanish and Italian banks suffered net withdrawals totaling close to €150bn, exacerbating their already considerable funding problems.

The US Panic of 2007–8

The Panic of 2007–8 was a banking panic in the sale and repurchase agreement (repo) market, a form of highly liquid short-term debt markets that shrank dramatically when the "depositors" withdrew their money (see Gorton 2010; Gorton and Metrick 2012; and Gorton, Laarits, and Metrick 2017). The crisis was a classic bank run like those in the National Banking Era, except that it did not involve lines of depositors at banks seeking to withdraw cash from their checking accounts or other banks withdrawing their deposit balances. Instead, it involved large institutions not rolling over their sale and repurchase agreements, a form of short-term collateralized debt. The crisis followed a credit boom, particularly in the housing market. And this boom involved securitization, turning portfolios of mortgages into bonds, much of which came to be the collateral for repo. When house prices stopped rising, the crisis began, and it became significantly worse when Lehman Brothers collapsed in September 2008.

The form of short-term bank debt in the US financial system started to change substantially starting in the late 1970s or early 1980s from a largely retail system to a wholesale system (see Gorton, Lewellen, and Metrick 2012). This change corresponds to other important changes in the global economy, including the rise of entities with large pools of cash to invest because of the enormous increase in global wealth: money managers, sovereign wealth funds, large pension funds, together with an integrated global financial network. Demand deposits, the dominant form of bank-produced short-term debt, declined as a percentage of total privately produced safe debt from 80 percent in 1952 and 70 percent in the late 1970s to about 30 percent. The items that grew in importance were those related to wholesale banking: repo, commercial paper, money market mutual funds, and AAA asset-backed and mortgage-backed securities (ABS and MBS).

A repo is a financial contract used by market participants to meet short-term liquidity needs. Repo transactions have two parties: the bank (or borrower) and the depositor (or lender). The depositor deposits or lends money to the bank, and in exchange for the cash, the bank pays interest on the loan and provides bonds as collateral to back the deposit. Repos are typically short-term, often overnight, transactions, so the money can be easily accessed by not renewing or "rolling" the repo. An important feature of the repo market is that the collateral often consisted of securitized bonds. These are the liabilities of a special-purpose vehicle, which finances a large portfolio of loans (e.g., home mortgages, auto loans, credit card receivables) by issuing tranches (bonds) in the capital markets. As the relative importance of demand deposits declined and the relative importance of the repo market grew, the bank loans were securitized creating bonds that could be used as collateral.

Securitization is the process of turning portfolios of bank loans (mortgages, auto loans, student loans, credit card receivables, etc.) into bonds, which can trade and be used as collateral for repo and derivative positions. (On securitization, see Gorton and Souleles 2006 and Gorton and Metrick 2013.) Securitization grew significantly because of a shortage of privately produced "safe" debt. As Bernanke, Bertaut, DeMarco, and Kamin (2011, 8) explain, "a large share of the highly rated securities issued by U.S. residents from 2003 to 2007 was sold to foreigners—55 percent. This share was even higher than in the 1998–2002 period—22 percent—even though total net issuance of apparently safe assets rose from $3.1 trillion in the first period to $4.5 trillion in the second [period]. (The net issuance of private label AAA-rated asset-backed outstanding, including MBS, rose from $0.7 trillion in the first period to $2 trillion in the second.)" As early as 2001, there were concerns in the United States that there was a shortage of collateral. In 2001 the Bank for International Settlements presciently noted that the use of collateral in financial markets had become so widespread that there was a looming problem: "With growth of collateral use so rapid, concern has been expressed that it could outstrip the growth of the effective supply of these preferred assets. . . . The increase in collateralized transactions has occurred while the supply of collateral with inherently low credit and liquidity risks has not kept pace. Securities markets continue to grow, but many major government bond markets are expanding only slowly or even contracting. The latter phenomenon was particularly evident in the United States in the second half of the 1990s" (2). Evidence of a shortage of collateral prior to the crisis can also be seen in repo fails. A repo fail occurs when either side of the transaction does not live up to its end of the bargain at maturity. In particular, at maturity it was increasingly the case that the lender, who has a bond as collateral, does not have the collateral to return to the borrower. This occurred when the collateral was US Treasuries. US Treasuries are valued as collateral and as a long-term store of value. Consequently, they have a convenience yield, a nonpecuniary return. Krishnamurthy and Vissing-Jørgensen (2012) found that the convenience yield was 73 basis points over 1926–2008. In other words, this is the amount saved by the US Treasury; US Treasury coupons are lower by this amount. Gorton and Muir (2016) show that repo fails were increasing as the convenience yield on US Treasuries was rising. That is, US Treasuries were increasingly scarce. The purpose of securitization is to produce safe debt for collateral. In fact, 85 percent of securitized portfolios become AAA/Aaa bonds (see Xie 2012).

This wholesale banking system, which came to be called shadow banking, was large, although there are no precise numbers. The average daily trading volume in the repo market was about $7.11 trillion in 2008, in comparison with the New York Stock Exchange, where the average daily trading volume in 2008 was around $80 billion. (On the repo markets, see Securities Industry and Financial Markets Association [SIFMA] 2008, 9; on the stock market, see "Daily NYSE Group Volume in NYSE Listed.")[10] The SIFMA number includes repo and reverse repo; half of $7.11 trillion would be $3.56 trillion.[11] According to Federal Reserve data, primary dealers reported financing $4.5 trillion in fixed-income securities with repos as of March 4, 2008.

There are no official statistics on the overall size of the repo market, but it is likely to be about $10 trillion, in comparison with the total assets in the US banking system of $10 trillion (see Gorton 2010). Hördahl and King (2008, 37) reported that the amount traded in repo markets had doubled since 2002, "with gross amounts outstanding at yearend 2007 of roughly $10 trillion in each of the US and euro markets, and another $1 trillion in the UK repo market." They also reported that the US repo market exceeded $10 trillion in mid-2008, including double counting. The firms that were the repo banks, the borrowers, were US broker-dealers (financial firms licensed to underwrite securities)—the old investment banks. It was a straightforward banking business: for example, borrow at 3 percent in the repo market and earn 6 percent on the collateral (which accrues to the borrower even though the collateral is in the hands of the lender). According to Hördahl and King, "the (former) top U.S. investment banks funded roughly half of their assets using repo markets, with additional exposure due to off-balance sheet financing of their customers" (39). The incentive to use repo financing was clear—it was a profitable exchange under the current circumstances. But the eventual costs and the implied risks of repo financing were less clear.

The shortage of collateral eventually led to the securitization of subprime mortgages in significant amounts. Subprime mortgages are structured so that they depend on house prices rising. There is an initial period of the mortgages, two or three years, during which the interest rate is fixed. But at the end of that initial period there is a jump up in the interest rate. The idea is that the borrower will refinance at the end of the initial period, with the view that equity will have been built up during that period. If house prices do not rise, or are not expected to rise, then subprime home owners will likely default, and the mortgage-backed securities based on those mortgages will suffer potential losses.

The crisis began in the first quarter of 2007. As shown in tranches of the ABX index, an index linked to subprime portfolios, the crisis started in January 2007 and the prices of subprime MBS show that the start was in March 2007 (Gorton et al. 2015a). The run started first in the asset-backed commercial paper programs, standalone entities that purchased a wide range of assets, but mostly ABS and MBS, and financed these assets with short-term commercial paper. Asset-backed commercial paper outstanding at the end of 2006 was $1.1 trillion. In summer 2007 holders of the commercial paper suddenly refused to roll over their paper or buy new commercial paper when their old paper matured. Maturities shortened for new issues, a phenomenon that became pervasive. (See Covitz, Liang, and Suarez 2013.)

As with other crises, the understanding of the financial market situation was foggy for the authorities. They were basically unaware of the extent to which the shadow banking system had expanded and developed. And the authorities did not observe any runs. But something was going on. Liquidity and trading of certain asset classes appeared to be faltering. So the Federal Reserve set up an emergency lending program, the Term Auction Facility in December 2007. But the broker-dealers were not eligible to borrow from this program, only commercial banks could borrow, an indication that the Federal Reserve did not understand completely where the problem was most critical. As a result, about 60 percent of the borrowed funds went to foreign banks (foreign banks do not have a distinction between commercial banks and broker-dealers). And foreign banks pledged ABS and MBS to the Federal Reserve as collateral to a much greater extent than did the US commercial banks. (See Benmelech 2012.)

In the first quarter of 2008 the crisis was ongoing with runs in the repo market as the key short-term debt at risk. But these runs were not visible unless the observer was on a trading floor and knew what he was seeing. Money market spreads and spreads in the interbank markets, however, were visible and were dramatically rising. The rating agencies were downgrading masses of MBS. In March the Federal Reserve opened two more emergency lending facilities, the Term Securities Lending Facility and the Primary Dealer Credit Facility to provide liquidity to markets over which it typically had only indirect influence. But, even with these new facilities, broker-dealers had to sell assets to raise cash to repay repo borrowers. To raise as much cash as possible, broker-dealers did not sell subprime (the assets considered suspect) but sold AAA ABS and MBS that might have had some subprime asset content. The result was that prices of these securities plummeted. Under mark-to-market accounting there was then a feedback effect as these low prices reduced capital. Banks had additional losses and were forced to reduce their capital levels to balance.

Still, without recognizing that there were severe ongoing runs, the Federal

Reserve was not sure how bad the situation had become (see Lowrey 2014). In April 2008 only four regional Federal Reserve Bank presidents used the word *recession* to describe the state of the economy. One Federal Reserve president put it this way: "While most analysts are in the process of downgrading their forecasts from skirting to actually having a mild recession, the risk of a more severe downturn is uncomfortably high."[12] Indeed, unbeknownst to the Federal Reserve and other outside observers, risk was building up in the financial system. The maturities of short-term debt was shortening and shortening, as if the forest was getting drier and drier. This shortening is documented by Brunnermeier (2009), Shin (2010), Krishnamurthy (2010), and Gorton, Metrick, and Xie (2015b). Krishnamurthy (2010, 18), for example, writes that "The maturity contraction . . . appears to have taken place across many different financing arenas."

This shortening of maturities created a huge vulnerability because the debt holders could all exit at once in a massive run. The accumulation of short-term debt had left the financial market exposed to just that kind of risk, a risk that resembles the type faced by the banks of the National Banking Era. So in 2008, the short-term debt was right in the repo market, and the holders did not have to run to get their cash. The ensuing credit collapse was going to be fast and furious. Still, to most outside observers—not seeing this vulnerability buildup—the characteristics in macroeconomic data looked like a mild recession.

But then came the collapse of Lehman Brothers, the lit match dropped on the forest floor. The failure of Lehman was a *systemic* event. "Of the twenty-five largest financial institutions at the start of 2008, thirteen failed (Lehman, WaMu), received government help to avoid failure (Fannie, Freddie, AIG, Citi, BofA), merged to avoid failure (Countrywide, Bear Stearns, Merrill-Lynch, Wachovia), or transformed their business structure to avoid failure (Morgan Stanley, Goldman)" (Geithner 2014, 255–56). Bernanke made the same point. The Financial Crisis Inquiry Commission report (2011, 354) quotes Ben Bernanke's testimony in which he says that during September and October 2008 "out of 13 of the most important financial institutions in the United States, 12 were at risk of failure within a period of a week or two." The vulnerability was such that there was essentially a hair-trigger for the credit collapse and if not for Lehman it likely would have been some other event that would have created the global financial crisis—"the imminent collapse of the global financial system" (Bernanke 2009b). Geithner (2008) said,

What we were observing in the U.S. and global financial markets was similar to the classic pattern in financial crises. Asset price declines—triggered by concern about the outlook for economic performance—led to a reduction in the willingness to bear risk and to margin calls. Borrowers needed to sell assets to meet the calls; some highly leveraged firms were unable to meet their obligations and their counterparties responded by liquidating the collateral they held. This put downward pressure on asset prices and increased price volatility. Dealers raised margins further to compensate for heightened volatility and reduced liquidity. This, in turn, put more pressure on other leveraged investors. A self-reinforcing downward spiral of higher haircuts forced sales, lower prices, higher volatility and still lower prices.

Just before Lehman filed for bankruptcy, the government had taken over the two large quasi-government mortgage lenders Fannie Mae and Freddie Mac.

The collapse of Lehman led to a run on US money market funds (MMFs), with holdings at the end of 2009 of $3.3 trillion, about 22 percent of GDP. (See Investment Company Institute 2009.) Here is another place where the short-term debt was held. The direct trigger for a run was that one MMF held a large volume of Lehman Brothers' commercial paper. Separately but importantly, the MMF industry participated actively in the repo market, and the run on the industry threatened further liquidity problems in that market.

MMFs in the United States originated in the 1970s from a desire by investors to escape Regulation Q, which set a ceiling on interest rates offered by deposit-taking institutions on demand deposits, and to avoid the reserve requirements imposed on depository institutions. MMFs are essentially banks, although they can invest only in securities with maturities of less than one year, and they have no capital. The MMF deposit contract is not legally debt but the funds maintain an implicit contract to not "break the buck," meaning that it will act like a debt contract. After Lehman, one fund did break the buck, causing a run on other funds (See McCabe 2015.) The US Treasury then announced an insurance fund for MMFs, effectively a blanket guarantee that removed the incentive to uncover information about specific MMFs.

The real effects of the crisis were deep and long. The unemployment rate in December 2007 was 5 percent; it had been at or below this rate for the prior 30 months. In June 2009 it was 9.5 percent. That amounts to a loss of about 8.7 million jobs. GDP contracted by 5.1 percent, the worst contraction since the Great Depression. Almost ten years later, GDP growth is still anemic.

Summary

Indonesia, Argentina, Spain, and the United States are just four of the many modern financial crises. Indonesia and Argentina involved runs on demand deposits, but these came amid the chaos as depositors waited to see what would transpire. Spain and the United States faced runs on wholesale debt. Indonesia and Spain experienced sudden stops. Short-term debt is the issue central to all these crises. But, as described above, the timing of the bank runs appears not to be consistent across these modern crisis episodes, unlike those during the National Banking Era, when the bank runs were regularly triggered by the arrival of information about the coming recession.

In this case, the contrast is more apparent than real. In fact, the timing of events in modern crises is essentially the same as the panics from history. The problem is more about the observation of crisis signals because the bank runs are silent runs. They do not necessarily appear in the press and the authorities may well not be aware of the runs. In studying crises, recall that researchers date the start of the crisis by looking for the date at which there is both financial distress and a visible response from the government or central bank. But this is not the start of the crisis. It is a response to an ongoing crisis. Boyd et al. (2009) show that modern crisis dating is indeed late. They show that there are large lending drops that can predict modern crisis start dates and that the true start date is *prior to* the date listed in crisis databases. Deposits, however, do not drop, as depositors wait to see what will happen. In other words, the government's actions are reactions to the real effects of the lending drop, even when the government is unaware of the latent run.

The results of Boyd et al. (2009) show why modern crises are difficult to understand. Modern financial panics (and many qualify as panics) do not appear to be the result of bank runs, but in fact the extensive depositor withdrawals—whether wholesale deposits or repo nonrenewal—start the crisis. The runs away from short-term debt do not appear in the same way as those of the National Banking Era, but the collapse of credit as a result of the runs is, to a significant extent, the key indicator that a panic has begun. This perspective and the results in Boyd et al. (2009) suggest that the postdating of the start of the crisis—identified with the date of the government intervention in reaction to the underlying events—is flawed. This makes studying these events difficult. To quote Boyd et al. (2009, 4):

> The problem is not limited to one of just systematically late dating [of the start of crises]. Equating the dating of a government response to banking distress to the dating of a systemic bank shock is like studying the evolution of a disease by dating the disease's onset when the patient enters a hospital. . . . [T]he researcher will be unable to disentangle the effects of an adverse shock to the banking industry from the effects of the restorative policy response. Disentangling these effects is key to understanding the mechanics of bank fragility.

As a result, the proximate source of the crisis—the trigger for the run and source of the credit contraction—is overlooked. Our explanation arises from repeated observations—both from historical panics and from modern crisis events—that short-term debt is central to all financial crises. All sorts of explanations are given for financial crisis episodes, each with a grain of truth, but most missing this true issue. Without that key insight in mind, policies to quell financial crises miss the opportunities for effective responses that arise soon after the onset of panic. In the next chapter, we suggest some guiding principles to keep in mind when faced with what looks like a financial panic.

Guiding Principles for Fighting Crises

The Panic of 2007–8 was completely unexpected, to the enduring embarrassment of economists and regulators.[1] There have been financial crises in the last thirty years, but they were in emerging economies. "[S]ince the 1980s emerging market economies . . . exhibit a long series of financial crises associated with major output collapse (for example, Argentina's GDP fell almost 20% from the peak to trough in the 2001/2 'corralito' crisis), those crises were easy to dismiss by the mainstream macroeconomist as stemming from institutional/political immaturity that will likely disappear once these economies embraced pro-market financial reform" (Calvo 2010, 1). As a result, not much is known about fighting crises because little attention was paid to the subject until the Panic of 2007–8. Knowledge from previous crises has been forgotten. So, in 2007–8 there was only Bagehot's 1873 rule. In this chapter we propose some crisis-fighting principles based on the analysis in earlier chapters.

What exactly is a crisis? A financial crisis arises when short-term debt becomes information-sensitive. The crisis is *systemic*. Short-term bank debt holders want their cash. The financial system is on the verge of collapse. Without a clear understanding of crises, they will recur. How can we get a clear understanding? History helps. The reason is that market economies have structural features that are always present, like the fact that demand curves slope down. Another structural feature is that market economies need short-term bank debt, but such debt is vulnerable to runs.

Bank runs are likely to happen again because the form of bank debt changes and this can go unnoticed. Studying the clearinghouse responses to panics during the US National Banking Era is useful for getting a clear picture of what is going on during a crisis. Indeed, it provides a clear picture of *what a crisis is* and how to fight it. To be clear, we are *not* advocating a return to the world of private bank clearinghouses. Central banks are essential for monetary policy. Clearinghouses were never able to prevent bank runs. But their experience can help us understand how to fight crises.

Guiding Principles for Fighting Crises

Bagehot's rule, namely that the central bank should lend against good (what would be good in normal times) collateral at a high (but not astronomical) rate relative to market rates, is the only policy to combat crises that appears consistently throughout modern and historical crises. Modern central banks follow Bagehot's rule in fighting crises even though it is old, dating from 1873. This suggests that crises have a common element. Doesn't Bagehot's rule work? It is part of a proper response, but application of Bagehot's rule alone does not by itself restore confidence. Indeed, it is not clear how this rule in isolation is supposed to end crises. The basic idea seems to be that the central bank, by lending cash against collateral, allows banks to get enough cash to hand out to depositors or other short-term debt holders so that the depositors would eventually realize that they could get their cash back. But what would cause them to later deposit their cash back into the banks? Surely, they realize that the cash came from the central bank and it has to be paid back to the central bank, at which point the assets used as collateral will return to the bank. The central bank does not *buy* the banks' collateral, but rather makes a temporary loan against the collateral. Emergency lending programs cannot by themselves reestablish confidence in the private markets. So what does?

What have we learned about fighting crises? First, in order to fight a crisis, it is imperative to know which firms are banks, that is, which firms are issuing the short-term debt that is under attack and, if possible, which firms or entities are holding the short-term debt. This is the first step because financial crises are always about short-term debt. Short-term debt is essential in an economy, but it is vulnerable to runs. Hence we describe our first guiding principle.

1. FIND THE SHORT-TERM DEBT

A financial crisis is always about short-term debt. Find it. That is our primary and most essential inference drawn from both history and modern financial crises episodes.

By definition, if there is a financial crisis, then short-term debt values become information-sensitive—that is, the value of an essential form of short-term debt becomes uncertain. In some modern cases, it was not clear where (and what) is the short-term debt. To fight a crisis, clearly it is important to know what and where the short-term debt is, where the banking system is. Although it seems simple, it is not. It is astounding in retrospect that during the financial crisis of 2007–8, authorities (both regulatory and academic) did not know what short-term debt was under attack and which firms were issuing it. The $10 trillion "shadow banking" system was literally not measured and therefore not seen. Consequently, a clear picture of the crisis emerged only slowly. And there seems no clear consensus about its causes even now.

Our first guiding principle is important even when the short-term debt is demand deposits, because modern crises have mostly involved demand deposits, and most involved bank runs. The results of Boyd, De Nicolò, and Loukoianova (2009), discussed in the previous chapter, show that there are silent runs prior to government and central bank reactions to the events. The authorities' actions are reactions to the effects of a silent run, even when the government is unaware of the actual run, which could be a steady drain of deposits out of the system. This is important because it shows that if regulators notice these drops in deposits, they would realize that a crisis has started—with a bank run. That Boyd et al. can predict the accepted start date of modern crises strongly suggests that in these crises the government and central bank do not have a concept of a crisis. So, the evidence indicates that key public authorities—governments and central banks—have not looked for the short-term debt. If they had, then in real time, they could have observed the same information used by Boyd et al. and see the crisis unfolding (and the ex post start date of the crisis would be accurate). From analyzing historical episodes, we see how the New York Clearing House Association at times took decisive action as the panic took hold. Although modern crises are complicated, policy-making institutions can aim resources to monitor short-term debt.

Like all financial crises, emerging markets' crises are also all about short-term debt. But, as Radelet and Sachs (1998b, 31) observe, "The biggest indicators of risk were financial, but generally ignored. Short-term debts to international banks had risen to high levels relative to foreign exchange reserves in Indonesia, Korea, and Thailand." Furman and Stiglitz (1998, 5) "argue that the evidence is consistent with the belief that large short-term debt exposure made the East Asian countries vulnerable to a sudden withdrawal of confidence." They analyzed a number of models for predicting financial crises and found that none was particularly good. But these models do not focus on short-term debt. When this type of variable is added, they find that "The ability of [the ratio of short-term debt to reserves], by itself, to predict the crises of 1997, is remarkable" (51). In fact, almost all the accounts of the Asian crisis have emphasized short-term debt. For example, Radelet and Sachs (1998a) find that the ratio of short-term debt to reserves is a statistically significant predictor of financial crisis in the period 1994–97 (also see Corsetti, Pesenti, and Roubini 1998 on this point). But this indicator was overlooked prior to the Asian crisis, and those crises were seen as unpredictable. There is a lesson here for current macroprudential policies.

2. MANAGE THE INFORMATION ENVIRONMENT (SUPPRESS BANK-SPECIFIC INFORMATION)

For both the clearinghouse and modern central banks, there is much more to the panic response than Bagehot's rule. What Bagehot left out is very important: secrecy of lending programs, specifically the anonymity of borrower identity and suppression of bank-specific information (as with short-sale constraints on the stock of financial firms) are critical to the response. In the most severe National Banking Era crises, as in the crisis of 2007–8, emergency lending programs were announced publicly, but the identities of the borrowing to banks (and the specific amounts borrowed) were kept secret. In addition, it is also important to "control the narrative" as key institutions take unusual actions to address the panic. At times, the New York Clearing House was masterful at focusing the narrative on what they could signal credibly— like the solvency of the banking system—with beneficial results to financial markets. But the success depends on whether the narrative is accurate and accessible to the public. In general, the authorities cannot articulate a coherent narrative of the crisis because they don't know what is going on—the fog former Treasury secretary Tim Geithner spoke of. Ironically, if the authorities could have articulated an accurate narrative during a crisis, there probably would not have been a crisis in the first place.

Secrecy limited the ability of short-term debt holders to use information to make inferences about which banks were weak and instead forced them to focus on the general solvency of the banking system as a whole. Specifically, the clearinghouse prohibited the publication of bank-specific information, which kept weak banks from being identified. Further, in the severe crises, the clearinghouse kept both the amounts of individual bank borrowing and their identities secret for the member banks that participated in their lending program, the clearinghouse loan certificates. During crises, saving the financial system requires a unified response, which means not letting weaker banks get picked off one by one. It is imperative to prevent sequential runs on banks that would begin first with the weakest bank, then the next weakest, and so on. That kind of event causes a dramatic contraction of credit and a liquidity drain comparable to a whirlpool around water draining from a bathtub. The key to preventing targeted bank runs is control of the information environment. What we learn from the National Banking Era is that suppressing bank-specific information shifts attention away from individual banks and makes the banking system the issue, which in fact it is. During crises, some banks need liquidity desperately. Lending to banks may be taken as a signal that the borrowing bank is in shaky financial condition, even if borrowing is only a reflection of its temporary liquidity condition. From historical experience, we learn that in general the identities of borrowing banks should not be revealed. Further, any information on specific banks that can be interpreted as signaling weakness should be suppressed (e.g., stock shorting). It may seem paradoxical for the clearinghouse and central banks to hide information during a crisis when the problem is that the holders of short-term debt precisely do not know which banks have bad assets. One might think that a policy of transparency is superior, because by revealing bank portfolios publicly the depositors can then figure out which banks are weak or insolvent. But this *cannot be done credibly*. The public cannot determine from the available information whether a bank is really in trouble, and in fact, neither the clearinghouse nor the central bank actually knows which banks are insolvent. The central bank and the public cannot assess the value of the opaque bank assets, especially in a crisis. The problem of bank asset opacity is likely the reason there was a (possibly silent) bank run in the first place. It is better to keep the financial system from unraveling as a sequence of banks perceived to be weak creates the prospect of runs. Tim Geithner (2014, 181) pointed out the potential serial unraveling of banks in 2007–8: "Merrill's stock had lost more than a third of its value in a week. If Lehman went the way of Bear, Merrill was widely understood to be the next-weakest investment bank, the next obvious target for a run"; "everyone on Wall Street knew that if Morgan [Stanley] went the way of Lehman, Goldman would be next" (204).

This potential unraveling of the banking system is related to "stigma," which refers generally to the cost to a bank of having publicly been revealed as having availed itself of central bank lending facilities, whether during a crisis or in normal times. By borrowing from a central bank lending facility, a bank reveals (if its identity comes out publicly) that it cannot feasibly borrow in the interbank markets. The revelation that a bank did borrow from an emergency lending facility can lead to a run on that bank, like Northern Rock. "Stigma was a real danger" (Geithner 2014, 235).

In response to stigma, the Federal Reserve created new anonymous lending programs during the 2007–8 financial crisis. Almost all of these programs were designed to use auctions to make loans secret, not publicly revealing borrowers' identities.[2] Bernanke (2010, 2) wrote that because of "the competitive format of the auctions, the TAF [Term Auction Facility] has not suffered the stigma of the conventional discount window." Armantier, Ghysels, Sarkar, and Shrader (2015) found that "banks were willing to pay a premium in excess of 44 basis points on average (143 basis points after the bankruptcy of Lehman Brothers) to avoid borrowing from the discount window. Discount window stigma is economically relevant as it significantly increased banks' borrowing costs during the crisis."

What is the point of designing anonymous lending programs if bank-specific information is revealed in the banks' stock prices? The US Securities and Exchange Commission and other agencies in Europe also acted to suppress bank-specific information that revealed the weak financial institutions by instituting short-sale bans on almost eight hundred financial firms starting on September 18, 2008.[3] This was not an issue for the clearinghouse in the National Banking Era because bank stock was very illiquid, largely owned by blockholders and insiders. This was not due to any regulation but happened endogenously (see Gorton 2014).

Appel and Fohlin (2010, 1) found that the short-sale bans that were implemented in several countries during the recent financial crisis "improved market liquidity or at least had a neutral impact." This result is consistent with preventing weak banks from being revealed. If they cannot be revealed by the trades of privately informed traders, then adverse selection is avoided and there is more liquidity.

The IMF has the opposite and not uncommon view, although we believe it is inaccurate. For example, Enoch, Baldwin, Frécaut, and Kovanen (2001, 116) write,

> Handling a banking crisis is made much more difficult if the public does not have full confidence in what the authorities are doing. [On this first point, we agree—confidence in the authorities is crucial.] If there is a lack of confidence in the banking system and no credibility in how the authorities will handle it, or whether they will protect depositors, a natural reaction will be flight from the banking system and maybe the currency. [Again, we agree with this point and on the projected response.] Particularly in this situation full transparency becomes critical. The authorities need to explain clearly to the public what they are doing and why. Decisions have to be on the basis of simple, uniform, credible, and defensible criteria.

In the quote above, there are some statements that we agree with fully. It is the final three sentences, however, that contradict our conclusions. From our perspective, the authorities cannot credibly explain clearly what is going on and what they are doing because in real time, they cannot know. There is no way to create "transparency." That is exactly the problem. If they could know in real time and do what they said they would do, there would not have been a crisis to start with. If there is one thing the examples of Indonesia and Argentina show, it is that the authorities cannot do this. The information on bank conditions is too fluid during a crisis—it is hard enough for the authorities to maintain a semblance that the banking system is safe and solvent, much less provide reliable information on the condition of individual banks. Authorities should be strategic about the release of information, and that information release should be aimed at the goal of ensuring the best outcomes for the banking system generally, not any specific bank.

Blanket deposit guarantees have been successful in the modern era and were unavailable to the New York Clearing House. In an attempt to control the information environment, the blanket deposit guarantee of the money market mutual funds in 2008 eliminated the incentive for depositors in money market mutual funds from acquiring information on individual institutions. Better to concentrate on system stability and use techniques to focus the public's attention on the system as an entity. Managing the information environment is central to that objective.

3. OPEN EMERGENCY LENDING FACILITIES (BAGEHOT'S RULE)

Emergency lending facilities have their origin in clearinghouse loan certificate issuance during panics and in the Bank of England discount facilities (see Flandreau and Ugolini 2011). The purpose of a central bank lending facility in a financial crisis is to prevent banks from being forced to dump assets in fire sales in order to raise cash to hand out to holders of short-term debt during runs. Fire sales exacerbate the crisis by causing asset prices to nosedive. And declining asset prices magnify the problem by forcing banks to sell more assets to raise the same amount of cash. Emergency lending facilities cannot by themselves end a financial crisis, but they can mitigate the effects of runs by attenuating the fire sales that accelerate the contractionary spiral of declining asset prices. So they are important. Follow Bagehot's rule. Sounds simple, but it is not.

Many questions must be answered to implement an emergency lending facility, and they depend on the legislation governing central banks, the structure of financial markets, and so on. Which firms are eligible to borrow from the emergency facilities? What is eligible collateral? What is "good" collateral? What percentage of collateral value will be available for the loan, that is, what are the haircuts on the collateral? How should the emergency facilities be designed—as auctions? What kind of auction? The answers to these questions changed during the Panic of 2007–8. (For overviews of these issues, see the Bank for International Settlements 2013, 2014; and Dobler et al. 2016.)

The major debate about emergency lending facilities today concerns whether there should be prespecified rules rather than a policy of deliberate ambiguity. This debate is framed around the usual moral-hazard point of view. From this vantage point, ambiguity prevents banks from relying on future assistance, since the rules are vague. On the other hand, it is argued that there are good reasons to clarify the rules in advance. One is that the rules may positively alter the incentives of banks. For example, they may hold more assets that are deemed good collateral. Second, it can minimize the political risk that comes from decisions during the crisis. (See Fischer 1999 and He 2000.)

This debate played out in the United States in the aftermath of the 2007–8 crisis. Section 13(3) of the Federal Reserve Act gave the board of governors of the Federal Reserve System the authority to extend credit to nonbank private firms in "unusual and exigent circumstances." This provision basically recognized that the circumstances of a financial crisis cannot be foreseen, and so the central bank needs to have some discretion. Indeed, Section 13(3) was invoked during 2007–8. But under the Dodd-Frank Act, this section was amended, removing this discretion and adding requirements for information production—including the identity of the borrowers (though with a two year lag). This condition conflicts with lending facilities with anonymous borrowers, something that has been critical in successful responses to crises. Further, it requires that emergency lending be only to participants with broad-based eligibility, rather than allowing for assistance to a single firm. Clearinghouse aid to a single firm was effective and successful in alleviating a crisis in 1884. The announcement of clearinghouse loans to a specific bank, Metropolitan National Bank, was credible because the New York Clearing House had announced the denial of loans and the closure of another member bank in the prior week. Metropolitan suffered massive depositor withdrawals and the clearinghouse loans helped the bank endure the panic and persist long enough for it to liquidate voluntarily after the panic was over.

Broadening the set of acceptable counterparties during a panic has precedents that are informative. During the Panic of 1907, the problem was that there were runs on trust companies, which were not members of the clearinghouse. The Knickerbocker Trust Company faced a run on its deposits and sought assistance through its clearing bank, the National Bank of Commerce, one of the largest banks in the New York Clearing House Association. The

National Bank of Commerce must have agreed that it was worthwhile because it requested a loan for Knickerbocker through the clearinghouse on Monday, October 21, 1907. The New York Clearing House chose to decline the request in order to retain its liquidity for its membership. Lending to Knickerbocker was the opportunity to contain the financial disturbance, but that opportunity was lost as Knickerbocker was run on the following day. After Knickerbocker disbursed $8 million in cash out of more than $40 million in deposits, it closed and the panic began in earnest. The clearinghouse still could have opened their emergency lending facilities to trusts during the panic, but it did not. The clearinghouse had weekly information on trust companies that cleared through clearinghouse members, but in real time they had no way of knowing just how strong each trust was. As nonmembers, trust companies were not part of the more rigorous, prepanic mutual monitoring system of clearinghouse members. Trusts could get liquidity by selling assets or liqui-dating deposit accounts with banks. Banks had an incentive to hold their own liquid balances, but clearinghouse loan certificates relaxed that constraint for banks during a crisis. The trusts could not be issued clearinghouse loan cer-tificates because they were not members of the clearinghouse. That barrier was an institutional hurdle, but there are limitations on central banks with respect to the counterparties with whom they can transact, and those con-straints hindered effective and timely actions in modern crises.

The reality is that effective rules cannot really be usefully written in ad-vance of crises anyway because the crisis will appear in some way that has not been imagined. For example, it may be that the firms that need access to the facility are not eligible because they were not officially banks. To widen the set of counterparties during a crisis, it is important to gather essential infor-mation from key new intermediaries as they become a larger portion of the market or highly interconnected. But there are likely to be surprises because there are many observed in history.

Another complication is that the potential collateral may be of a different form. For example, during the Panic of 2007–8 it was not allowable to deliver a super senior credit default swap as collateral at an emergency lending facility. A super senior credit default swap is a synthetic risk transfer (via a derivative security) of the risk of loss due to default on a portion (called a "tranche") of a portfolio that is senior to the most senior AAA/Aaa-rated tranche. Central banks need to ensure that their collateral requirements evolve along with the developments in the financial sector.

Who is eligible to borrow at the emergency lending facility? What is a bank? Broker-dealers? Flandreau and Ugolini (2011) discussing the English Overend-Gurney Panic of 1866: There was "a marked contrast between nor-

mal times lending and crisis lending in that main financial intermediaries
and the 'shadow banking system' only showed up at the Bank's window during crises" (abstract). In 1866 the Bank of England found itself rescuing a
shadow banking system of nonbank, limited liability, money market institutions called bill brokers. And Bagehot (1873) famously quotes one of the Bank
of England's more senior directors, Mr. Harman, that, during the Panic of
1825, the Bank of England "lent by every possible means and modes we have
never adopted before" (Bagehot 1873, 51–52).

The issue of what collateral constitutes "good collateral" (or "eligible collateral") is a sticky one. The key issue is to provide liquidity to prevent the fire
sales, and there are clear examples in history of the extent to which the range
of collateral forms was expanded in order to ensure that liquidity was available (like the artwork provided by George Seney for Metropolitan National
Bank—see chapters 5 and 6).

The value of financial assets can become increasingly dependent on the
perceived ability of financial institutions to fund positions. In turn, the funding market access of financial market institutions can be impaired by uncertainty about asset values and firm insolvency. Paradoxically, the decision
about what assets are eligible can determine a firm's solvency, since if it cannot fund those assets, it will die. But if it cannot fund those assets, then they
are not "good" assets because their value has fallen.

Further, if banks need to sell assets in a crisis, they sell their best assets,
reasoning that these will raise the most cash. But all banks reason the same
way and, as a result, the best assets' prices get crushed and these assets then
become "bad" assets.

4. PREVENT SYSTEMICALLY IMPORTANT INSTITUTIONS FROM FAILING DURING THE CRISIS

During a crisis it is not possible to declare, with full credibility, that a bank
is solvent or insolvent. Consequently, letting banks fail during a crisis creates
uncertainty about whether other banks will also be allowed to fail. And this
uncertainty will accelerate the runs. We saw this during the Indonesian crisis.
And we saw this with Lehman Brothers. But the dynamic is not widely understood. For example, Rohdé (2011, 1) writes that "Letting banks fail [in a crisis]
is a necessary disciplinary factor." And Rohdé is not alone in thinking this
way. It was partly the logic behind letting Lehman fail (though not the articulated logic of Bernanke and Geithner). Our argument is not that banks should
not face discipline; our point is that the middle of a crisis is not the time for

large or interconnected banks to fail. Goodhart (2008) made the same point in the midst of the Panic of 2007–8. There may be some clearly insolvent banks, but closing only those banks (without a blanket deposit guarantee) causes runs on the remaining banks. The system begins to unravel.

This lesson is not new. Perhaps the first example of this mistake was the failure of Overend, Gurney and Company in England in June 1866, during what became known as the Overend-Gurney Crisis. The crisis began in May 1866 when "For several months it had been suspected that some of the Finance Companies had practically exhausted their means; and the suspension of the Joint Stock Discount Company supplied obvious proof of it. . . . The fall of the Joint Stock Discount led to talk about every other Discount Company . . . and to talk about all Finance Companies, and some banks too. [Increases in the Bank of England's discount rate] were made for the protection of the Bank's reserves, which was run upon" (*Bankers' Magazine*, June 1866, 638–39). The term "finance companies" refers to financial intermediaries that were not banks but took deposits and discounted bills. They were called discount houses or bill brokers. These firms were at the center of the English financial system. Discount houses could borrow from the Bank of England, and in the crises of 1857 and 1866 they had borrowed heavily from the bank. (See King 1935 and Flandreau and Ugolini 2011, 2014.)

Overend, Gurney was not a bank, but a discount house or bill broker. It was, however, the largest discount house by far. In May, Overend, Gurney and Company applied to the Bank of England for help. But the Bank of England refused to help Overend, Gurney and it failed. The result was a Lehman-like disaster. *Bankers' Magazine* of June 1866 explained that the crisis began

> on the morning of Thursday, May 10th, when the great house of Overend, Gurney & Co., Limited, applied for help [from the Bank of England] to the amount of £400,000. Their securities not being satisfactory, the application was . . . refused with very sincere regret, and with full knowledge of the consequences that must inevitably follow. About half-past three o'clock in the afternoon the great house at the "corner," of wider European fame, shut its doors, and made confession of insolvency. It is impossible to describe the terror and anxiety which took possession of men's minds for the remainder of that and the whole succeeding day. No man felt safe. A run immediately commenced upon all the banks, the magnitude of which . . . can hardly be conceived.

Flandreau and Ugolini (2011, 4) observe the

> fascinating parallel between the way the Bank of England found itself involved in rescuing a "shadow banking system" of non-bank, limited liability, money

market institutions known as bill brokers (or . . . "discount houses" . . .) despite its initial insistence on not supporting it because it saw it as a source of speculation and financial vulnerability. But when markets learned of the failure of Overend, Gurney, which the Bank had refused to help, liquidity seized and a violent panic set in. The Bank of England was forced to resume support to the shadow banking system. The analogy with the Fed's refusal to help Lehman in September 2008 and the events that followed is not only tempting; it is legitimate.

The Bank of England learned the lesson. The bank did rescue Barings Brothers in 1890. In other words, the Bank of England did "distinctly acknowledge that it is its duty" to lend in times of crisis. Fetter (1965, 257–83) called it "the victory of the Bagehot Principle."[4]

The New York Clearing House Association also understood guiding principle 4. As we discussed in chapter 6, the clearinghouse rescued the Metropolitan National Bank in 1884. The clearinghouse policy applied to large, important banks (too big to fail), not to all banks. As discussed in chapter 6, the clearinghouse let the National Bank of the Commonwealth fail in the Panic of 1873 (though the depositors were paid in full); it was not significantly interconnected. It is important to note that because of the incentive-compatible mutual monitoring of member banks, the credibility of the clearinghouse was strong. There was a credible selection mechanism in place before the crisis: the clearinghouse members were the too-big-to-fail banks. So, when there was no crisis, the clearinghouse would let large banks fail, as with the Ocean Bank in 1871.

Of course, the rule that banks should not be allowed to fail in a crisis runs up against the dogma of "too big to fail," which we discussed in chapter 6. Opposition to too-big-to-fail policies arise from "who pays" for the potential losses from aiding those institutions. During the National Banking Era, the clearinghouse banks agreed to share losses arising from unpaid clearinghouse loan certificates. In modern crises, the gray area between taxpayer liabilities and, say, Federal Deposit Insurance coffers, leads to confusion. Staunch opposition to "too big to fail" is a viewpoint without a concept of a crisis and without an estimate of the costs associated with the counterfactual of a panic without too-big-to-fail policies. As a result, that opposition is without any historical context of the costs to the taxpayer arising from what we see as far more costly crises. It is a view that would recommend that we have an Overend, Gurney event and a Lehman event in every crisis. If that viewpoint rules the day, then this lesson within guiding principle 4 has not yet been learned.

5. LAWS AND REGULATIONS NEED NOT
APPLY DURING A FINANCIAL CRISIS

A financial crisis is different from normal times. Joplin (n.d., 29) asserts that "There are times when rules and precedents cannot be broken; others, when they cannot be adhered to with safety." A fundamental problem is that a financial crisis is an event that is not verifiable; it is not contractible. In other words, it is not possible to describe a financial crisis in a precise enough way that the concept could be used in contracts. It is a case of "you know it when you see it." The court in the case of *Livingston v. the Bank of New York*, discussed in chapter 3, was clear about this: When all banks have suspended convertibility, it is not evidence that any single bank is insolvent. When all banks have suspended convertibility, then it is clear that there is a financial crisis. As a result, we see instances where debt contracts are not enforced, where governments break private contracts, and where private agents take actions that they are not contractually obligated to take. The nonverifiability of crises is the logic behind the original Section 13(3) of the Federal Reserve Act (which Dodd-Frank diluted). That section gave the board of governors of the Federal Reserve System the authority to extend credit to nonbank private firms in "unusual and exigent circumstances."

Guiding principle 5 can be phrased as "consider temporary relaxation of laws and regulations during a crisis, even those that would be unquestionable during normal times." In US history, suspension of convertibility always occurred in pre–Federal Reserve crises. Suspension of convertibility means that demand deposit contracts were not enforced. The contract says that the depositor has the right to withdraw cash any time the bank is open. So, suspension was illegal, but the law was never enforced in widespread suspensions. In fact, it was often openly welcomed because it prevented fire sales. In other words, debt contracts were not enforced during the panics of the pre–Federal Reserve era. The same is true of the United Kingdom. This is an old lesson. Speaking of a panic in England in 1797, Poor (1877, 196) noted that "With the announcement of suspension the panic instantly subsided." But the working knowledge of the history of suspension of convertibility and of not enforcing debt contracts was lost in the twentieth and twenty-first centuries (although banking holidays, which are closely related, have been used in emerging market crises). That knowledge was lost because financial crises were not supposed to happen in advanced economies. Clearly, such a policy would provide legal and logistical challenges to implement today, but active investigation into the feasibility and implementation of such actions could be beneficial. Consider the policies akin to "circuit breakers" that are presently in place on numerous stock exchanges.

Similarly, mortgage moratoriums were declared by many US states during the Great Depression, and in fact regularly during crises in previous US history, and these were upheld by the US Supreme Court in the Blaisdell case.[5] The decision in *Blaisdell* was based on US states having emergency powers. These powers were almost always used only during wartime. But during the Great Depression, Supreme Court Justice Louis Brandeis wrote that the Great Depression was "an emergency more serious than war."[6] (See Fliter and Hoff 2012 and Gorton 2012.) The Blaisdell case was cited by Argentina's highest court to uphold the pesification of dollar deposits, which was in violation of the deposit contracts.[7] Depositors viewed pesification as confiscation. The Argentine court in the case of Bustos, invoking *Blaisdell*, wrote as follows:

> [I]t is evident that the prolonged maintenance of an artificial value equivalence between the Argentine peso and the U.S. dollar . . . led to a process of worsening of the national productive apparatus . . . , to a threat of bank run that the Government tried to avert . . . and finally to a certain risk that that threat really should occur or start, which were the determinants of the measures adopted by the Executive Branch and the Congress with the goal of impeding the generalized insolvency of the banking system and the subsequent ruin of the set of depositors. (quoted in Spector 2008, 142–43)

President Franklin Delano Roosevelt declared a national bank holiday on March 5, 1933, during the US Great Depression. This declaration had no real legal basis, although he claimed wartime emergency powers as the basis, and ex post his action was legalized. (See Gorton 2012.) On June 5, 1933, Roosevelt signed legislation that made gold clauses in public and private bonds unenforceable. These contract features had been almost universally included in debt contracts because of inflation during the US Civil War. The clause indexed the payments to creditors to the value of gold; creditors could demand payment in gold or the gold equivalent in dollars. In order to go off the gold standard, Roosevelt needed to delink the dollar from gold. The US Supreme Court upheld the government's abrogation of the gold clauses. (See Krozner 1999.) This action lightened the burden of debt for the federal government and contributed to the recovery from the depression (see Jacobson, Leeper, and Preston 2017).

Another example of crisis actions concerns implicit contracts in securitization. Securitization is the process of taking bank loans and turning them into bonds that can be traded and used as collateral. The purpose of securitization is to create safe debt: 85 percent of a typical securitized loan portfolio is AAA/Aaa bonds. "Safe debt" means information-insensitive debt. Securitization requires setting up a legal entity called a special-purpose vehicle (SPV). The SPV buys the loan portfolio from the financial firm that originated the loans, financing that purchase by issuing asset-backed and mortgage-backed securities (ABS and MBS) in the capital markets. The SPV buys loans from a single financial firm repeatedly over time, and each time issuing new ABS or MBS. The SPV is legally separate from the originator and the originator has no legal obligations to the SPV once the loan portfolio has been sold.

It is profitable for financial firms to securitize because the 85 percent that is viewed as safe has a convenience yield, which refers to the nonpecuniary returns that the holder of the ABS or MBS can receive. The term "convenience yield" comes from thinking about cash. Cash bears no return and yet we hold it—because it is convenient for many transactions. The same is true for privately produced safe debt. In order to make this safe debt, securitizations involve homogeneous loan portfolios, for example portfolios of auto loans, credit card receivables, or home mortgages. Asset classes are never mixed because this would create an incentive to produce information about the correlations of the returns on the different asset classes.

Prior to the recent crisis, financial firms employed securitization to remain competitive as it was a cheap source of funding.[8] The firms had the incentive to choose portfolios efficiently and without adverse selection because without that source of funding, financial firms were not profitable. During the Panic of 2007–8, banks took extralegal actions to bail out their SPVs in order to assure investors in the ABS and MBS that the portfolios were not adversely selected. According to Robertson (forthcoming, 1): "Between mid-2008 and late 2009, over $350 billion in credit card securitization programs were bailed out by their sponsors." Robertson studied twelve public credit card securitization programs amounting to almost half a trillion dollars in outstanding receivables. Of these, eight engaged in some type of bailout.

Examples of these bailouts include Bank of America, American Express, and JP Morgan Chase. The bailouts were accomplished by having the SPV issue junior securities to the sponsoring bank. This amounts to a cash donation from the bank to its trust. It is a donation in that the sponsoring bank is not contractually required to support its SPV. According to the *Financial Times* of June 24, 2009,

> Although they are not obligated to support the pools of credit card receivables when losses mount, banks have done so to ensure investors continue to buy

such securities. . . . Banks have been supporting card trusts by issuing—and then buying—bonds that would absorb the first layer of losses in the underlying loans. This is designed to provide a protective buffer for existing bondholders. B of A bought $8.5bn of junior debt from one of its trusts in the first quarter and put aside $750m to cover losses on the investment. Citi bought $265m of so-called junior debt from one of its credit card trusts in October and an additional $2.3bn of junior debt from the same trust in April, according to a regulatory filing.

So, it seems that the banks' SPVs were too big to fail from the perspective of their sponsors.

And there are many other examples, including others from the Panic of 2007–8. But the main point is that because a financial crisis is not verifiable event, it is not feasible to prespecify contractually permissible actions that may be taken during a crisis. Nevertheless, societies have allowed deviations from contracts, rules, and laws during a crisis.

Similar issues arose with respect to actions taken during the Panic of 2007–8. For example, using the US Treasury Exchange Stabilization Fund to insure money market funds was of dubious legality, but no one has seriously questioned this action. A lawsuit about the Federal Reserve's bailout of AIG has challenged the Federal Reserve's powers and the limits of its discretion during a financial crisis. This has yet to go to the US Supreme Court, and may not.

The Purpose of the Guiding Principles

The goal of presenting guiding principles is to raise our main point to the top priority: to protect the banking system from collapsing. In a crisis—even if the event is not thought to be a "banking" crisis—it is paramount to ring-fence and protect the banking *system*. The financial system is about to collapse. The situation is dire. Recall Bernanke's point about twelve of the largest thirteen financial firms in the United States about to fail. And this was after Lehman's collapse—the crisis had actually started more than a year earlier, as noted earlier.

The goal of protecting the banking system seems simple. It is not. The confusion usually concerns other goals. One big problem is the charge of "moral hazard," the critique that attempts to save the banking system will cause bankers to take more risk in the future—"the line had to be drawn somewhere." It seems clear that even if this is a problem (which is in itself not clear), during a financial crisis is not the time to let the banking system collapse, as emphasized by Goodhart in the *Financial Times* on September 19, 2008.

And, rather than focus on the banking system, the IMF focuses on a broad array of reforms. The IMF perspective makes sense because fiscal and institutional problems—not crises—are what the IMF had faced in a number of its previous challenges. For example, Lane and Schulze-Ghattas (1999, 1) write that "these crises . . . were rooted mainly in financial sector fragilities, stemming in part from weaknesses in governance in the corporate, financial, and government sectors, which made these economies increasingly vulnerable to changes in market sentiment, a deteriorating external situation, and contagion. . . . IMF-supported programs, structural reforms, particularly in the financial sector and related areas, assumed a central role. These reforms were intended to address the root causes of the crisis, with a view to restoring market confidence." This quote reflects in the IMF what remains widespread in the economics profession—there is no concept of a crisis here, rather the crisis is attributed to just about everything. And so just about everything has to be fixed to "restore confidence." But a banking crisis is not the time to worry about "moral hazard" or implementing new bank regulations or worrying about bankers' bonuses or forcing structural reforms of the economy. All of this can be dealt with, if necessary, *after* confidence has been restored. As Radelet and Sachs (1998b, 7) say: "Financial panic is rarely the favored interpretation of [an emerging market] financial crisis. . . . [Analysts] are much more prone to look for weightier explanations." If the central bank and government are trying to do too much, there will be no credibility in their efforts to restore confidence in the banking system. All these actions will seem confused, because they will be confused.

And David Scott (2002, 13) writes, "The ability to restore depositor confidence so as to stabilize liquidity rapidly can be an important milestone in minimizing the damage caused by financial crises. The relatively positive results in Korea and Thailand stand in contrast to the experiences in Indonesia (and more recently Ecuador). A key distinguishing characteristic seems to be the *relatively early adoption of extensive bank liability guarantees* in Korea and Thailand and the limited credibility of the guarantee eventually adopted in Indonesia" (emphasis added). Early intervention with extensive guarantees is an example of decisive action to save the banking system.

The Problem of the Counterfactual

A major problem with fighting crises is that the authorities cannot convincingly argue the counterfactual. What would happen if the panic-fighting measures are not undertaken? What would have happened if Continental Illinois had not been bailed out? Imagine trying to argue that letting Lehman fail would be a disaster. No one would listen much less be convinced (although ex post it seems that those very same people thought letting Lehman fail was a big mistake!). Yet it was a disaster. Unless such counterfactuals can be argued convincingly, a crisis must go on and get worse until there is a consensus that it is really bad, really a crisis.

The most common way to try to stop bank runs is with a blanket or extensive guarantee of the bank debt. Laeven and Valencia (2008) analyze forty-two financial crises in which there were fourteen cases in which blanket guarantees were issued; they find that blanket guarantees are largely successful in reducing liquidity pressures on banks. But there are two problems with authorities proposing a blanket guarantee or a similar action. First, there is a cost to such guarantees. And the counterfactual of what would happen without the guarantee cannot be persuasively argued. And this is also true of any type of bailout of banks. It is not possible to show what the costs to society would have been had these actions not been taken. The case of letting Lehman Brothers fail shows the difficulties. Having seen what happened after the Lehman failure, would society have preferred to have saved Lehman? It is not clear. What should be clear is that it would have been better for Lehman to fail in a more orderly manner after the crisis had subsided.

What we can say is that governments and central banks—and clearinghouses—have never allowed the banking system to collapse completely in a financial crisis. Actions have always been taken to save the banking system. And these actions have *always* been costly and controversial. It seems that the revealed preference of society is to save the banking system and live with the costs and the controversy. In a subtle inference from history, early crisis interventions generate lower costs but that requires accurate diagnosis of the problem, a challenge in modern crises.

Second, a major problem with thinking about a policy during a crisis is the charge of moral hazard, discussed earlier. The concern with moral hazard comes up over and over again. That it does is surprising, as the same charge was made in 1933 when deposit insurance was being considered in the United States. The claim was that this insurance would cause moral hazard: "Banks get the upside but not the downside." But deposit insurance worked effectively to reduce the incidence of bank runs. The downside was perhaps not recognizing the expansion of the asset risk profile of commercial banks and adjusting the deposit insurance premiums appropriately. These adjustments can be made during nonpanic periods. Where is the moral hazard? Are banks aiming to fail? No. Are they gaming the system to maximize their benefit from the provision of insurance? Perhaps, and that is a regulator and supervisory challenge. Nevertheless the charge of moral hazard is repeated even if it is exaggerated.

This concern about moral hazard is related to the first point about the costs. Imagine that no bailout actions are undertaken to avoid a systemic collapse and a systemic collapse occurs—unlike what we observed in 2007–8. What would that cost be? We cannot know. Yet, in every crisis, the government and central bank have chosen to save the banking system. Blustein (2001, 77–78) provides an example from Thailand during the Asian crisis, when the IMF was considering various policies:

> Lindgren, a Finnish national, contended that closing insolvent finance companies meant that the Thais also had to take drastic steps to protect the surviving institutions. Otherwise depositors would become worried that more institutions might be closed, and total panic might set in, toppling bank after bank. Accordingly, he supported a plan for the Thai government to guarantee the claims of depositors and creditors in all banks and finance companies. But this idea outraged many top Fund officials back at headquarters who saw the guarantee as a giveaway to rich investors who had gambled on high-yielding deposits in shaky financial institutions. It would be a classic case of "moral hazard," they argued. . . . But Lindgren persisted, asserting that although the guarantee might be costly, the cost of not issuing one would likely be higher. . . . Lindgren won. On August 5, the Thais suspended the operations of a total of fifty-eight finance companies, and a comprehensive guarantee was issued on deposits and liabilities of financial institutions. That decision now appears wise and farsighted, for the runs gradually abated.

In the 2007–8 financial crisis, Geithner (2014) writes of frustration with the "moral hazard fundamentalists" who criticized every proposal to mitigate the crisis because of moral hazard. "[O]ur critics didn't seem to have feasible plans of their own" (325).

Summary

We could have written a book about how to prevent financial crises, but we did not because financial crises are here to stay. Short-term debt backed by long-term debt is inherent in market economies. The form of the debt changes over time. Bills of exchange, private banknotes, demand deposits, money market funds, repo, asset-backed commercial paper, and other forms of short-term debt appear and disappear and new forms will appear again. These forms of debt are vulnerable to runs.

Why can't we see these new forms of short-term debt and act to prevent runs? The problem is that while financial crises happen repeatedly in market economies, they do not happen so often that we learn lessons from the experience. Expertise cannot be developed overnight.

We don't have a pithy one-sentence summary of the principles for fighting crises. But if we had to sum up the principles in one sentence, it would be this: Find the short-term debt and protect the banking system fast with whatever means are necessary.

Appendix A: Details of Table 8.1

Introductory Comments

The dating for the dates of the panic start (column 1), the date of suspension of convertibility (column 4), and the date of resumption of convertibility (column 7) are not as clear as the tables indicate. There are no clear-cut dates for these events. The literature usually defines the panic start date as the date of the first failure of a large bank that led to other related suspensions. Independent suspensions before this date were not considered part of the crises. With regard to the suspension and resumption dates, it is important to differentiate between the various forms of suspension of cash payment (in other words, convertibility) that took place in various crises. Wicker (2000) and Sprague (1910) highlight the difference between restricting payments in New York City and shipments to the interior. Restriction within New York City was always partial and took the form of "checks had to be certified through the CH" and/or advance notice of withdrawal for savings banks. The *Times* and the *Chronicle* often do not mention the exact form and extent of suspension. The resumption dates are also somewhat vague. In general, initial events are somewhat chaotic at the start of the panic. And resumption seems to happen quietly. There are no clearinghouse announcements of suspension or resumption of convertibility. Each date is discussed further below.

Details of Table 8.1

Please refer to table A.1, which corresponds to each cell in table 8.1. Each cell is discussed below.

TABLE A.1. Details for tables 8.1 and 8.2

Panic of	1 Panic start date	2 Date CH stopped publishing bank-specific information	3 Date of first CH loan certificates	4 Date of suspension of convertibility	5 First date at which currency premium was positive	6 Date at which currency premium was zero	7 Date of resumption of convertibility	8 Date of last CH loan certificate issue	9 Date that individual bank info resumed	10 Date of final cancellation of loan certificates
1873	A1	A2	A3	A4	A5	A6	A7	A8	A9	A10
1884	B1	B2	B3	B4	B5	B6	B7	B8	B9	B10
1890	C1	C2	C3	C4	C5	C6	C7	C8	C9	C10
1893	D1	D2	D3	D4	D5	D6	D7	D8	D9	D10
1907	E1	E2	E3	E4	E5	E6	E7	E8	E9	E10

PANIC OF 1873

A1. Although other companies failed before this date, subsequent runs began on other banks and brokerage houses in New York City and the interior only after Jay and Cooke and Company's failure. Wicker (2000, 20) agrees, saying that "but the shock that gained national attention was the failure of Jay Cooke and Co. on September 18th."

"The suspension [of stock brokers Kenyon, Cox and Company] was of far less general influence than that of Messrs. Jay Cooke and Co., which occurred on Thursday [September 18], which was followed by the failures of a number of smaller stock brokerage firms" (*Commercial and Financial Chronicle*, September 20, 1873, 382).

A2. The last individual and aggregate bank data were published for September 20. They were not published after that date (*New York Times Financial Affairs*, September 21, 1873; *Commercial and Financial Chronicle*, September 27 and October 4, 1873).

A3. The official announcement issued by the New York Clearing House Association on September 20 was printed in the *New York Times* and the *Chronicle* (*Commercial and Financial Chronicle*, September 27, 1873; *New York Times*, September 21, 1873). The 1907 *Annual Report* of the US comptroller of the currency gives the date as September 22, 1873 (66).

A4. The clearinghouse decided on September 22 that all checks from New York Clearing House Association member banks must be certified through the New York Clearing House. The clearinghouse announced on September 24 that all checks when certified by any bank should also be first stamped or written "Payable through the Clearing House" (*New York Times*, September 25, 1873; *New York Times Financial Affairs*, September 23, 1873).

The adoption of this resolution involved the partial suspension of cash payments by the banks. It did not signify that no money would be paid out to the depositors, but it placed the dwindling supply of currency more within the control of the New York Clearing House Committee. In fact, suspension too was limited to New York City, currency was paid to the interior as freely as before (see Wicker 2000, 21, 32; also see Sprague 1910, 54).

The equalization and pooling of reserves policy was also announced on September 20, 1873.

A5. Sprague 1910, 57.

A6. Sprague 1910, 57.

A7. On October 24, the New York Clearing House Association announced the end of the reserve pooling arrangement from November 1 onward. Certificates continued to be in use until natural retirement. It is not clear whether complete payment of cash also was implemented on that day (*Commercial and Financial Chronicle*, November 1, 1873, 589; *New York Times*, October 24, 1873).

Wicker also says that the resumption of cash payment was on November 1, but there was no mention of resumption of cash payment or certification of checks in the *Chronicle* or the *New York Times*.

A8. *Annual Report* of the US comptroller of the currency, 1907, 66.

A9. Only the total bank statement for November 15 and November 22 was published in the November 29 issue (*Commercial and Financial Chronicle*, November 29, 1873, 715).

Individual bank statements for the week of December 6 were issued again for the first time in the December 13 issue (*Commercial and Financial Chronicle*, December 13, 1873, 799).

A10. *Annual Report* of the US comptroller of the currency, 1907, 66.

PANIC OF 1884

B1. The Marine National Bank (a New York Clearing House Association member) and the Wall Street brokerage firm of Grant and Ward failed on Tuesday, March 6 (*Commercial and Financial Chronicle*, May 10, 1884, 563; "Wall Street Startled," *New York Times*, May 7, 1884, 1).

The $3 million fraud committed by the president of the Second National Bank (a New York Clearing House Association member) was made public on Wednesday, March 14, before the stock market opened (*Commercial and Financial Chronicle*, May 17, 1884, 589; "Two Millions Absorbed," *New York Times*, May 14, 1884, 1).

The closing of Metropolitan Bank (a New York Clearing House Association member) on Wednesday, March 14, was the "final shock" and the "immediate event which started the panic" (*Commercial and Financial Chronicle*, May 17, 1884, 582, 589; "On the Verge of a Panic," *New York Times*, May 14, 1884, 1).

B2. The detailed weekly bank statement for May 17 was published. While the Metropolitan and Second National banks were listed, the Marine bank was not shown (*Commercial and Financial Chronicle*, May 24, 1884, 617).

The detailed weekly bank statement for May 24 was not published. Instead, the May 17 statement was republished (*Commercial and Financial Chronicle*, May 31, 1884, 644).

B3. Authorized May 14 (Sprague 1910, 113, quoting the *Annual Report* of the comptroller of the currency, 1884, 33; *Commercial and Financial Chronicle*, May 17, 1884, 589; "On the Verge of a Panic," *New York Times*, May 14,

1884, 1). The 1907 *Annual Report* of the US comptroller of the currency gives the date as May 15 (66).

B4. "There was no suspension of gold and currency payments at any point" (Sprague 1910, 114, quoting the *Annual Report* of the comptroller of the currency, 1884, 33).

B5. *New York Times, New York Tribune,* and *Wall Street Journal.*

B6. Not applicable.

B7. Not applicable. See **B2.**

B8. *Annual Report* of the US comptroller of the currency, 1907, 66.

B9. The detailed weekly bank statement for May 31 was published. While Metropolitan National and Second National banks were listed, Marine National Bank was not shown (*Commercial and Financial Chronicle*, June 7, 1884, 670).

The *Chronicle* commented that resumption of the detailed weekly bank statement was "one fact which contributed to the restoration of confidence" (*Commercial and Financial Chronicle*, June 7, 1884, 668).

B10. *Annual Report* of the US comptroller of the currency, 1907, 66.

PANIC OF 1890

C1. After leaving the discount rate unchanged at its regular weekly meeting Thursday, November 6, the Bank of England unexpectedly raised the discount rate from 5 percent to 6 percent on Friday, November 7. This action was "unusual" and created a feeling of "uneasiness" (*Commercial and Financial Chronicle*, November 8, 1890, 624; "Financial Affairs," *New York Times*, November 8, 1890, 6).

On Monday, November 10, a false report circulated at the New York Stock Exchange that the Bank of England had raised the discount rate to 7 percent (*Commercial and Financial Chronicle*, November 15, 1890, 667).

C2. The detailed weekly bank statement for November 15 was published (*Commercial and Financial Chronicle*, November 22, 1890, 705). But the detailed weekly bank statement for November 22 was *not* published. Instead, the November 15 statement was republished (*Commercial and Financial Chronicle*, November 29, 1890, 741).

C3. Clearinghouse loan certificates were authorized on Tuesday, November 11 (Sprague 1910, 141– 42; *Commercial and Financial Chronicle*, November 15, 1890, 667; "Firms Fail, Banks Shaken," *New York Times*, November 12, 1890, 1). The 1907 *Annual Report* of the US comptroller of the currency gives November 12 as the first date of issuance (66).

C4. "The issue of loan certificates was not followed by the suspension of payments by the banks" (Sprague 1910, 145).

C5. Not applicable.

C6. Not applicable.

C7. Not applicable. See **C2**.

C8. *Annual Report* of the US comptroller of the currency, 1907, 66.

C9. The *Chronicle* noted that on March 7, the clearinghouse banks "resumed the publication of their detailed statement, which publication has been suspended since November 15" (*Commercial and Financial Chronicle*, March 14, 1891, 406).

C10. *Annual Report* of the US comptroller of the currency, 1907, 66.

PANIC OF 1893

D1. Sprague (1910, 418) refers to Sunday, June 4, as the "week when panic may be said fairly to have begun."

D2. The detailed weekly individual bank statements for June 10 were published (*Commercial and Financial Chronicle*, June 17, 1893, 999). But the detailed weekly individual bank statements for June 17 were *not* published. Instead, the June 10 statement was republished. The aggregate bank statement continued to be published (*Commercial and Financial Chronicle*, June 24, 1893, 1046, 1048; "Financial and Commercial," *New York Times*, June 18, 1893, 14).

D3. Loan certificates were authorized on Thursday, June 15 (Sprague 1910, 170, 409–10; *Commercial and Financial Chronicle*, June 17, 1893, 997; "Certificates to Be Issued," *New York Times*, June 16, 1893, 8). The 1907 *Annual Report* of the US comptroller of the currency gives the date of first issuance as June 21 (66).

"The NYCH on June 15 took the unusual step of authorizing CH certificates even though there was no banking disturbance in NYC" (Wicker 2000, 64).

D4. "On August 3, the New York banks severely restricted, though they did not completely halt, the shipment of currency" (Wicker 2000, 77).

The presidents of almost all New York savings banks met on July 28* and recommended that the bank trustees begin to enforce legal notice of withdrawals "when need of such action arises." This action was "unexpected and caused some uneasiness." While each bank would establish its own policy, a common rule was that withdrawals over $100 required 30 days' notice, while withdrawals over $300 required 60 days' notice ("Banks May Hold Deposits," *New York Times*, July 29, 1893, 1; and "Financial and Commercial," *New York Times*, July 30, 1893, 14).

Sprague (1910, 177–78, 181–82) indicates that a partial suspension of cash payments began with the New York banks on August 1 or 2, but that suspension was "at no time complete."

The *Chronicle* indicates that the New York savings banks began to enforce "legal notice for the withdrawal of deposits" during the week ended August 5 (*Commercial and Financial Chronicle*, August 5, 1893, 196).

*The date of decision was Friday, July 28. The date of enforcement ranges from August 1 to August 3.

D5. Sprague 1910, 187.

D6. Sprague 1910, 187.

D7. Sprague (1910, 189–90) indicated his certainty that the banks that regained the 25 percent reserve ratio by September 2 "then removed all restrictions upon payments."

The *Chronicle* states that the "30-day notices required by the savings banks of [New York] for the withdrawal of deposits expired in many cases on Thursday [August 31], and payment was made either with gold or checks payable through the Clearing House, as depositors chose" (*Commercial and Financial Chronicle*, September 2, 1893, 356).

The *Times* noted the August 31 expiration date and indicated that there was "no longer difficulty" in cashing checks under $5,000 (see "Financial and Commercial," *New York Times*, September 1, 1893, 6).

D8. *Annual Report* of the US comptroller of the currency, 1907, 66.

D9. The *Chronicle* noted in each issue that the detailed weekly bank statement would not be issued as long as any clearinghouse loan certificates remained outstanding.

The last certificate was canceled on November 1, and the detailed statement was again published for the following Saturday, November 4, in the November 11 issue. In the November 4 issue, the June 10 statement was published again (*Commercial and Financial Chronicle*, November 4 and November 11, 1893, 754 and 800; "Financial and Commercial," *New York Times*, November 5, 1893, 14).

Several earlier reports in the *Chronicle* also point to this date:

- "Boston . . . last certificates canceled today; while in NYC the amount is down to 2,785,000, and this will be extinguished in a few days" (*Commercial and Financial Chronicle*, October 21, 1893, 668).
- "[C]ancellation of CH certificates this week have been 1,255,000, reducing the amount outstanding to 1,525,000. The expectation now is that all the certificates will be retired October 31" (*Commercial and Financial Chronicle*, October 28, 1893, 701).

D10. *Annual Report* of the US comptroller of the currency, 1907, 66.

PANIC OF 1907

E1. This date is debatable. On October 16, 1907, rumors about treachery among United Copper Board of Directors became known, setting off speculations that these directors may be involved in bad business elsewhere, leading to a series of other temporary runs and failures, such as Mercantile National Bank. United Copper itself was not, however, a firm of prime importance and it could be argued that the crises actually began on October 22, when the prime trust company Knickerbocker Trust suspended, leading to a series of trust company suspensions. (See *New York Times*, October 17 and 23, 1907.) Wicker marks the start of the crisis with the failure of the Knickerbocker Trust on October 22. Earlier events were marked as "prepanic" since it only concerned the copper market related banks without general loss of confidence (see Wicker 2000, 9, 88).

E2. The last individual bank statements (for both member and nonmember banks) were published for October 26 in the *Chronicle*. On November 1, they were announced not to be published again for the following week, that is, November 2 in the *Times*. The aggregate statements continued to be published (*Commercial and Financial Chronicle*, November 2, 1907, 1124; *New York Times*, November 1, 1907).

E3. Clearinghouse certificates were authorized on October 26 (Sprague 1910, 271; *New York Times*, October 27, 1907).

E4. According to Sprague (1910, 260), cash payments were suspended together with the authorization of clearinghouse certificates, which is October 26. Saving banks began to enforce legal notice of withdrawals for 60 or 90 days (*New York Times*, October 26, 1907).

E5. Sprague 1910, 280–82.

E6. Sprague 1910, 280–82.

E7. "Cash payments were not completely resumed until the beginning of January. For exactly two months, money was regularly bought and sold at a premium in NYC" (Sprague 1910, 278). Wicker cites the date of resumption as January 1 (Wicker 2000, 9).

E8. *Annual Report* of the US comptroller of the currency, 1908, 65.

E9. Individual bank statements (for both member and nonmember banks) were published for February 8 onward in the February 15 *Chronicle* issue. As a new measure, nonmember state and national banks' aggregate statement was published in addition to the aggregates of member banks (*Commercial and Financial Chronicle*, February 15, 1908, 403; *New York Times*, February 9, 1908, 13).

E10. *Annual Report* of the US comptroller of the currency, 1908, 65.

Details of Table 8.2

Please refer to table A.1, which corresponds to each cell in table 8.2. Each cell is discussed below.

PANIC OF 1873

A1. The failure of Jay Cooke and Company: *Philadelphia Bulletin*, September 18, 1873; *Philadelphia Inquirer*, September 19, 1873, 1; and *Philadelphia Record*, September 19, 1873.

A2. *Philadelphia Record*, September 30, 1873; *Philadelphia Bulletin*, September 29, 1873. The *Philadelphia Inquirer* published bank-specific information on page 6 of its September 30, 1873, issue, however, and started withholding such information the following issue, on October 7, 1873. In the September 30, 1873, issue, the *Philadelphia Record* reported that "The clearing house made no statement of the condition of the banks yesterday. We think this policy is a mistake."

A3. *Philadelphia Inquirer*, September 24, 1873, 1, reported that "The clearances of the Gold Exchange Bank are completed, and balances will be paid as usual. $1,500,000 of loan certificates have been issued by the clearing house today. It is probable that the whole ten millions of loan certificates will be taken up, and the clearing house association will increase the amount." *Philadelphia Record*, September 26, 1873, reported that "The Loan Committee of the Clearing House Association decided to issue an additional $10,000,000 of loan certificates. These are available for the immediate use of the banks connected with the association. The clearing house committee issued $2,500,000 in loan certificates yesterday, making a total thus far of $12,500,000. The banks have also agreed to buy up $10,000,000 of government bonds of individual holders, at the value say of 3 or 1 per cent above the government price, and, turning them in to the treasury at their own cost, to draw out the green backs for the public uses." *Philadelphia Record*, September 27, 1873, reported that "The clearing house commenced the issue of loan certificates yesterday, the amounts of which were in sums of 5 thousand and 20 thousand and are to be used only in the settlements between the banks."

Cannon (1910a, 86–88) quotes as follows:

> In like manner the Philadelphia association now, for the first time, entered upon the plan so successfully followed in New York since 1860, by appointing a loan committee, with authority to issue clearing-house loan certificates. Such certificates were authorized by resolution adopted September 24, 1873, and amended October 18, 1873, to read as follows:

For the purpose of enabling the banks, members of the Philadelphia Clearing House Association, to afford proper assistance to the mercantile and manufacturing community, and also to facilitate the inter-bank settlements resulting from their daily exchanges, we, the undersigned, do bind ourselves by the following agreement on the part of our respective banks, namely:

First. That the clearing-house committee be, and that they are hereby, authorized to issue to any bank, member of the association, loan certificates bearing 6 per cent interest on the deposits of bills receivable and other securities to such an amount and to such percentage thereof as may in their judgment be advisable. These certificates may be used in settlement of balances at the clearing house, and they shall be received by creditor banks in the same proportion as they bear to the aggregate amount of the debtor balances paid at the clearing house. The interest that may accrue upon these certificates shall be apportioned monthly among the banks which shall have held them during that time.

Second. The securities deposited with the said committee shall be held by them in trust as a special deposit, pledged for the redemption of the certificates issued thereupon, the same being accepted by the committee as collateral security, with the express condition that neither the clearing-house association, the clearing-house committee, nor an member thereof shall be responsible for any loss on said collaterals from failure to make demand and protest, or from any other neglect or omission other than the refusal to take some reasonable step which it said depositing bank may have previously required in writing.

Third. On the surrender of such certificates, or any of them, by the depositing bank, the committee will indorse the amount as a payment on the obligation of said bank held by them, and will surrender appropriate amount of securities, except in cases of default of the bar in any of its transactions through the clearing house, in which case the securities will be applied by the committee, first to the payment of outstanding certificates with interest; next to the liquidation of any indebtedness of such bank to the other banks, members of the clearing house association.

Fourth. The committee shall be authorized to exchange any portion of said securities for others, to be approved by them, and shall have power to demand additional securities at their own discretion.

Fifth. That the clearing-house committee be authorized to carry in full effect this agreement, with power to establish such rules and regulations for the practical working thereof as they may deem necessary and any loss caused by the nonpayment of loan certificates shall be assessed by the committee upon all the banks in the ratio of capital.

Sixth. The expenses incurred in carrying out this agreement shall be assessed upon the banks in equal proportion to their respective capitals.

Seventh. That the clearing-house committee be and they are hereby authorized to terminate this agreement upon giving thirty days' note thereof at any stated meeting of the clearing-house association.

The issue of certificates made in conformity with the foregoing resolution reached the maximum amount outstanding at one time, namely, $6,285,000, on December 1, 1873.

A4. *Philadelphia Record,* September 22, 1873; the Union Banking Company and E W Clark and Company closed doors.

A5. *Philadelphia Inquirer,* September 26, 1873, 1; *Philadelphia Record,* September 26, 1873, 4. According to the *Inquirer:* "The banks in the Clearing House Association are pooling their greenbacks, as agreed yesterday. One or two, which stood exceptionally strong, refused at first to put their legal tenders in, but finally concluded to do so rather than be expelled from the association. Money is still unquotable; greenbacks have been exchanged today for certified checks all the way from 1 to 3.5% premium. The loan committee of the clearing house issued up to this evening $17,000,000 of certificates."

A6. The *Philadelphia Record* on October 25, 1873, indicated that currency was on par with certified checks first on October 24, 1873. According to the *Philadelphia Inquirer,* however, there was likely a positive currency premium by at least as late as October 27, 1873. "How the payment of currency in Philadelphia, when it is at a premium in NY, would cause money to flow from us until our banks were drained of their cash resources, and the disastrous results of such a policy, may be readily imagined by a tyro in financial matters" (6).

A7. *Philadelphia Inquirer,* November 18, 1873, 6, stated that "Money was quite as abundant and easy at the resumption of business yesterday as at the close of last week."

A9. *Philadelphia Inquirer,* December 2, 1873, 6; *Philadelphia Record,* December 2, 1873; *Philadelphia Bulletin,* December 1, 1873.

PANIC OF 1890

C1. Cannon (1910a), 91; *Philadelphia Inquirer,* November 12, 1890, 1–2; *Philadelphia Record,* November 12, 1890, 1 and 8; *Press,* November 12, 1890, 1.

C2. *Philadelphia Inquirer,* November 18, 1890, 7; *Philadelphia Record,* November 18, 1890.

C3. Cannon (1910a), 94. *Philadelphia Inquirer,* November 19, 1890, 7, wrote, "The Philadelphia Clearing House Association yesterday took such action in regard to the money market as the condition of the case seemed to warrant. It was decided to issue to the banks making appellation therefor certificates to be used in settling balances between themselves. This is precisely the action that has been taken by the Clearing House Association of NY and Boston and binds the Clearing House banks closely together. The credit of one is now the credit of all. Any bank having in its vaults good collateral or acceptable mercantile paper can obtain credit with all the other banks. That is a bank upon which a check is drawn need not pay the collecting bank in cash, but may pay in a due bill secured by ample credit. In this way the resources of all the banks in the Clearing House Association are practically at the command of each bank."

C4. Barker Brothers and Company suspended on November 20, 1890, but no widespread suspension ensued in the city. (See *Philadelphia Inquirer*, November 21, 1890, 7.)

C5. Does not apply.

C6. Does not apply.

C7. Does not apply.

C8. Does not apply.

C9. *Philadelphia Inquirer*, February 17, 1891, 10; *Philadelphia Record*, February 17, 1891, 8.

C10. See **C3**.

PANIC OF 1893

D1. *Philadelphia Inquirer* report on June 16, 1893, 5.

D2. *Philadelphia Inquirer*, June 20, 1893, 5; *Philadelphia Record*, June 20, 1893.

D3. *Philadelphia Inquirer*, June 16, 1893, 5.

D4. *Philadelphia Inquirer* on August 8, 1893, 6, wrote, "There is very general complaint among the banks in the interior of the State over the unsatisfactory course pursued by the banks of this city. The banks here not only refuse to send currency into the interior, but the officials decline to commit themselves as to their policy in case difficulties arise. In other words, the country banks can neither get their cash nor any assurance that money will be sent in case of a run. Such a course as this is not at all likely to disarm apprehensions as to the future. Another matter that has caused general and unfavorable comment is the refusal of the Clearing House to make known the amount of certificates issued. In all other cities the information is cheerfully published, but in Philadelphia the secret is regarded as too awful to be published and is disclosed only to the elect. The only clue as to the amount outstanding is conveyed in the reports to the Comptroller of the Currency under date of July 12, where an item 'other liabilities' is given as $5,870,000, whereas the same item on May 4 was $510,000. In times like the present secrecy only arouses suspicion, while a plain statement alone will dissipate distrust. The banks have asked much from their depositors, and all they have asked has been cheerfully granted, but surely the banks owe something to the public. No harm has resulted from the publication of the issue of certificates in other cities, and it would puzzle the depositories of the awful secret in Philadelphia finance to tell what harm would result from giving out the information here. The time has come when this matter ought to be made known; further secrecy can only lead to the conclusion that the amount is so large the Clearing House officials do not want it to become known."

D5. *Philadelphia Inquirer*, August 10, 1893, 5; *Philadelphia Bulletin* on August 9, 1893, 1, wrote, "A Third Street banking house displays the sign 'United States gold and currency purchased at a premium.' The firm offers 1 1/2 per cent. premium for gold and currency. It has several large orders for funds which it is undertaking to fill in this way, and it is expected that the premium of $15 per thousand will bring cash out of tin boxes where it has been secluded. The person who thus sells his money is paid by a check upon a bank, and upon presentation of the check at the bank he will receive a Clearing House due bill, which he may deposit in his own bank, where it will be credited as cash."

D6. See **D7.**

D7. *Philadelphia Inquirer*, September 6, 1893, 5.

D8. *Philadelphia Inquirer* on November 21, 1893, wrote, "The Clearing House authorities have restored the publication of the detailed bank statement, which was suspended after June 12. At last reports all but a few of the Clearing House certificates had been canceled, and these maybe retired anyday."

D9. *Philadelphia Inquirer*, November 21, 1893, 5; *Philadelphia Record*, November 21, 1893.

D10. *Congressional Record*, 53rd Congress, 2nd Session, vol. 26 (Washington, DC: Government Printing Office), June 2, 1894, 5675.

PANIC OF 1907

E1. The 1907 crisis spread from New York City, as reflected in the *Philadelphia Inquirer* report on October 22, 1907, 1, and the *Philadelphia Bulletin* report on October 22, 1908, 1.

E2. *Philadelphia Inquirer*, November 5, 1907, 15; *Philadelphia Record*, November 5, 1907, 14.

E3. No direct news or announcement. On November 4, 1907, the *Philadelphia Inquirer* mentioned the "Clearing House's plan of issuing loan certificates," and on November 5, 1907, there is the announcement that "[d]uring the time that Clearing House certificates are outstanding, the Philadelphia National banks following the New York precedent, will issue only a summarized statement." However, there was mention of "The situation in financial circles was helped by the action of the banks in issuing Clearing House certificates and the test companies in paying depositors with checks upon their banks payable through the Clearing House only" on October 29, but it is not clear whether this news pertains to situations in New York or in Philadelphia.

E4. See **E3.**

E5. *Philadelphia Inquirer*, November 5, 1907, 15: "Pending the arrival of gold imports, money is exceedingly scarce. Indeed, actual currency is very difficult to secure in large amounts in this city. Already it is bringing a premium of from 2 to 4%, and brokers are gathering it up to sell to concerns and manufacturers who have large pay rolls which must be met with cash. If relief does not come before the week is over it is likely that cashier's checks for $5, $10 and $20 will be in circulation. The local bank statement accounts for the scarcity of funds here, showing large decreases in deposits and reserves."

E6. *Philadelphia Inquirer*, December 11, 1907, 11, indicated there was a zero currency premium on the street on December 10, 1907. But on January 7, 1908, the news reads, "There seemed to be an accumulation of buying orders in the stock market at the opening yesterday, which was due largely to the better bank statement published Saturday, and the promise of further ease in the monetary situation, as shown by the elimination of the premium on currency and the prospects of passing away of the Clearing House certificates." This indicates there might have been currency premium by as late as January 6, 1908. In addition, the *Philadelphia Record* of December 28–30, mentioned a decline in currency premium. On December 30, an article read, "The source of anxiety was clearly indicated by the brisk rebound in stocks at the end of the week, induced by the decisive decline in the premium on currency."

E7. *Philadelphia Inquirer*, January 8, 1908, 11.

E8. *Philadelphia Inquirer*, February 11, 1908, 11, read, "For the first time since Oct 29th the Philadelphia Clearing House Association yesterday issued a detailed statement of the figures of the associated banks, as on Saturday the last of the clearing house certificates were retired."

E9. See **E8.**

E10. *Philadelphia Inquirer*, February 11, 1908, 11; *Philadelphia Record*, February 11, 1908, 12.

Appendix B: The Check Collection Process at Clearinghouses

The clearing of checks at the clearinghouse (from Squire 1888, 8–9):

Each bank member of the association sends daily to the Clearing House two clerks, one designated as delivery clerk, the other as settling clerk, the delivery clerk to distribute the exchanges, the settling clerk to receive the exchanges from the delivery clerks. They assemble a little before ten o'clock, at which hour (promptly) the operation of clearing begins.

Upon entry of the settling clerk, he furnishes the Manager with a credit ticket, showing the amount of exchanges brought by his bank. At ten o'clock the manager takes his position on the platform with his Assistant Manager and staff, one of whom is a Proof Clerk, who has a Proof Sheet, upon which he enters the Credit Tickets. After the exchanges are made, each Settling Clerk sends the result of the exchanges of his bank on tickets called Debit Tickets, to the Proof Clerk, who enters them on his sheet. After footing the total of the Proof Sheet the amount brought (Credit Tickets), and the amount received (Debit Tickets), should be the same and the resulting balances should also prove. . . .

At the tap of a gong, the Settling Clerks occupy their respective desks, with their settling sheets before them, upon which, opposite the names of the various banks of the association, is entered the amounts brought in exchanges against each bank. The Delivery Clerks with the exchanges in boxes arranged in consecutive order for delivery, in front of their desks, have a receipt list (or as it is termed, Delivery Clerk's Statement), with the amount of exchanges opposite the name of each bank set down in delivery order.

The manager upon the first stroke of the gong, surveys the assembled clerks to see that all are present. The second stroke is a signal for the clearings to begin.

Each Delivery Clerk advances to the next desk at which he delivers the exchanges and receipt list; each Settling Clerk upon receipt of the exchange, receipts for it, and enters it on his settling sheet opposite the name of the bank from which he received it; thus the exchanging continues until every bank has been visited, and the Delivery Clerk has returned to the desk occupied by his bank. . . . In about ten minutes the exchanges have been made, and the Settling Clerk has entered on his settling sheet, opposite the name of the banks, the various exchanges he has received, thus having a record on his sheet, of the amount brought, and the amount received from each bank. . . . [H]e foots up the aggregate he has received from various banks, and then makes a ticket called Debit Ticket, which is sent to the Proof Clerk on the platform. . . . The differences are generally announced in about half an hour. . . . By three o'clock the settlements of the transactions are completed.

Appendix C: The Effect of a Currency Premium on Gold Points and Gold Imports

The analysis of gold export and gold import points describes "average" circumstances. The points are a function of the relevant interest rate, the costs of shipping, the cost of insuring the cargo (gold), and so on.

The fluctuations of such costs during brief time intervals were minimal in contrast to the effect of a currency premium on the profitability of gold imports into the United States. The panic periods were of short duration and the currency premium varied over time. For clarity, we illustrate the effect on gold import points of a 1 percent currency premium and a 4 percent currency premium.

EXAMPLE: The US Dollar–UK Pound Exchange Rate[1]
Mint parity value for the US dollar per UK pound exchange rate: $4.86656
Gold import point (below this value, it was profitable to import gold into
United States): $4.835
Gold export point (exchange rates above this value, profitable to export
gold): $4.899

Suppose the market exchange rate is $4.82 (per pound), which is below the gold import point. Then, the gold importer would pay $4.82 in dollars for a British pound, take it to the Chancellor of the Exchequer for $4.86656 worth of gold, and ship that gold to the United States, making a profit of $4.86656 − $4.82 = $0.04656, or less than 5 cents, which is a 0.966 percent return on the $4.82 investment.

Currency premium of 4 percent:
Mint parity:	$4.86656*(1 + 0.04) = $5.061
Gold import point:	$4.835*(1 + 0.04) = **$5.028**
Gold export point:	$4.899*(1.04) = $5.095

How does this affect the gold import and export points? The purchase of gold at any value below the adjusted gold import point (adjusted for the value of the gold in terms of US dollars in the New York City money market) will provide a profit opportunity to the gold importer. Notice that the adjusted gold import point of $5.028 is above the normal gold export point ($4.899).

Currency premium of 1 percent:
Mint parity: $4.86656*(1 + 0.01) = $4.915
Gold import point: $4.835*(1 + 0.01) = **$4.883**
Gold export point: $4.899*(1.01) = $4.948

Any market exchange rate below the effective gold import point (the line with diamond markings in figure C.1) would make gold imports into the United States profitable during the crisis period. The most notable aspect of this mechanism is that during a crisis that involves a currency premium, market exchange rates that would normally trigger gold exports were instead consistent with gold imports. At a 4 percent currency premium, any exchange rate below $5.028 offers a profit opportunity for the import of gold.

In the adjusted gold point example, the gold importer pays, say, $4.86656 for a UK pound—the mint parity value—exchanges that pound for gold, ships the gold to the United States, exchanges the gold for $4.86656 in dollars and then sells the dollars for $4.86656*(1 + currency premium). The profit

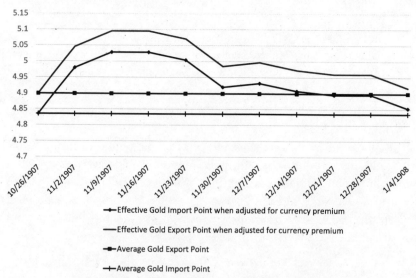

FIGURE C.1. Chart for "effective" gold import and export points during Panic of 1907
Source: Data from Officer (2008); currency premium data from *New York Times* and *New York Tribune* (various issues).

in the two currency premium cases comes from the ability to sell a dollar of gold for a percentage premium.

$$\$4.86656^*(1 + 0.04) - \$4.86656 = \$5.061 - \$4.86656 = \$0.1944$$
$$\text{or nearly 20 cents (a 4\% return)}$$

The returns are not annual percentage rates but returns that accrue over a span of a few weeks for the transactions to take place and for the gold to get shipped overseas.

Note that the profits from these transactions would clearly be altered by the level of the market interest rates. But the example and the chart using 1907 data demonstrates that the mechanism generates substantial profit opportunities from gold importation.

Appendix D: Currency Composition in the United States, 1860–1914

The currency supply of the United States from 1860 to 1914 was composed of various forms of payment media. In normal periods, all forms of coinage and currency traded at par during day-to-day exchanges. The variegated currency supply in the United States is important because the New York Clearing House Association held rigid standards for what it would consider as final payment media. This is only an outline of the acceptable media and not a rigorous analysis of the reasons for their choices.

During the Panic of 1873, the New York Clearing House considered only legal tender ("greenbacks") acceptable as a final payment medium. After 1879 and the return to the gold standard, gold coin (specie) and legal tender could be used for final payment at the New York Clearing House. During the gold standard era, greenbacks were redeemed for gold by the US Treasury, despite the fact that the Treasury had the option to redeem US notes with gold or silver. The Gold Standard Act of 1900 made the redemption in gold mandatory.

It is notable that national banknotes were never accepted for final payment at the New York Clearing House. Neither were silver certificates, which became a sizable component of the hand-to-hand money supply in the 1880s and 1890s.

In figure D.1, the first four components of the currency supply—gold coin, gold certificates, US notes, and other US currency—constituted the supply of currency for what the New York Clearing House would consider final payment.

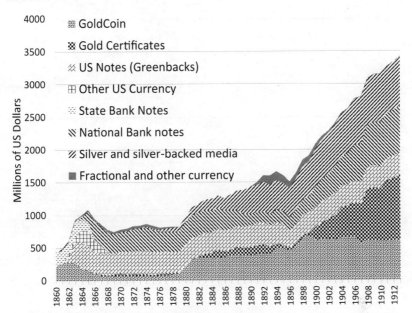

FIGURE D.1. Composition of the currency supply, 1860–1914

Source: Data from Banking and Monetary Statistics, 1914–41, 408, table 109, "Currency in Circulation—by Kind," 1860–1913.

Notes

Chapter 1

1. See Bernanke (2009a) for more specific information about the lending programs. On "stigma" during the financial crisis see Armantier, Ghysels, Sarkar, and Shrader (2015). Also see Anbil (2017).

2. See SEC Release 34-58592, http://www.sec.gov/rules/other/2008/34-58592.pdf: "Emergency order pursuant to section 12(k)(2) of the Securities Exchange Act of 1934 taking temporary action to respond to market developments," September 18, 2008. Similar bans were put in place in England and in many European and other developed market regulators temporarily banned the short selling of the stock of financial firms after September 2008. Also, on May 19, 2010, the German Federal Financial Supervisory Authority (BaFin) prohibited naked short sales of euro-denominated government bonds, naked CDSs based on those bonds, and also naked short sales of the stock of Germany's ten largest financial institutions. "Naked" short selling means selling a security when the seller has not borrowed the security. Such a ban prevents short selling in excess of the existing supply of securities available to borrow and can be viewed as a method to restrain "excessive" short sales. See Gruenewald, Wagner, and Weber (2010) for a list of worldwide short-sale bans that were instituted during the financial crisis. Appel and Fohlin (2010) argue that the short-sale prohibition created liquidity. But Beber and Pagano (2013) find the opposite result. In Europe naked CDS on sovereign debt also was banned (EU Short Selling Regulation 236/2012).

3. See http://www.federalreserve.gov/bankinforeg/stress-tests-capital-planning.htm. On the information effects of the stress tests see Peristian, Morgan, and Savino (2014) and Bayazitova and Shivdasani (2012).

4. The currency premium during these nineteenth-century panics also has a counterpart in modern financial crises. The currency premium arises because cash and certified checks are not perfect substitutes. People prefer cash. Cash has a higher "convenience" yield. The counterpart in the modern area is also any measure of the convenience yield on US Treasuries. For example, the spread between the interest rate paid on general collateral repo, repo backed by a US Treasury bond as collateral, and the yield on the same Treasury bond. See, e.g., Xie (2012). Such measures spiked during the Panic of 2007–8 because US Treasuries were preferred over privately produced assets. This is the flight to quality.

Chapter 2

1. On US clearinghouses generally, see Gibbons (1859), Squire (1888), Curtis (1898), Bolles (1903), Cannon (1910a), Gorton (1984), Timberlake (1984), Gorton (1985), Gorton and Mullineaux (1987), and Gorton and Huang (2006) for theory.

2. Article VI, Section 5, New York Clearing House Constitution, 1908—the same point is highlighted below as an amendment accepted in 1884.

3. For an extensive examination of the New York City banks as the "clearinghouse" of the United States, see James and Weiman (2010).

4. Bank stocks did change owners and stock prices and transactions are listed in newspapers. But transactions are fairly sparse and the prices are often described as from the last transaction, which may have been sometime considerably earlier.

5. The one and only "bank" stock that appears in 1883 and 1884 in Goetzmann et al. (2001) is the Manhattan (s216) in the underlying data, which turns out to be the Manhattan Elevated based on our other sources, more of a transportation company. The *New York Times* calls it "Manhattan," while the *Chronicle* uses "Manhattan Elevated." The Manhattan price in the Goetzmann et al. (2001) data is ~50 for 1883–84, which matches the Manhattan Elevated price in the *Chronicle*, while the Manhattan bank quotes were ~150.

6. Results are similar for the panics of 1873 and 1907.

7. Also, the National Bank Act in 1864 established double liability for bank stock. State-chartered banks faced double liability in some states. See Marquis and Smith (1937) and Macey and Miller (1992). This may have made stocks less liquid; there have been no studies of this in the United States. Acheson, Hickson, and Turner (2010) studied nineteenth-century British banking and found that liability rules appeared not to affect stock liquidity.

8. This is also true today. The results of bank examinations in the United States are kept confidential.

9. Throughout, references to *Minutes* refer to the Clearing House *Minutes* in the New York Clearing House Association Archives.

10. Other examples include April 6, 1872, examination of the Tenth National Bank; April 26, 1873, investigation of the Gallatin National Bank; April 29, 1873, examination of the Continental National Bank; May 1, 1873, examination of the Manufacturers' and Merchants' Bank; December 10, 1877, examination of the Ninth National Bank; January 30, 1888, examination of the Grocers' Bank; January 28, 1880, examination of the German American Bank.

11. Printed verbatim in the article, "Weekly City Bank Statements," *New York Daily Times*, April 18, 1853, 8.

Chapter 3

1. See Gorton, Metrick, and Xie (2015a) who econometrically date the start of the Panic of 2007–8.

2. See Calomiris and Gorton (1991). And, in the modern era of active central banks, a financial crisis is an event in which there is large-scale intervention by the central bank or government.

3. The US Treasury became more active in each panic. In 1873, it played a part and was crucial in keeping 1890 from becoming a worse disruption. We know that the balance was limited in 1907, but the deposit of $35 million in NYC banks was still important.

4. The other panics of the National Banking Era also had large failures that were pointed to as particularly important: Jay Cooke and Company 1873; Decker, Howell and Co. 1890; The National Cordage Co. 1893; The Knickerbocker Trust 1907.

5. Alexander D. Noyes would later become the *New York Times* financial editor and probably the most respected financial journalist of the era.

Chapter 4

1. Alternative strategies to identify panics, as in Jalil (2015), arrive at similar conclusions.

2. In those instances, the currency premium on certified checks (discussed in chapter 7) appeared when extensive cash withdrawals (widespread liquidity drains) spurred a general suspension of convertibility of deposits into currency.

3. A predetermined agreement described how losses on unpaid clearinghouse loan certificates would be shared by the membership—in essence, the payment of clearinghouse loan certificates was guaranteed by mutual assurance.

4. See Timberlake (1993, 199–200) and Redlich (1951, 158–59). See also Swanson (1908a, 1908b).

5. See, e.g., Sprague (1910), Laughlin (1912), and Kemmerer (1910). See also Muhleman (1908) and Conant (1909).

6. Goodhart (1969) emphasizes the balance of trade between New York City and the interior of the country, arguing that Sprague (1910), Kemmerer (1910), and Laughlin (1912) concentrate entirely on the capital flows.

7. Muhleman (1908) and Sprague (1910) emphasize similar points about the source of the cash drain. Hagen (1932) also highlights the cash drain from banks by its trust company depositors during the 1907 panic.

8. The description of a panic has similarities to those of Wicker (2000) and Kindleberger (2005), and also fits with the general framework of asymmetric information as described by Calomiris and Gorton (1991).

9. See Wicker (2000, 32–33). He notes that the New York Clearing House was comfortable going so low in aggregate reserves in 1873 because they also engaged in reserve pooling in their efforts to combat that panic. Used in 1860 and 1861 panics, the New York Clearing House was unable to forge a willingness to implement that technique in later crises.

10. For some transactions, legal constraints required a specific form of payment (gold for international transactions, legal tender for payments, etc.) or prohibited other forms of payment (e.g., silver certificates). Still, the par for various forms of currency and deposit values held for many transactions.

11. Clearinghouse loan certificates in the form we discuss were first issued in 1860—see Swanson (1908a, 1908b). Redlich (1947) discusses the issuance of "metropolitan certificates" in 1857 as a comparable liquidity vehicle, but the nature of the liability is sufficiently different to warrant a separate denotation. After the initial issuance in 1860, clearinghouse loan certificates were again issued in 1861, 1863, and 1864—1863 and 1864 are apparently not considered important—see Sprague (1910, 46, note b). They were not issued again until the Panic of 1873. Cannon (1910a) provides more detail on loan certificates. Moen and Tallman (2015) present the distribution of clearinghouse loan certificates among several borrowing banks in New York City for each of the panics from 1873 to 1907.

12. Losses on clearinghouse loan certificates would be paid through assessments on all surviving clearinghouse member banks in proportion to their capital and surplus relative to the total capital and surplus of the membership.

13. This is discussed by Timberlake (1984), Gorton (1985), Gorton and Mullineaux (1987). Gorton and Huang (2006) provide a theoretical explanation of the incentive compatibility of this transformation.

14. Cannon (1910a, 83) writes that while weak banks may need clearinghouse loan certificates and strong banks may not, still, the strong banks also take them out. Moen and Tallman (2015), however, could not verify the accuracy of those statements mainly because data are insufficient to indicate the liquidity requirements of the borrowing banks. Cannon's intimation could be correct, but Moen and Tallman found Cannon's argument about universal borrowing by clearinghouse member banks during panics to be incorrect.

15. Friday, May 16, 1884. A report circulated that the Clearinghouse Loan Committee decided to lend money against government bonds at par, instead of applying the customary 25 percent haircut ("The Ebb of the Panic," New York Times, May 17, 1884, 1).

16. See Wicker (2000, 42) and Sprague (1910, 139). Wicker (2000, 44) describes how the US Treasury injected funds in August 1890 by offering to redeem bonds with full interest through August 31, 1891. The actions, however, did not reduce the stringency in New York City because the offer to buy $15 million resulted in purchases of $9 million in bonds from all over the country (see Sprague 1910, 137). In contrast, the September 17, 1890, US Treasury action to buy bonds added about $21 million in cash—that action bought bonds that were held by a syndicate of New York institutions, so that the proceeds went directly into New York City banks (see Sprague 1910, 139).

17. Suspension was announced in New York City in the Panic of 1857, but that was a suspension of bank currency redemption for specie (gold).

Chapter 5

1. The Heinze-Morse-Thomas group of banks was associated with the failed corner of a copper stock, which was considered the proximate trigger for the panic by contemporaries like Sprague (1910), as well as by more recent treatments as in Tallman and Moen 1990 and Bruner and Carr 2007. See the former for further discussion of those events.

2. New York Clearing House Minutes, May 14, 1884.

3. Marine National Bank was closed and, after an examination indicated malfeasance and insufficient assets of quality, the New York Clearing House made clear it had no intention of aiding that bank.

4. From Tallman (2013, 51): "Trusts competed effectively for retail deposits with national banks in New York City. Yet trusts were not considered part of the high-volume check-clearing part of the payments system, because deposits at trust companies did not turn over at rates similar to national banks. As a result, trust companies did not seek membership in the New York Clearing House when membership was offered in 1903."

5. Charles W. Morse was described by Sprague (1910, 258) as someone "whose activities in the industrial and banking world had been of an extreme character, even when judged by American speculative standards."

6. Also recall that North River Bank was closed by the New York superintendent of banks on November 12, 1890.

Chapter 6

1. See the 1984 congressional hearing "Inquiry into Continental Illinois Corp. and Continental Illinois National Bank," Regulation and Insurance of the Committee on Banking, Finance and Urban Affairs, House of Representatives, 98th Cong., 2nd Sess. (September 18, 19, and October 4, 1984), 300.

2. On the emergency liquidity facilities of clearinghouses during crises, see, e.g., Moen and Tallman (2000, 2015).

3. We identified New York Clearing House member banks from the *Bankers' Magazine*, *Commercial and Financial Chronicle*, and Bailey (1890).

4. The Atlantic Bank was expelled from the New York Clearing House Association on April 28, 1873, and subsequently failed on September 22, 1873, in the midst of the Panic of 1873. See Clearing House Committee *Minutes*, October 1, 1873, and *New York Times*, April 28, 1873, 5.

5. The Metropolitan received clearinghouse loan certificates of around $3 million; see Wicker (2000, 37).

6. *Annual Report* of the comptroller of the currency, 1883.

7. The loss to Columbia Bank was $90,000, which was about one quarter of the capital and surplus at National Bank of Deposit. See *New York World*, May 23, 1893. According to the 1893 *Annual Report* of the comptroller of the currency: Capital of $300K, currency outstanding of $45K; dividends issued August 4, 1893, $204K; October 24, $199.8K (notice that both payments took place after the failure).

8. *New York Evening World*, May 23, 1893, 3.

9. The loans were actually clearinghouse loans, which were like emergency loans from the New York Clearing House (as opposed to clearinghouse loan certificates). The loans were nontransferable but were changed to clearinghouse loan certificates after the crisis took hold.

Chapter 7

1. Reported by Andrew (1908b, 299).

2. It also reflects a risk premium, but this is ignored in our calculation for simplicity.

Chapter 8

1. Officer (1986) and Silber (2008, 28–32 and 43–47) describe the mechanisms in more detail and with further context. See also Officer (2008). The shipping costs were notably higher over the period 1891–1900 than the period 1901–10.

2. This rough forecast turned out to be a relatively precise estimate of the gold inflows that accumulated through the New York City arrivals. They are generally in line with official measures available (on monthly frequency) that total approximately $40.6 million during the month of August 1893 for the entire United States.

3. Rodgers and Payne (2014) argue that early (and unusual) specie payment by the Banque de France to the United States in November 1907 was the catalyst for a recovery from the Panic of 1907.

4. Sprague (1910, 59–60) says that the gold movements had nothing to do with the currency premium, arguing that "exchange rates and the gold premium moved up and down with changes in the currency premium, since they were both expressed in terms of depreciated certi-

fied checks." Inflows of gold did not affect the currency premium because of the nonmonetary role of gold in a fiat money standard. We cannot rule out that the currency premium (and related gold premium on certified checks) affected the inflow of gold. It is still important as measured capital inflow.

5. The currency premium data are the averages of daily figures calculated from newspaper reports and remain preliminary as we look to fill in missing observations. At present, missing observations are skipped rather than assumed to be zero.

Chapter 9

1. It is reasonable to conclude, however, that the demise of Metropolitan National Bank in 1884, though officially categorized as "voluntarily liquidated," is essentially a bank closed by extended depositor runs. What we find notable is that the bank—having deposits contract from $7.4 million (May 17) to $1.2 million (June 21) in just over a month—was able to continue its operations until mid-November. The key point is that the closure did not occur in the midst of the panic. The delay of that outcome was essential to the strategy of the New York Clearing House.

2. Metropolitan National Bank requested a reduction in the interest rate on their outstanding clearinghouse loan certificates in early 1886, a request that was granted by the New York Clearing House.

Chapter 10

1. Bagehot did not mention secrecy because "a key feature of the British system, its in-built protective device for anonymity was overlooked [by Bagehot]" (Capie 2007, 313). In England, geographically between the country banks and the Bank of England was a ring of discount houses. See Capie (2002, 2007). If a country bank needed money, it could borrow from its discount house, which in turn might borrow from the Bank of England. As a result, it was not known where the money from the Bank of England was going. King (1936) provides more discussion on the industrial organization of British banking in the nineteenth century. Also see Pressnell (1956). The Bank of England did not always get along with the discount houses, and there is a complicated history to their interaction. See, e.g., Flandreau and Ugolini (2011).

Chapter 11

1. For example, in the *Financial Times* on September 18, 2008, in an op-ed piece discussing the run on Northern Rock in the United Kingdom, Charles Goodhart noted, "Now is not the time to agonise over moral hazard."

2. Laeven and Valencia (2012, 4) wrote, "We consider policy interventions in the banking sector to be significant if at least three out of the following six measures have been used: (1) extensive liquidity support (5 percent of deposits and liabilities to nonresidents), (2) bank restructuring gross costs (at least 3 percent of GDP), (3) significant bank nationalizations, (4) significant guarantees put in place, (5) significant asset purchases (at least 5 percent of GDP), (6) deposit freezes and/or bank holidays."

3. In the Mexican tequila crisis of 1994–95, investors did not want to roll over the dollar-denominated Mexican government debt (called "tesobonos"). This was also true in the Russian

crisis of 1998 in which the government was unable to roll over short-term zero-coupon government debt called GKOs (Gosudarstvennoye Kratkosrochnoye Obyasatyelstov).

4. There is a large literature on the Asian crisis (see the references in Grenville 2004, for example).

5. See http://www.imf.org/external/np/loi/103197.htm.

6. Jack Boorman, director of the IMF's policy development and review department, "asked whether the decision to close the 16 banks was a mistake, said the IMF 'agonized greatly' over the closures, and the impact of the move was 'one of the most difficult questions' for the review committee. He defended the closures on the grounds that in a country with Indonesia's 'history—or lack of history' in dealing with problem banks, 'the line had to be drawn somewhere'" (*Wall Street Journal*, January 20, 1999).

7. Information about the Argentinian crisis is drawn from Hausmann and Velasco (2002), Powell (2002), Bortot (2003), de la Torre, Yeyati, and Schmukler (2003a, 2003b), Perry and Servén (2003), and Calvo and Talvi (2005). IMF (2003) provides a brief review of the academic literature on the Argentine crisis.

8. This figure is from de la Torre, Yeyati, and Schmukler (2003a) and we thank them for sharing it. It is calculated with the one-month nondeliverable forward (NDF) discount, the forward exchange rate minus the spot rate. (Also see Schmukler and Servén 2002.)

9. *Reuters*, February 23, 2017, wrote, "Former International Monetary Fund chief Rodrigo Rato was sentenced to 4-1/2 years in prison by Spain's High Court on Thursday following a scandal over the widespread misuse of company credit cards during his tenure at lender Bankia."

10. "Daily NYSE Group Volume in NYSE Listed, 2009" http://www.nyxdata.com/nysedata/asp/factbook/viewer_edition.asp?mode=table&key=3002&category=3.

11. For every repo there is a reverse repo, which is the other side of the transaction. So, counting repo and reverse repo would be double counting.

12. Eric Rosengren, Board of Governors, Federal Reserve System, Transcripts of the Federal Open Market Committee, March 18, 2008.

Chapter 12

1. Academics dismissed bank runs as a thing of the past. For example, Mankiw (2011, 636), a typical textbook, states, "Today, bank runs are not a major problem for the U.S. banking system or the Fed. The federal government now guarantees the safety of deposits at most banks, primarily through the Federal Deposit Insurance Corporation (FDIC)." (Note the date of the textbook.)

2. The Primary Dealer Credit Facility, introduced during the recent crisis in the US, was a standing facility like the Fed's discount window.

3. See SEC Release 34-58592, http://www.sec.gov/rules/other/2008/34-58592.pdf. See Gruenewald, Wagner, and Weber (2010) for a list of worldwide short-sale bans that were instituted during the financial crisis. In Europe, naked CDS on sovereign debt was also banned (EU Short Selling Regulation 236/2012).

4. See the discussion in Wood (2003) and Flandreau and Ugolini (2014).

5. *Home Building & Loan Association v. Blaisdell et al.*, 290 US 426 (1934).

6. *New State Ice Co. v. Liebmann*, 285 US 306 (1932).

7. See Corte Suprema de Justicia de la Nación [National Supreme Court of Justice],

7/12/1934, "Avico, Oscar Agustín c. de la Pesa, Saúl C. / recurso extraordinario," Colección Oficial de Fallos de la Corte Suprema de Justicia de la Nación (1935-172-21).

8. Because of the scarcity of safe debt, there was a demand for privately produced safe debt. The AAA/Aaa tranches of securitizations amounted to 85 percent of each securitized portfolio (see Xie 2012). These tranches had a convenience yield, which was the source of the cheap funding. See Gorton (2017).

Appendix C

1. Coleman (2007) emphasizes that the triparty relationships among leading European nations effectively eliminated this kind of arbitrage trading between the United States and the United Kingdom by 1905. Hence, the example is not meant to mimic the actual transactions in that period. Rather, it uses as convention the United States–United Kingdom transactions as a pedagogical device.

References

Primary Sources

American Review of Reviews, various issues.

Attorney General of the State of New York, *Annual Reports*, various years.

Bankers' Magazine, various issues.

Board of Governors, Federal Reserve System, transcripts of the Federal Open Market Committee, March 18, 2008.

Bradstreet's, various issues.

Commercial and Financial Chronicle, various issues.

Dun's Review, various issues.

Evening World, various issues.

The Financier, various issues.

Forum, various issues.

New York Clearing House Association. Clearing House Committee *Minutes*, various dates. Archives of the New York Clearing House Association, New York.

New York Clearing House Association. 1873. *Report to the New York Clearing House Association of a Committee upon Reforms in the Banking Business.* New York: W. H. Arthur.

New York Clearing House Association. 1903. *Constitution of the New York Clearing House Association, with Amendments.* Arthur Mountain.

New York Daily Times, various issues.

New York Sun, various issues.

New York Times, various issues.

New York Times Financial Affairs, various issues.

New York Tribune, various issues.

Philadelphia Bulletin, various issues.

Philadelphia Inquirer, various issues.

Philadelphia Record, various issues.

Superintendent of the Bank Department of the State of New York, *Annual Reports*, various years.

US Comptroller of the Currency. *Annual Report*, various years. Washington, DC: Government Printing Office.

US Comptroller of the Currency. *Call Reports of Condition and Income*, various dates. Washington, DC: Government Printing Office.

US Government Accountability Office. 2010. *Troubled Asset Relief Program: Bank Stress Test Offers Lessons as Regulators Take Further Actions to Strengthen Supervisory Oversight.* GAO-10-861.

Wall Street Journal, various issues.

Secondary Sources

Acheson, Graeme, Charles Hickson, and John Turner. 2010. "Does Limited Liability Matter? Evidence from Nineteenth Century British Banking," *Review of Law and Economics* 6: 247–73.

Ahmed, Javed, Christopher Anderson, and Rebecca Zarutskie. 2015. *Are the Borrowing Costs of Large Financial Firms Unusual?* Board of Governors of the Federal Reserve System Finance and Discussion Series, Working Paper 2015-024.

Anbil, Sriya. 2017. "Managing Stigma During a Financial Crisis," Finance and Economics Discussion Series 2017-007, Board of Governors of the Federal Reserve System, *Journal of Financial Economics.*

Andrew, A. Piatt. 1908a. "Hoarding in the Panic of 1907." *Quarterly Journal of Economics* 22(4): 290–99.

———. 1908b. "Substitutes for Cash in the Panic of 1907." *Quarterly Journal of Economics* 22(2): 497–516.

———. 1910. *Statistics of Banks and Banking in the United States.* Washington, DC: National Monetary Commission.

Angert, Eugene. 1908. "Liability of Banks for Refusal to Pay Checks in Currency." *Bankers' Magazine,* January, 22–27.

Appel, Ian, and Caroline Fohlin. 2010. "Shooting the Messenger? The Impact of Short Sale Bans in Times of Crisis." Emory University, working paper. https://papers.ssrn.com/sol3/papers.cfm?abstract_id=1595003.

Argüero, Luis Ignacio. 2013. "Regional Currencies and Employment Creation: The Case of Argentina, 2001–2003." Research Note, University of Belgrano.

Armantier, Olivier, Eric Ghysels, Asani Sarkar, and Jeffrey Shrader. 2015. "Discount Window Stigma During the 2007–2008 Financial Crisis." *Journal of Financial Economics* 118, 317–35.

Bagehot, Walter. 1873. *Lombard Street: A Description of the Money Market.* London: Henry S. King.

Bailey, Dudley. 1890. *The Clearing House System.* New York: Homans.

Bank for International Settlements. 2009. "An Assessment of Financial Sector Rescue Programmes." Monetary and Economic Department, Bank for International Settlements Papers No. 48. https://www.bis.org/publ/bppdf/bispap48.pdf.

———. 2013. *Central Bank Collateral Frameworks and Practices.* A Report of a Study Group by the Markets Committee.

———. 2014. "Re-Thinking the Lender of Last Resort." Bank for International Settlements Papers No. 79.

Batunanggar, Sukarela. 2002. "Indonesia's Banking Crisis Resolution." Centre for Central Banking Studies, Bank of England, working paper.

Bayazitova, Dinara, and Anil Shivdasani. 2012. "Assessing TARP." *Review of Financial Studies* 25: 377–407.

Bayles, W. Harrison. 1917. "A History of the Origin and Development of Banks and Banking." In

McMaster's Commercial Cases and Business Intelligence for Bankers, Treasurers, Credit Men and Others, vol. 20, 249–76. New York: McMaster.

Beber, Alessandro, and Marco Pagano. 2013. "Short-Selling Bans around the World: Evidence from the 2007–09 Crisis." *Journal of Finance* 68: 343–81.

Beck, Thorsten, Asli Demirgüç-Kunt, and Ross Levine. 2006. "Bank Concentration, Competition, and Crises: First Results." *Journal of Banking and Finance* 30: 1581–1603.

Benmelech, Efraim. 2012. "An Empirical Analysis of the Fed's Term Auction Facility." *Cato Papers on Public Policy* 2: 1–42.

Bernanke, Ben S. 2009a. "The Federal Reserve's Balance Sheet: An Update." Speech at the Federal Reserve Conference on Key Developments in Monetary Policy, Washington, DC.

———. 2009b. "Reflections on a Year of Crisis." Speech at the Federal Reserve Bank of Kansas City's Annual Economic Symposium, Jackson Hole, Wyoming, August 21.

———. 2010. "Causes of the Recent Financial and Economic Crisis." Testimony before the Financial Crisis Inquiry Commission. http://1.usa.gov/9XW4fi.

———. 2014a. "Central Banking after the Great Recession: Lessons Learned and Challenges Ahead: A Discussion with Federal Reserve Chairman Ben Bernanke on the Fed's 100th Anniversary." Brookings Institution, January.

———. 2014b. "The Federal Reserve: Looking Back, Looking Forward." January 3. http://www.federalreserve.gov/newsevents/speech/bernanke20140103a.htm.

Bernanke, Ben S., Carol Bertaut, Laurie Pounder DeMarco, and Steve Kamin. 2011. "International Capital Flows and the Returns to Safe Assets in the United States, 2003–2007." *Banque de France Financial Stability Review*, February, 13–26.

Bluedorn, John, and Haelim Park. 2016. "Stopping Contagion with Bailouts: Micro-Evidence from Pennsylvania Bank Networks during the Panic of 1884." Office of Financial Research working paper. Forthcoming, *Journal of Banking and Finance*.

Blustein, Paul. 2001. *The Chastening: Inside the Crisis That Rocked the Global Financial System and Humbled the IMF*. New York: Public Affairs.

Boies, William Justus. 1908. "The Story of the Hoarders." *American Review of Reviews* 37: 82–84.

Bolles, Albert. 1903. *Practical Banking*. 11th ed. Indianapolis: Levey Brothers.

Bortot, Francesco. 2003. "Frozen Savings and Depressed Development in Argentina." *Savings and Development* 27: 161–202.

Boyd, John, Gianni De Nicolò, and Elena Loukoianova. 2009. "Banking Crises and Crisis Dating: Theory and Evidence." International Monetary Fund, Working Paper WP/09/141.

Browning, Reuben. 1869. *The Currency, with a View to the Effectual Prevention of Panics*. London: E. and F. N. Spon.

Bruner, Robert F., and Sean D. Carr. 2007. *The Panic of 1907: Lessons Learned from the Market's Perfect Storm*. Hoboken, NJ: John Wiley.

Brunnermeier, Markus. 2009. "Deciphering the Liquidity and Credit Crunch 2007–2008." *Journal of Economic Perspectives* 23: 77–100.

Burns, Arthur, and Wesley Mitchell. 1946. *Measuring Business Cycles*. Cambridge, MA: National Bureau of Economic Research.

Caballero, Julián. 2016. "Do Surges in International Capital Flows Influence the Likelihood of Banking Crises?" *Economic Journal* 126: 281–316.

Calomiris, Charles, and Gary Gorton, with Charles Calomiris. 1991. "The Origins of Banking Panics: Models, Facts, and Bank Regulation." In *Financial Markets and Financial Crises*, edited by Glenn Hubbard. Chicago: University of Chicago Press.

Calvo, Guillermo. 2003. "Explaining Sudden Stop, Growth Collapse, and BOP Crisis: The Case of Distortionary Output Taxes." *IMF Staff Papers* 50: 1–20.

———. 2010. "Looking at Financial Crises in the Eye: Some Basic Observations." Columbia University, School of International and Public Affairs, working paper.

Calvo, Guillermo A., Alejandro Izquierdo, and Ernesto Talvi. 2006. "Phoenix Miracles in Emerging Markets: Recovering without Credit from Systemic Financial Crises." Inter-American Development Bank Research Department, Working Paper 570.

Calvo, Guillermo, and Ernesto Talvi. 2005. "Sudden Stop, Financial Factors and Economic Collapse in Latin America: Learning from Argentina and Chile." National Bureau of Economic Research, NBER Working Paper 11153.

Camp, William. 1892. "The New York Clearing House." *North American Review* 154: 684–90.

Cannon, James Graham. 1910a. *Clearing Houses.* Washington, DC: Government Printing Office.

———. 1910b. "Clearing House Loan Certificates and Substitutes for Money Used during the Panic of 1907." Speech delivered at the Finance Forum, New York City, March 30. New York: Trow Press.

Capie, Forest. 2002. "The Emergence of the Bank of England as a Mature Central Bank." In *The Political Economy of British Historical Experience, 1688–1914,* edited by Donald Winch and Patrick O'Brien, 295–315. Oxford: Oxford University Press.

———. 2007. "The Emergence of the Bank of England as a Mature Central Bank." In *The Lender of Last Resort,* edited by Forrest Capie and Geoffrey Wood, 297–316. London: Routledge.

Carlson, Mark, and Jonathan Rose. 2016. "Can a Bank Run Be Stopped? Government Guarantees and the Run on Continental Illinois." Finance and Economics Discussion Series 2016-003. Washington: Board of Governors of the Federal Reserve System, http://dx.doi.org/10.17016/FEDS.2016.003.

Chang, Roberto, and Andrés Velasco. 1998. "The Asian Liquidity Crisis." Federal Reserve Bank of Atlanta, Working Paper 98-11.

Clews, Henry. 1888. *Twenty-Eight Years in Wall Street.* New York: Irving.

Coleman, Andrew. 2007. "The Pitfalls of Estimating Transactions Costs from Price Data: Evidence from Trans-Atlantic Gold-Point Arbitrage, 1886–1905." *Explorations in Economic History* 44: 387–410.

Conant, Charles A. 1909. *A History of Modern Banks of Issue. With an Account of the Economic Crises of the Nineteenth Century and the Panic of 1907.* New York: G. P. Putnam.

Corsetti, G., Paolo Pesenti, and Nouriel Roubini. 1998. "Paper Tigers? A Preliminary Assessment of the Asian Crisis." Paper prepared for NBER Bank of Portugal International Seminar on Macroeconomics, Lisbon, June 14–15.

Covitz, Daniel, Nellie Liang, and Gustavo Suarez. 2013. "The Evolution of a Financial Crisis: Collapse of the Asset-Backed Commercial Paper Market." *Journal of Finance* 68: 815–48.

Curtis, Charles. 1898. "Clearing House Loan Certificates, How Issued and Why." *Yale Review* 6: 251–66.

Dang, Tri Vi, Gary Gorton, and Bengt Holmström. 2013. "Ignorance, Debt and Financial Crises." Yale School of Management, working paper.

Dang, Tri Vi, Gary Gorton, Bengt Holmström, and Guillermo Ordoñez. 2017. "Banks as Secret Keepers." *American Economic Review* 107: 1005–29.

de la Torre, Augusto, Eduardo Levy Yeyati, and Sergio Schmukler. 2003a. "Argentina's Financial Crisis: Floating Money, Sinking Banking." World Bank, working paper.

———. 2003b. "Living and Dying with Hard Pegs: The Rise and Fall of Argentina's Currency Board." *Economía* (Spring): 43–106.

Dewey, Davis Rich. 1922. *Financial History of the United States*. 8th ed. New York: Longmans, Green.

Dobler, Marc, Simon Gray, Diarmuid Murphy, and Bozena Radzewicz-Bak. 2016. "The Lender of Last Resort Function after the Global Financial Crisis." International Monetary Fund, Working Paper WP/16/10.

Draghi, Mario. 2013. "Building Stability and Sustained Prosperity in Europe." Speech at the event "The Future of Europe in the Global Economy," hosted by the City of London, May 23. http://www.bis.org/review/r130524a.pdf?frames=0.

Eichengreen, Barry, Ashoka Mody, Milan Nedeljkovic, and Lucio Samo. 2012. "How the Subprime Crisis Went Global: Evidence from Bank Credit Default Swap Spreads." *Journal of International Money and Finance* 31(5): 1299–1318.

Englund, Peter. 2015. "The Swedish 1990s Banking Crisis: A Revisit in the Light of Recent Experience." Stockholm School of Economics, working paper.

Enoch, Charles. 2000. "Interventions in Banks during Banking Crises: The Experience of Indonesia." International Monetary Fund, Policy Discussion Paper PDP/00/2. https://www.imf.org/external/pubs/ft/pdp/2000/pdp02.pdf.

Enoch, Charles, Barbara Baldwin, Olivier Frécaut, and Arto Kovanen. 2001. "Indonesia: Anatomy of a Banking Crisis." International Monetary Fund, Working Paper WP/01/52.

Evrensel, Ayşe. 2008. "Banking Crisis and Financial Structure: A Survival-Time Analysis." *International Review of Economics and Finance* 17: 589–602.

Fetter, Frank. 1965. *The Development of British Monetary Orthodoxy, 1797–1875.* Cambridge, MA: Harvard University Press.

Financial Crisis Inquiry Commission. 2011. *The Financial Crisis: Inquiry Report*. Washington, DC: Government Printing Office.

Fischer, Stanley. 1999. "On the Need for an International Lender of Last Resort." *Journal of Economic Perspectives* 13: 85–104.

Flandreau, Marc, and Stefano Ugolini. 2011. "Where It All Began: Lending of Last Resort and the Bank of England during the Overend-Gurney Panic of 1866." Norges Bank, Working Paper 2011-03.

———. 2014. "The Crisis of 1866." Graduate Institute of International and Development Studies, Working Paper 10/2014.

Fliter, John, and Derek Hoff. 2012. *Fighting Foreclosure: The Blaisdell Case, the Contract Clause, and the Great Depression*. Lawrence: University Press of Kansas.

Friedman, Milton, and Anna Schwartz. 1963. *A Monetary History of the United States*. Princeton, NJ: Princeton University Press.

Furman, Jason, and Joseph Stiglitz. 1998. "Economic Crises: Evidence and Insights from East Asia." *Brookings Papers on Economic Activity* 2: 1–135.

Garicano, Luis. 2012a. "Five Lessons from the Spanish Cajas Debacle for a New Euro-wide Supervisor." In *Banking Union for Europe: Risks and Challenges*, edited by Thorsten Beck, 77–84. A VoxEU.org Book, Centre for Economic Policy Research.

———. 2012b. "Five Lessons from the Spanish Cajas Debacle for a New Euro-wide Supervisor." CEPR Vox, http://voxeu.org/article/five-lessons-spanish-cajas-debacle-new-euro-wide-supervisor.

Gassiot, John. 1867. *Monetary Panics and Their Remedy, with Special Reference to the Panic of May 1866*. London: Effingham Wilson.

Geithner, Timothy. 2008. "Actions by the New York Fed in Response to Liquidity Pressure in Financial markets." Testimony before the U.S. Senate Committee on Banking, Housing and

Urban Affairs, April 3. http://www.newyorkfed.org/newsevents/speeches/2008/gei080403
.html.

———. 2014. *Stress Test: Reflections on Financial Crises.* New York: Crown.

Gibbons, J. S. 1859. *The Banks of New York, Their Dealers, the Clearing House, and the Panic of
1857.* New York: D. Appleton.

Giglio, Stefano. 2011. "Credit Default Swap Spreads and Systemic Risk." Harvard University,
Department of Economics, working paper.

Gilpin, William, and Henry Wallace. 1904. *New York Clearing House Association, 1854–1905.* New
York: Moses King.

Goetzmann, William N., Roger G. Ibbotson, and Liang Peng. 2001. "A New Historical Database
for the NYSE 1815 to 1925: Performance and Predictability." *Journal of Financial Markets*
4(1): 1–32.

Goodhart, Charles A. E. 1969. *The New York Money Market and the Finance of Trade, 1900–1913.*
Cambridge, MA: Harvard University Press.

———. 2008. "Now Is Not the Time to Agonise over Moral Hazard." *Financial Times,* September 18.

Gorton, Gary. 1984. "Private Bank Clearinghouses and the Origins of Central Banking." *Business
Review—Federal Reserve Bank of Philadelphia,* January–February, 3–12.

———. 1985. "Clearinghouses and the Origin of Central Banking in the United States." *Journal
of Economic History* 45(2): 277–83.

———. 1988. "Banking Panics and Business Cycles." *Oxford Economic Papers* 40(4): 751–81.

———. 1996. "Reputation Formation in Early Bank Note Markets." *Journal of Political Economy*
104(2): 346–97.

———. 1999. "Pricing Free Bank Notes." *Journal of Monetary Economics* 44: 33–64.

———. 2010. *Slapped by the Invisible Hand: The Panic of 2007.* Oxford: Oxford University
Press.

———. 2012. *Misunderstanding Financial Crises: Why We Don't See Them Coming.* Oxford: Oxford University Press.

———. 2014. "The Development of Opacity in U.S. Banking." *Yale Journal of Regulation* 31:
825–51.

———. 2015. "Stress for Success: A Review of Timothy Geithner's Financial Crisis Memoir."
Journal of Economic Literature 53(4): 975–95.

———. 2017. "The History and Economics of Safe Assets." *Annual Review of Economics* 9:
547–86.

Gorton, Gary, and Lixin Huang. 2006. "Banking Panics and Endogenous Coalition Formation."
Journal of Monetary Economics 53(7): 1613–29.

Gorton, Gary, Toomas Laarits, and Andrew Metrick. 2017. "The Run on Repo and the Fed's
Response." Yale School of Management, working paper.

Gorton, Gary, Stefan Lewellen, and Andrew Metrick. 2012. "The Safe-Asset Share." *American
Economic Review: Papers and Proceedings* 102 (May): 101–6.

Gorton, Gary, and Andrew Metrick. 2012. "Securitized Banking and the Run on Repo." *Journal
of Financial Economics* 104: 425–51.

———. 2013. "Securitization." In *Handbook of the Economics of Finance,* edited by George Con-
stantinides, Milton Harris, and René Stulz, 2A: 1–70. New York: Elsevier.

Gorton, Gary, Andrew Metrick, and Lei Xie. 2015a. "An Econometric Chronology of the Financial Crisis of 2007–2008." Yale School of Management, working paper.

———. 2015b. "The Flight from Maturity." Yale School of Management, working paper.

Gorton, Gary, and Tyler Muir. 2016. "Mobile Collateral versus Immobile Collateral." Yale School of Management and UCLA, working paper.

Gorton, Gary, and Don Mullineaux. 1987. "The Joint Production of Confidence: Endogenous Regulation and Nineteenth Century Commercial Bank Clearinghouses." *Journal of Money, Credit and Banking* 19(4): 458–68.

Gorton, Gary, and Guillermo Ordoñez. 2014. "Collateral Crises." *American Economic Review* 104(2): 343–78.

Gorton, Gary, and George Pennacchi. 1990. "Financial Intermediation and Liquidity Creation." *Journal of Finance* 45(1): 49–72.

Gorton, Gary, and Nicholas S. Souleles. 2007. "Special Purpose Vehicles and Securitization." In *The Risks of Financial Institutions*, edited by René Stulz and Mark Carey, 549–602. Chicago: University of Chicago Press.

Gorton, Gary, and Ellis Tallman. 2016. "Too-Big-to-Fail before the Fed." *American Economic Review* 106(5): 528–32.

Gouge, William. 1837. *An Inquiry into the Expediency of Dispensing with Bank Agency and Bank Paper in the Fiscal Concerns of the United States*. Philadelphia: William Stavely.

Grenville, Stephen. 2004. "The IMF and the Indonesian Crisis." International Monetary Fund, Independent Evaluation Office, BP/04/3.

Gruenewald, Serainan, Alexander Wagner, and Rolf Weber. 2010. "Emergency Short-Selling Restrictions in the Course of the Financial Crisis." University of Zurich, SSRN working paper.

Hagen, Everett Einar. 1932. "The Panic of 1907." MA thesis, University of Wisconsin–Madison.

Hammond, Bray. (1957) 1991. *Banks and Politics in America from the Revolution to the Civil War*. Princeton, NJ: Princeton University Press.

Harvie, Charles. 1999. "Indonesia: Recovery from Economic and Social Collapse." University of Wollongong, Faculty of Business, working paper.

Hausmann, Ricardo, and Andrés Velasco. 2002. "The Argentine Collapse: Hard Money's Soft Underbelly." Harvard Kennedy School, working paper.

He, Dong. 2000. "Emergency Liquidity Support Facilities." International Monetary Fund, Working Paper WP/00/79.

Holland Martin, Robert. 1910. "The London Bankers Clearing House." In *The English Banking System*, edited by Hartley Withers, 267–91. Senate Doc. No. 492, 61st Cong., 2nd Sess. Washington, DC: Government Printing Office.

Hördahl, Peter, and Michael King. 2008. "Developments in Repo Markets during the Financial Turmoil." *BIS Quarterly Review*, December, 37–53.

International Monetary Fund. 2000. "Recovery from the Asian Crisis and the Role of the IMF." https://www.imf.org/external/np/exr/ib/2000/062300.htm#II.

———. 2003. "Lessons from the Crisis in Argentina." Prepared by the Policy Development and Review Department, working paper.

———. 2012. "Spain: The Reform of Spanish Savings Banks Technical Notes." International Monetary Fund, Country Report No. 12/141.

Investment Company Institute. 2009. *2009 Investment Company Fact Book*. 49th ed. Washington, DC: Investment Company Institute.

Jacobson, Margaret M., Eric M. Leeper, and Bruce Preston. 2017. "Recovery of 1933." Unpublished manuscript, Indiana University.

Jalil, Andrew. 2015. "A New History of Banking Panics in the United States, 1825–1929: Construction and Implications." *American Economic Journal: Macroeconomics* 7: 295–330.

James, John, Jamies McAndrews, and David Weiman. 2013. "Panics and the Disruption of

Private Payments Networks: The United States in 1893 and 1907." Unpublished working paper. https://gc.cuny.edu/CUNY_GC/media/CUNY-Graduate-Center/PDF/Programs/Economics/Seminar%20papers/James-McAmdrews-Weiman.pdf.

James, John, and David F. Weiman. 2010. "From Drafts to Checks: The Evolution of Correspondent Banking Networks and the Formation of the Modern U.S. Payments System, 1850–1914." *Journal of Money, Credit and Banking* 42(2–3): 237–65.

Joplin, Thomas. N.d., after 1832. *Case for Parliamentary Inquiry into the Circumstances of the Panic* [of 1825], *a Letter to Thomas Giscourne, Esq., M.P.* London: James Ridgeway and Sons.

Kane, Thomas. 1922. *The Romance and Tragedy of Banking.* New York: Bankers Publishing.

Kaufman, George. 2004. "Too Big to Fail in U.S. Banking: Quo Vadis?" In *Too-Big-to-Fail: Policies and Practices,* edited by Benton Gup, 153–68. Santa Barbara, CA: Praeger.

Kemmerer, Edwin R. 1910. *Seasonal Variations in the Relative Demand for Money and Capital in the United States.* Washington, DC: Government Printing Office.

Kindleberger, Charles. 2005. *Manias, Panics, and Crashes: A History of Financial Crises.* Hoboken, NJ: Wiley.

King, Mervyn. 2010. "Banking—from Bagehot to Basel, and Back Again." Speech at the Second Bagehot Lecture, Buttonwood Gathering, New York, October 25. http://www.bis.org/review/r101028a.pdf?frames=0.

King, W. T. C. 1935. "The Extent of the London Discount Market in the Middle of the Nineteenth Century." *Economica* 2: 321–26.

———. (1936) 1972. *A History of the London Discount Market.* London: Routledge.

Kniffin, William. 1916. *The Practical Work of a Bank.* New York: Bankers Publishing.

Kress, Wilson. 1896. *Pennsylvania State Reports,* vol. 173, containing cases adjudged in the Supreme Court of Pennsylvania. New York: Banks and Brothers.

Krishnamurthy, Arvind. 2010. "How Debt Markets Have Malfunctioned in the Crisis." *Journal of Economic Perspectives* 24(1): 3–28.

Krishnamurthy, Arvind, and Annette Vissing-Jørgensen. 2012. "The Aggregate Demand for Treasury Debt." *Journal of Political Economy* 120: 233–67.

Krozner, Randall. 1999. "Is It Better to Forgive Than to Receive? Repudiation of the Gold Indexation Clause in Long-Term Debt during the Great Depression." University of Chicago, Booth School of Business, working paper.

Laeven, Luc, and Fabián Valencia. 2008. "The Use of Blanket Guarantees in Banking Crises." International Monetary Fund, Working Paper WP/08/250.

———. 2012. "Systemic Banking Crises Database: An Update." International Monetary Fund, Working Paper WP/12/163.

Lane, Timothy, and Marianne Schulze-Ghattas. 1999. "IMF-Supported Programs in Indonesia, Korea, and Thailand: A Preliminary Assessment." International Monetary Fund Occasional Paper 178.

Laughlin, J. Laurence. 1912. *Banking Reform.* Chicago: National Citizens' League.

Lowrey, Annie. 2014. "How the Fed Saw a Recession and Then Didn't." *Economix* (*New York Times* blog), February 21. https://economix.blogs.nytimes.com/2014/02/21/how-the-fed-saw-a-recession-then-didnt-then-did/.

Macey, Jonathan, and Geoffrey Miller. 1992. "Double Liability of Bank Shareholders: History and Implications." *Wake Forest Law Review* 27: 31–62.

Mankiw, Gregory. 2011. *Principles of Economics.* Mason, OH: South-Western Cengage Learning.

Marquis, Ralph, and Frank Smith. 1937. "Double Liability for Bank Stock." *American Economic Review* 27: 490–502.

Martin-Aceña, Pablo. 2014. "The Savings Bank Crisis in Spain: When and How." Asociación Española de Historia, Documentos de Trabajo No. 1404.

McCabe, Patrick. 2015. "The Cross Section of Money Market Fund Risks and Financial Crises." Board of Governors of the Federal Reserve System, working paper.

McLeod, Ross. 2004. "Dealing with Bank System Failure: Indonesia, 1997–2003." *Bulletin of Indonesian Economic Studies* 40: 95–116.

Moen, Jon, and Ellis Tallman. 2000. "Clearinghouse Membership and Deposit Contraction during the Panic of 1907." *Journal of Economic History* 60: 145–63.

———. 2015. "Close but Not a Central Bank: The New York Clearing House and Issues of Clearing House Loan Certificates." In *Current Policy under the Lens of Economic History*, edited by Owen Humpage, 102–25. New York: Cambridge University Press.

Muhleman, Maurice Louis. 1908. *Monetary and Banking Systems.* New York: Monetary Publishing.

Noyes, Alexander. 1894. "The Banks and the Panic of 1893." *Political Science Quarterly* 9(1): 12–30.

———. 1901. *Thirty Years of Finance.* New York: G. P. Putnam's Sons.

———. 1909. "A Year after the Panic of 1907." *Quarterly Journal of Economics* 23: 185–212.

Officer, Lawrence. 1986. "The Efficiency of the Dollar-Sterling Gold Standard, 1890–1908." *Journal of Political Economy* 94: 1038–73.

———. 2008. "Gold Standard." EH.Net Encyclopedia, edited by Robert Whaples. March 26. http://eh.net/encyclopedia/gold-standard/.

O'Sullivan, Mary. 2007. "The Expansion of the U.S. Stock Market, 1885–1939: Historical Facts and Theoretical Fashions." *Enterprise and Society* 8: 489–542.

Parker, Randall. 2002. *Reflections on the Great Depression.* Northampton, MA: Edward Elgar.

———. 2008. *The Economics of the Great Depression.* Northampton, MA: Edward Elgar.

Peristian, Stavros, Donald Morgan, and Vanessa Savino. 2014. "The Information Value of the Stress Test and Bank Opacity." *Journal of Money, Credit and Banking* 46(7): 1479–1500.

Perry, Guillermo, and Luis Servén. 2003. "The Anatomy of a Multiple Crisis: Why Was Argentina Special and What Can We Learn from It?" World Bank Policy Research, Working Paper 3081.

Poor, Henry V. 1877. *Money and Its Laws.* New York: H. V. and H. W. Poor.

Powell, Andrew. 2002. "Argentina's Avoidable Crisis: Bad Luck, Bad Economics, Bad Politics, Bad Advice." *Brookings Trade Forum*, 1–58.

Pressnell, Leslie. 1956. *Country Banking in the Industrial Revolution.* Oxford: Clarendon Press.

Radelet, Steven, and Jeffrey D. Sachs. 1998a. "The East Asian Financial Crisis: Diagnosis, Remedies, Prospects." *Brookings Papers on Economic Activity* 1: 1–90.

———. 1998b. "The Onset of the East Asian Financial Crisis." National Bureau of Economic Research, NBER Working Paper 6680.

Redlich, Fritz. 1947. *The Molding of American Banking.* New York: Hafner.

———. 1951. *The Molding of American Banking, Men and Ideas. Part II, 1840–1910.* New York: Hafner.

Reinhart, Carmen M., and Kenneth S. Rogoff. 2009. "The Aftermath of Financial Crises." *American Economic Review* 99(2): 466–72.

Robertson, Adriana. Forthcoming. "Shadow Banking, Shadow Bailouts." *Delaware Journal of Corporate Law.*

Rodgers, Mary Tone, and Berry Wilson. 2011. "Systemic Risk, Missing Gold Flows, and the Panic of 1907." *Quarterly Journal of Austrian Economics* 14: 158–87.

Rodrik, Dani, and Andrés Velasco. 1999. "Short-Term Capital Flows." National Bureau of Economic Research, NBER Working Paper 7364.

Rohdé, Lars. 2011. "Lessons from the Last Financial Crisis and the Future Role of Institutional Investors." *OECD Financial Market Trends* 1(1): 1–6.

Santos, Tano. 2017a. "Antes del Diluvio: The Spanish Banking System in the First Decade of the Euro." In *After the Flood: How the Great Recession Changed Economic Thought*, edited by Edward Glaeser, Tano Santos, and Glen Weyl. Chicago: University of Chicago Press.

———. 2017b. "El Diluvio: The Spanish Banking Crisis, 2008–2012." Columbia University, Department of Finance, working paper.

Schmukler, Sergio, and Luis Servén. 2002. "Pricing Currency Risk under Currency Boards." *Journal of Development Economics* 69: 367–91.

Schwert, G. William. 1990. "Indexes of United States Stock Prices from 1802 to 1987." *Journal of Business* 63: 399–426.

Scott, David. 2002. "A Practical Guide to Managing Systemic Financial Crises: A Review of Approaches Taken in Indonesia, The Republic of Korea, and Thailand." http://unpan1.un.org/intradoc/groups/public/documents/APCITY/UNPAN021162.pdf.

Securities Industry and Financial Markets Association (SIFMA). 2008. "Repo Average Daily Amount Outstanding Increases in the First Quarter." *Research Quarterly* 3(8): 9. https://www.sifma.org/wp-content/uploads/2017/05/us-research-quarterly-2008-q2.pdf.

Shin, Hyun. 2009. "Reflections on Northern Rock: The Bank Run That Heralded the Global Financial Crisis." *Journal of Economic Perspectives* 23: 101–19.

———. 2010. "Macroprudential Policies beyond Basel III." In *Macroprudential Regulation and Policy*, Bank for International Settlements, BIS Papers, No. 60, 5–15.

Silber, William. 2008. *When Washington Shut Down Wall Street: The Great Financial Crisis of 1914 and the Origins of America's Monetary Supremacy.* Princeton, NJ: Princeton University Press.

Smith, Gordon. 1908. "Clearing-House Examinations." *Bankers' Magazine* 76: 177–78.

Spector, Hector. 2008. "Constitutional Transplants and the Mutation Effect." *Chicago-Kent Law Review* 83: 129–44.

Sprague, O. M. W. 1908. "The American Crisis of 1907." *Economic Journal* 18(71): 353–72.

———. 1910. *History of Crises under the National Banking System.* Senate Doc. No. 538, 61st Cong., 2nd Sess. Washington, DC: Government Printing Office.

Squire, Newton. 1888. *The New York Clearing House, Its Methods and Systems, and a Description of the London Clearing House, with Valuable Statistics and Other Information.* New York: Arthur & Bonnell.

Swanson, William Walker. 1908a. "The Crisis of 1860 and the First Issue of Clearing-House Certificates: I." *Journal of Political Economy* 16(2): 65–75.

———. 1908b. "The Crisis of 1860 and the First Issue of Clearing-House Certificates: II." *Journal of Political Economy* 16(4): 212–26.

Tallman, Ellis W. 2013. "The Panic of 1907." In *The Handbook of Major Events in Economic History*, edited by Randall E. Parker and Robert Whaples, 50–66. New York: Routledge.

Tallman, Ellis W., and Jon R. Moen. 1990. "Lessons from the Panic of 1907." *Federal Reserve Bank of Atlanta Economic Review* 75(3) (May/June): 2–13.

———. 2012. "Liquidity Creation without a Central Bank: Clearing House Loan Certificates in the Banking Panic of 1907." *Journal of Financial Stability* 8: 277–91.

Thrall, Jerome. 1916. *The Clearing House.* New York: American Bankers Association.

Timberlake, Richard. 1984. "The Central Banking Role of Clearinghouse Associations." *Journal of Money, Credit and Banking* 16: 1–15.

———. 1993. *Monetary Policy in the United States: An Intellectual and Institutional History.* Chicago: University of Chicago Press.

Warner, John De Witt. 1895. "The Currency Famine of 1893." *Sound Currency* 2: 1–20.

Wicker, Elmus. 1966. *Federal Reserve Policy, 1917–1933.* New York: Random House.

———. 2000. *Banking Panics of the Gilded Age.* Cambridge: Cambridge University Press.

Wood, John. 2003. "Bagehot's Lender of Last Resort: A Hollow Hallowed Tradition." *Independent Review* 7: 343–51.

Xie, Lei. 2012. "The Seasons of Money: ABS/MBS Issuance and the Convenience Yield." Yale School of Management, working paper.

Index

Page numbers in italics refer to figures and tables.

INDEX